David Alan Herzog
with Douglas French

THOMSON
PETERSON'S

Australia • Canada • Mexico • Singapore • Spain • United Kingdom • United States

About The Thomson Corporation and Peterson's

With revenues of US$7.2 billion, The Thomson Corporation (www.thomson.com) is a leading global provider of integrated information solutions for business, education, and professional customers. Its Learning businesses and brands (www.thomsonlearning.com) serve the needs of individuals, learning institutions, and corporations with products and services for both traditional and distributed learning.

Peterson's, part of The Thomson Corporation, is one of the nation's most respected providers of lifelong learning online resources, software, reference guides, and books. The Education Supersite℠ at www.petersons.com—the Internet's most heavily traveled education resource—has searchable databases and interactive tools for contacting U.S.-accredited institutions and programs. In addition, Peterson's serves more than 105 million education consumers annually.

For more information, contact Peterson's, 2000 Lenox Drive, Lawrenceville, NJ 08648; 800-338-3282; or find us on the World Wide Web at www.petersons.com/about.

ISBN 0-7689-1070-6

Printed in the United States of America

10 9 8 7 6 5 4 3 2 1 05 04 03

CONTENTS

CONTENTS

PART II—MATH REVIEW

CONTENTS

BEFORE YOU GET STARTED

Directions: Choose from (A), (B), (C), or (D) the words that make the completed sentence most accurate.

High Stakes tests are

(A) performed by supermarkets to ensure the highest quality beef for their customers.

(B) administered by vampire slayers to ensure the demise of their enemies.

(C) very tall poles.

(D) taken by students to determine whether they are ready to graduate from high school.

We're going to take a wild guess that you chose **(D)** as the correct answer.

All kidding aside, we refer to the exit-level proficiency exams as "**high stakes**" **tests** because your high school diploma is *at stake*. Your diploma is probably the most valuable piece of paper you'll ever have in your hands. Without it, you may be limited in the kind of work you can do as an adult, and you also won't earn as much money as people who have diplomas. So, unless you're the next Britney Spears or one of those lucky people who wins the million-dollar lottery, these tests *are* high stakes for you.

We're not going to lie to you. Most of the test questions on your exit-level exams will not be as easy to answer as the question above. We're sure you already know that. But we'd bet that you *don't* know what kind of questions will pop up on these exams. And this is one case where what you don't know *can* hurt you.

But not to worry. We have diligently studied the standards for **math, reading, writing,** and **science** skills set by the state educational professionals, as well as the test questions that appear on these exams. We're not only going to tell you what you will be tested *on* but also *how* you will be tested. So, whether your state is going to use multiple-choice questions, essays, or open-ended response, if you've got a *High Stakes* skill book in your hands, we've got you covered.

So that's the good news . . .

But here's even better news! Unlike the SAT, which tests "critical thinking," the state proficiency exams test only what you've learned in school. It's actually pretty hard to study for something as vague as *critical thinking,* which is why you'll find that most SAT test-prep books are full of tricks on how to squeeze out a couple of hundred more points on the test. But the exit-level proficiency exams test **real subject knowledge**. That's not vague, that's simple! And if you've bought this book, we're going to assume you're prepared for some review. So, the bottom line is that if you study the material we give you in this book (which is not that big, right?), you can do more than just pass these exams—you can score high!

Let's Get Organized

The organization of this book is really straightforward. The book is divided into three parts:

Part I provides a short guide to the state exit-level exams and a chapter on strategies and tips to help you plan your study and alleviate test anxiety.

Part II reviews all the topics that will be covered on your state exam.

Part III contains lots of practice questions to help you get comfortable answering the test questions on high stakes exams. We also give you answers and explanations to make sure you understand everything.

Now that you know you can rely on us to help you succeed, we hope we've reduced your stress level. So . . . sit down, take a deep breath, and . . . *relax.* We're going to take you step-by-step through everything you need to know for test day.

PART I

INTRODUCTION

ALPHABET CITY

Have you checked out the shaded bands on the top of the pages in this book? You'll see some pretty odd combinations of letters, such as TAAS, BST, FCAT, OGT, CAHSEE, and MEAP.

> MEAP? What the heck is that? Sounds like Martian for salad or something.

More likely you've recognized some of the letters because they are *acronyms,* which means they are letters that stand for the name of your state exam. MEAP, by the way, stands for Michigan Educational Assessment Program. You have to admit that *Meap* rolls off the tongue a bit more easily.

In this chapter, we list all sixteen states that require exams for graduating high school. Each of the high-stakes states (can you say that 5 times fast?) sets its own rules for the exams, and you'll find some students may appear to have it easier than others. North Carolina tests its students in reading and math only, and the question types are multiple choice only. Students in Minnesota, however, are tested in reading, math, *and* writing, and the question types include multiple choice, short answer, *and* essays! But don't worry, beginning in 2005, students in North Carolina will be tested in reading, math, science, social studies, English, *and* grammar. Perhaps that's why the official state beverage of North Carolina is milk . . . those students will need their strength!

The point is that you should look carefully at the rules for your own state. For example, if you're one of those lucky North Carolinians taking the test in 2003 or 2004, you can skip any practice question that is not multiple choice. As we said earlier, it's our job to make sure we cover all the bases for everyone, but you only have to study what you're actually being tested on.

You may have to take other subject tests in high school, which are not required for graduation. Some tests are for advanced diplomas (such as the Regents Math B). Other tests are actually testing your teachers and your school system. We're here to help you graduate, and we focus only on the tests where the stakes are high for *you.*

Log on to www.petersons.com/highstakes for your Graduation Checklist, which will highlight information you need to have on your state's scoring, test dates, required topics of study, and more!

The following list of states is in alphabetical order.

Alabama

Exit-Level Exam: Alabama High School Graduation Exam (AHSGE)

State Education Department Website: www.alsde.edu

Students take the AHSGE in eleventh grade. Beginning with the graduating class of 2003, students must pass all subject-area tests in order to graduate. Students have six opportunities to take these exams.

Test	# Questions	Time	Question Type
Reading	84	approx. 3 hrs.	multiple choice
Language	100	approx. 3 hrs.	multiple choice
Science	100	approx. 3 hrs.	multiple choice
Math	100	approx. 3 hrs.	multiple choice
Social Studies	100	approx. 3 hrs.	multiple choice

California

Exit-Level Exam: California High School Exit Exam (**CAHSEE**)

State Education Department Website: www.cde.ca.gov

Students take the CAHSEE in tenth grade. As of the 2003–04 school year, students are required to pass both parts of the CAHSEE. Students have multiple opportunities to retake one or both portions of the exam.

Test	# Questions	Time	Question Type
English-Language	82	untimed	multiple choice
English-Language	2	untimed	short essays (includes written response to text and prompt)
Math	80	untimed	multiple choice

Florida

Exit-Level Exam: Florida Comprehensive Assessment Test (**FCAT**)

State Education Department Website: www.firn.edu/doe/sas/fcat

Students take the FCAT in tenth grade and must pass the reading and math parts of the exam in order to graduate. Students have multiple opportunities to retake the exams.

Test	# Questions	Time	Question Type
Reading	105	untimed	multiple choice
Math	100	untimed	multiple choice

Georgia

Exit-Level Exam: Georgia High School Graduation Tests **(GHSGT)**

State Education Department Website: www.doe.k12.ga.us/sla/ret/ghsgt.asp

Students take the GHSGT in eleventh grade and must pass each of the 5 tests in order to graduate. Students have five opportunities to take each of the tests before the end of twelfth grade.

Test	# Questions	Time	Question Type
English/ Language Arts	50	3 hrs. max	multiple choice
Math	60	3 hrs. max.	multiple choice
Social Studies	80	3 hrs. max.	multiple choice
Science	70	3 hrs. max.	multiple choice
Writing	1	90 mins.	essay

Louisiana

Exit-Level Exam: Graduation Exit Examination for the 21st Century **(GEE 21)**

State Education Department Website: www.doe.state.la.us

Students take the GEE 21 in the tenth grade (English language arts *and* mathematics) and must pass them both to graduate. Students also take the GEE 21 in the eleventh grade (science *or* social studies) and must pass one of these to graduate. Students have multiple opportunities to retake each portion of the exam.

Test	# Questions	Time	Question Type
English / Language Arts	61	untimed	multiple choice and essay

Math	60	untimed	multiple choice and short answer
Science	44	untimed	multiple choice and short answer
Social Studies	64	untimed	multiple choice and short answer

Massachusetts

Exit-Level Exam: Massachusetts Comprehensive Assessment System (**MCAS**)

State Education Department Website: www.doe.mass.edu/mcas

Students take the MCAS in the tenth grade and must pass the English Language Arts and Math portions of the exam in order to graduate. Students have multiple opportunities to retake both portions of the test.

Test	# Questions	Time	Question Type
Math	51	untimed	multiple choice, short answer, and open response
English/ Language Arts	55	untimed	multiple choice and writing prompt

Michigan

Exit-Level Exam: Michigan Educational Assessment Program High School Tests (MEAP HST)

State Education Department Website: www.meritaward.state.mi.us/mma/meap.htm

Students take the MEAP HST in eleventh grade and must pass all parts of the exam in order to graduate. Students have the opportunity to retake portions of the exam in the twelfth grade.

Test	# Questions	Time	Question Type
Math	43	100 min.	multiple choice and open response
Reading*	29	80 min.	multiple choice and open response
Science	50	90 min.	multiple choice and open response
Social Studies	42	80 min.	multiple choice and open response
Writing*	2	120 min.	open response

**As of the 2003–04 school year, Reading and Writing will be combined into an English Language Arts test along with a Listening test.*

Minnesota

Exit-Level Exam: Basic Skills Test (**BST**)

State Education Department Website: http://cflapp.state.mn.us/CLASS/stds/assessments/bst/index.jsp

Students take the math and reading portions of the BST in eighth grade and the writing portion in tenth grade and must pass all portions of the exam in order to graduate. Students have multiple opportunities to retake each section of the exam.

Test	# Questions	Time	Question Type
Reading	40	120–150 min.	multiple choice and short answer
Writing	several	90–120 min.	short essays
Math	68	120–150 min.	multiple choice and short answer

New Jersey

Exit-Level Exam: High School Proficiency Assessment **(HSPA)**

State Education Department Website: www.state.nj.us/education

Students take the HSPA in eleventh grade and must pass both sections in order to graduate. In 2004–05, a social studies assessment will be phased in, and in March 2005, science will be added. Students have two additional opportunities to retake each portion of the exam in their senior year.

Test	# Questions	Time	Question Type
Language Arts/ Literacy	55	4 hrs.	multiple choice and open ended
Mathematics	48	2 hrs.	multiple choice and open ended

New York

Exit-Level Exam: Regents Exams

State Education Department Website: www.emsc.nysed.gov/deputy/Documents/alternassess.htm

Students take the Regents in tenth and eleventh grades and must pass the five Regents Examinations listed below to graduate. In general, students in the tenth grade are tested in science, math, and global history and geography. Students in the eleventh grade are tested in English language arts, and U.S. history and government. Students who fail portions of the exam twice are required to pass a component test for that portion in order to graduate.

Test	# Questions	Time	Question Type
English	29	3 hrs.	multiple choice and essay
Math	35	3 hrs.	multiple choice and open ended

Global History and Geography	60–62	3 hrs.	multiple choice and open ended
U.S. History and Government	60–62	3 hrs.	multiple choice and open ended
Science	62–94	3 hrs.	multiple choice and open ended

North Carolina

Exit-Level Exam: North Carolina Competency Tests (**NCCT**)

State Education Department Website: www.ncpublicschools.org/accountability/testing/policies/

Students take the NCCT in eighth grade. Students who do not pass may retake portions of the test three times each year in grades 9–11 and four times in twelfth grade in order to graduate. Passing scores in both portions of the exam are needed in order to graduate.

Test	# Questions	Time	Question Type
Reading	156	1 hr. 40 mins.	multiple choice
Math	165	1 hr. 40 mins.	multiple choice

Ohio

Exit-Level Exam: Ninth Grade Proficiency Tests and Ohio Graduation Tests (**OGT**)

State Education Department Website: www.ode.state.oh.us

Students take the Ninth Grade Proficiency Tests and must pass all of the portions to graduate. Beginning in the 2003–04 school year, students will take the exams (to be renamed OGT) in the tenth grade and are also required to pass all portions of the exam to graduate. Students have multiple opportunities to retake portions of both the Ninth Grade Proficiency Tests and the OGT.

Test	# Questions	Time	Question Type
Writing	2	2.5 hrs.	essay
Reading	49	2.5 hrs.	multiple choice and open response
Math	50	2.5 hrs.	multiple choice and open response
Science	50	2.5 hrs.	multiple choice and open response
Citizenship	52	2.5 hrs.	multiple choice and open response

South Carolina

Exit-Level Exam: Basic Skills Assessment Program (**BSAP**) and Palmetto Achievement Challenge Tests (**PACT**)

State Education Department Website: www.myscschools.com/offices/assessment

Students take the BSAP in tenth grade and must pass all portions to graduate. Students may retake portions of the test once in eleventh grade and twice in the twelfth grade. The PACT will be given to tenth graders in the spring of 2004 and will test in English language arts, mathematics, and social studies.

Test	# Questions	Time	Question Type
BSAP Reading	60	untimed	multiple choice
BSAP Math	50	untimed	multiple choice
BSAP Writing	1	untimed	essay

Texas

Exit-Level Exam: Texas Assessment of Academic Skills (**TAAS**)

State Education Department Website: www.tea.state.tx.us

Students take the TAAS in tenth grade and must pass all three portions to graduate. Students have multiple opportunities to retake each portion of the exam.

Note that students who will be in the eleventh grade in spring 2004 or later and plan to graduate in spring 2005 or later will take a new test: the Texas Assessment of Knowledge and Skills (TAKS). This will cover English language arts, mathematics, science, and social studies.

Test	# Questions	Time	Question Type
Reading	40	untimed	multiple choice/essay
Writing	48	untimed	multiple choice/essay
Mathematics	60	untimed	multiple choice

Virginia

Exit-Level Exam: Standards of Learning (**SOL**)

State Education Department Website: www.pen.k12.va.us

Students must pass two SOL end-of-course English tests and any other four SOL end-of-course tests to graduate. Students entering ninth grade in 2003–04 must pass two English tests, one math test, one history test, one science test, and one test of their choosing in order to graduate. Students have multiple opportunities to retake portions of the exam.

The SOL tests are different from other exit-level exams in that there is no specific test for each subject area. Instead, numerous tests are offered in the required disciplines (i.e., biology and physics are tests offered in the science discipline). Listed below are the discipline areas where passing test scores are required for graduation.

Discipline Area	Time	Question Type
English	untimed	multiple choice and short answer
Math	untimed	multiple choice and short answer
Science	untimed	multiple choice and short answer
History & Social Sciences	untimed	multiple choice and short answer
Fine or Practical Arts	untimed	multiple choice and short answer
Health & Physical Education		
Electives		
Student Selected Test		

Washington

Exit-Level Exam: Washington Assessment of Student Learning (**WASL-10**)

State Education Department Website: www.k12.wa.us/assessment

Students take the WASL-10 in the tenth grade and are required to pass all subject-area tests to graduate. Students have multiple opportunities to retake portions of the exam. As of the 2003–04 school year, science will also be a required test.

Test	# Questions	Time	Question Type
Reading	40	untimed	multiple choice, short answers, extended answers
Math	42	untimed	multiple choice, short answers, extended answers
Writing	2	untimed	essay
Communication	8	untimed	multiple choice, short answers, extended answers

TEST-TAKING TIPS AND STRATEGIES

How to Be Successful and Beautiful

Well, okay, so maybe reading this book won't make you beautiful, but it *will* help you to succeed on your exit-level math exam. This exam will test your knowledge of basic math principles and procedures that you've already learned in school, so you don't have to be a math wizard to do well on the test. But if you use specific test-taking tips and strategies, you *can* score high. That's where we come in; we provide you with the tools you need to be successful on your test.

And yes, you should try to get a good night's sleep before the test, try to eat a healthy breakfast, and try to stay calm and focused. Any book will tell you that. These tips are great advice for preparing for any test. But the tips and strategies we provide in this chapter are designed—and proven—to help you score higher on your state exit-level math exam. And keep in mind that the biggest key to scoring well on any standardized test is to become familiar with the test itself, including the format, types of questions, and, yes—even the directions.

Your Study Plan

The best way to prepare for your exit-level math exam is to set up a good study plan, and then stick to it. Ideally, you should start prepping a month or two before the test. We don't mean that you should devote every waking moment of the next four to eight weeks to studying, nor should you let studying interfere with your normal life. Don't sacrifice time you would normally spend on homework, at soccer practice, or hanging out with your friends. Instead, set aside just 30 minutes a day for your preparation.

> Scientists have shown that students have an easier time remembering what they've studied when they don't cram. So don't wait until the night before your exam to hit the books. Spread your studying out over a couple of weeks or months.

You should focus on one subject review in this book each week and one topic each day. Don't push yourself to cover more than one topic a day because if you cram too much in at one time, you aren't likely to remember much of it later. Read the topic carefully, and then try the practice questions that follow. If there's anything that you have trouble with, review the lesson again and don't move on to the next topic until you feel totally comfortable with what you've just studied.

Once you've finished all of the review chapters and pop quizzes, jump to the last part of the book and try the final review questions. Afterward, you'll find the correct answers, but even more important, you'll find detailed answer explanations. The most important step in the study plan process is actually following the plan. Don't get so relaxed (or paralyzed by panic) about the test that you don't study every night. And don't fall into the trap of thinking that you can spend 4 hours on Sunday night working on the exercises instead of doing a little bit every day. It's much more effective to study for shorter periods every day than to do long sessions every now and then. Believe us, we know about these things.

The Night before Your Test

It's probably obvious that you shouldn't go out partying the night before the exam and come home an hour before you have to leave for school. But we're telling you not to do that anyway. On the other hand, you shouldn't spend the night before the test frantically cramming. In fact, cramming may actually hurt your performance on the test by causing anxiety and erasing some of the other stuff in your short-term memory (like what time the test starts).

A better way to use your time the night before the test is to do something that relaxes you—something that makes you laugh is even better. Rent a funny movie, watch it, and go to bed at a decent time. You'll wake up in a better mood and will be set to conquer your exit-level math test.

Your Test-Day Strategy

Now for the obvious stuff you have probably heard before when you were about to take a big test. Here's the condensed version:

- Get up with plenty of time to get ready.
- Eat a good breakfast and stick to your normal routine as much as possible.
- If you have time, do a little stretching to relax your body.
- Try to get to the test site early so you don't have to rush.
- Avoid sitting near a window or door so you are not distracted.

> Bring a watch (without an alarm) to your exam. Lay it on the desk next to your test booklet, so you can keep an eye on the time.

Many test takers waste precious time by losing their place on the answer sheet. To avoid having this happen to you, place your test booklet on top of the answer sheet and use it as a placeholder. Keep the top of the booklet just below the next answer space. That way, you won't have to stop working to figure out where the next answer gets marked. Also, if you decide to skip a question, make sure you leave it blank on your answer sheet, or lightly circle it so you'll remember to come back to it later. Before you hand in your exam, however, be sure to completely erase anything you circle on the answer sheet. The machine might misread a stray or forgotten mark as a wrong answer.

Get the point? Then let's move on to the tips and strategies in the rest of the chapter.

General Test Info

Although the emphasis on each area of math on the exit-level math tests may vary from state to state, we cover every possible area that will appear on your test. Note that the test consists of multiple-choice questions, and some questions also ask you to write short answers. The next few pages give you tips on reading and understanding the test directions, pacing yourself, and when to use or not to use a calculator.

North, South, and Other Directions

The directions for most exit-level math examinations are pretty much the same. By having an understanding of what the directions are and what may be asked of you, you will be one step ahead of the game. The directions on your state's exit-level math test may resemble the following:

> **Directions:** Solve each problem below and mark the oval representing the correct answer on your answer sheet.
>
> **Directions:** Use the space in your test book to do your work on the multiple-choice and grid-in response questions, but be sure to put your answers in the answer book.
>
> **Directions:** Which algebraic equation corresponds to the problem below?
>
> **Directions:** Which inequality describes the interval graphed on the number line above?
>
> **Directions:** Diagrams that accompany problems may or may not be drawn to scale. Unless otherwise indicated, you may assume that all figures shown lie in a plane and that lines that appear straight are straight. Mark the oval representing the correct answer on your answer sheet.

Also, be on the lookout for little words that make a huge difference in what a question is really asking. Consider the following three words: *which, following*, and *true.* Now examine these three questions:

1. Which of the following *may be* true?
2. Which of the following *must be* true?
3. Which of the following *may not be* true?

The words *may, must,* and *may not* have different meanings. As we mentioned, be sure to read all directions and questions so you know what is required for the answer. The directions give you the information that you need to determine what is being asked in each question.

> You should reread the directions carefully so you understand them—you'd be surprised at the number of top students who read the directions quickly, misunderstand one point, and get even the easiest question wrong.

Slow and Steady Wins the Race

Because you have a limited amount of time to complete the exam, pace yourself. Don't spend too much time on any one problem, especially the beginning ones. You can use the test booklet itself as scratch paper to work out your calculations.

Timing is critical. Say you have 60 minutes to answer approximately 60 questions. That's one minute per question. Timing shouldn't be a problem since you should be able to answer many questions in just 15 or 30 seconds. That should leave more than enough time for you to spend on the more involved questions, for which you might need 2 or 3 minutes.

According to My Calculations . . .

Some state exit exams allow you to use calculators on certain sections of the test, while others will not. It does not matter what your calculator can do or how dexterous you are at pushing buttons. The purpose of the exam is to test your mathematical reasoning and knowledge of the correct formulas. Remember that the actual mathematical computations are usually easy, and this book gives you the advice you need to work through them.

If a calculator is permitted and you decide to use one, here are some tips:

- If you are in a tricky computation that uses big numbers and calls for many successive computations on your calculator, stop and begin again with a clear mind. You're probably overlooking a simple shortcut or formula that you can find in this book that would make the calculation unnecessary.

- You may be susceptible to certain errors with a calculator, such as hitting the wrong key, hitting the right key twice, and jamming keys. So make sure you don't rush and that you press the buttons with accuracy. If you use a calculator, you will not have a visible paper trail that you can go back and retrace with your eyes in case of a silly error.
- Use a calculator if you must (if it is permitted), but don't rely upon it. Calculators work best for arithmetic calculations, square roots, and percentages. If you must use one, use it for those calculations.
- Be sure to use a calculator with which you're familiar. Don't decide to break in a new one on test day.
- Most important—if you use a calculator, make sure you put a fresh battery into it the night before the test.

What's *Really* on the Math Assessment Test?

OK. Here are the basics. The exit-level math assessment tests your knowledge of specific math facts, formulas, techniques, and methods and your ability to apply that knowledge by solving problems. For you to succeed on this exam, you need to know the rules and procedures of math and be able to apply those rules to nonroutine, or real-world, situations. You can't play a game if you don't know the rules. The purpose of this book is to make you more comfortable with your exam. The more you know about what is covered, the better armed you will be.

> You can't play a game if you don't know the rules.

The following specific topics are covered in this book to make sure you are completely prepared for your exit-level math test:

- **Numerical concepts:** addition, subtraction, multiplication, division, working with fractions and decimals, figuring out averages, and more
- **Pre-algebra, elementary and intermediate algebra:** basic algebraic operations, including solving equations, using negative numbers and square roots, and factoring
- **Coordinate, plane, and some solid geometry:** properties of triangles, circles, and quadrilaterals and procedures such as determining the areas and volumes of simple figures

- **Trigonometry**: solving trigonometric equations, graphing functions, and understanding the values and properties of functions
- **Measurement**: differentiating among units of distance, weight, and capacity and working with traditional and metric quantities.
- **Interpreting and displaying data**: reading and drawing line, bar, and circle graphs and histograms

The bulk of most exit-level math tests consists of multiple-choice questions. There are, however, some questions that will require you to write in a short answer and some that test your in-depth grasp of a subject by requiring you to write a paragraph or construct a table or a graph. The different problem types include:

- Straight arithmetic problems
- Word problems
- Problems in reading and interpreting graphs and charts
- Algebra problems
- Geometry problems with and without diagrams
- Trigonometry problems

Tips to Ace the Test

Here are some specific tips to help you ace your exit-level math test. Once you understand these tips and the reasoning behind them, you will be able to apply them to the questions on your test.

Read Between the Lines

It's important to read each question fully and make sure you know what's *really* being asked. Most problems include a series of interrelated facts. The kinds of facts vary depending on the kind of question.

Here's an example:

> Hailee has a block of wood in the form of a rectangular solid that is 14 inches long with a square base that's 6 inches on each side. A right circular cylinder is drilled out of the block, as shown below. What is the volume of the block remaining, to the nearest cubic inch?

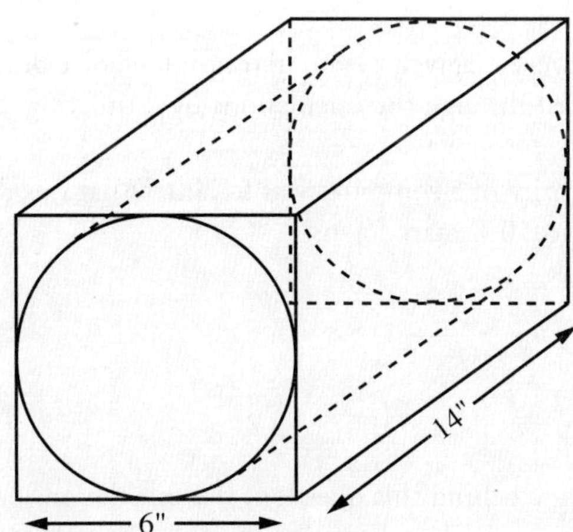

(A) 54
(B) 108
(C) 396
(D) 485

The key to solving a problem like this is to make sure you know which fact is being asked about and what form the answer should take. If you skim the question hastily, you might assume that you are being asked something different from what the test makers want you to focus on. In the above problem, instead of asking the obvious question about the volume of either the cylinder or the rectangular block for which you have figures, they have asked about the volume of the odd-shaped region that is the difference between the cylinder and the block. You have to subtract; therefore, the correct answer is (B).

It is important to read and understand exactly what is needed for the correct answer. A common error is to give the answer in terms of the wrong unit. For example, the answer you calculate is 2 quarts. However, because the question asked for gallons, the correct answer is really ½ (4 quarts = 1 gallon). One way to avoid this type of error is to begin the problem by converting the units into the units demanded by the answer. In other words, if you see that the answers are all stated in terms of square feet, while the numbers in the problem are in square yards, change them to square feet before beginning your work. (1 square yard equals 9 square feet.)

When it comes to graph problems, spend 30 seconds "reading" or analyzing the graph(s) before even looking at the questions. Look at the structural features, labels, and basic content. This will help you find the relevant information and separate it from the mass of other information in which it is embedded. You can always return to the graph later for the details.

Your Best Estimate

Believe it or not, the answers are given to you in multiple-choice questions! With that in mind, you can often speed through the calculations by estimating. Here's an example:

> The original price of a computer was $1200. What was the price of the computer after two 10% markdowns?
>
> (A) $960
> (B) $972
> (C) $980
> (D) $1072

If you understand the logic behind this question, the calculations aren't difficult. If you are unsure, check the review in Chapter 3. You can figure out the answer in two steps:

1. Subtract 10 percent from the original cost of $1,200. This gives you $1,200 – $120 = $1,080.
2. Subtract 10 percent of this new price of $1,080. This gives you $1,080 – $108 = $972.

Using either your calculator or pencil and paper, the math isn't hard.

However, if you had only minutes left in which to do five more math problems, estimating would be a more useful strategy. Instead of subtracting 10 percent twice in two steps, you could simply subtract 20 percent from $1,200 at once in your head, which gives you $960. Since you know the answer must be higher than that, you can quickly eliminate choice (A). Then do the first step: Mentally subtract 10 percent from the original cost

($1200 – 100 = 1100 – 20), giving you $1080. You can eliminate choice (D), as $1072 is too close to $1080 (the second 10 percent hasn't been subtracted yet). Ten percent of $1080 is $108, close enough to a hundred that you could subtract a hundred from $1080 for an estimate of $980. Because the actual answer will be lower, and you've already eliminated $960 as too low, the answer must be $972. So, the correct answer is (B).

> Estimating isn't necessary on all test items. In some cases, the numbers used are so few and so simple that you do not need to estimate.

You should never (and we mean *never)* estimate when the choices are very close together. For example, if your five choices are 270, 272, 275, 278, and 282, you're going to need a precise answer that only a full calculation can give. On the other hand, if your five choices are 110, 292, 348, 512, and 721, you can estimate. Here, you have more than enough room for the "error" that's built into estimating. Though it's not always the best route to a solution, estimating is a handy method to use when time is short.

Rounding numbers to the nearest whole can sometimes save you valuable time, and it's a practice that goes hand-in-hand with estimating. Once again, if the answer choices are bunched close together, or precise to the hundredths place, rounding isn't a useful technique. But, in other situations, rounding can help you find the answer quickly, so you can move on.

The Elimination Game

Remember that one of the answer choices given for each test question has to be right. If you have no idea about how to solve a problem, try one answer choice and work backward. If it doesn't lead you to the correct answer, it can at least alert you to one or two that can be eliminated. In other words, eliminate the answer choices that are incorrect. Here's a very simple example:

> Margaret had a test average of 88% in math after having taken 4 exams. What grade would she need to score on her next exam to bring her test average to 90%?
>
> (A) 92
>
> (B) 94
>
> (C) 96
>
> (D) 98

Because in many cases answers are put in numerical order, choices (B) and (C) are always the middle answers and the most logical ones to use if you're trying out possibilities. For an average of 88 on four exams, Margaret must have a total of $4 \times 88 = 352$. Adding 96 to 352 gives 448, and dividing that by 5 gives 89.6, which means it isn't high enough. By trying one number, you eliminated choices (A), (B), and (C). You can now try choice (D) if you have time; if you have no time, just choose it—it has to be right, since the others are all wrong—and move on to the next question. And yes, the correct answer is (D).

English to Math Translations

If word problems are your downfall—if your eyes start to glaze at the mere mention of planes heading east, gallons of paint being used up, or workers working together at two different speeds—translate the unfamiliar into the familiar. Turn the words into numbers and build an equation to find the answer you want.

Surprisingly, the math in most word problems is not difficult. You might have a few fractions to multiply or divide or a simple equation to solve, but the computations will usually be easy. Turning the words into numbers is usually the most difficult part. How do you do that? Check out these three tips; you're gonna love them:

- **What you don't know is *x*.** If the question asks, "What fraction of the entire job will be completed after 3 hours?" begin writing your equation with $x =$, where x represents that fraction of the job. On the other hand, if the question asks, "How many hours will it take to do $\frac{3}{7}$ of the entire job?" then x represents the hours of work needed. This way, after you've solved the equation, you'll automatically have your answer with no further conversions needed. Even better—instead of x, use j for the job and t for the time. These hints are easier to remember and help you focus on what you're really looking for.

- **Break each phrase into a numerical expression.** Divide the problem into its smallest parts. If the part has a known number (such as *3 gallons of paint*), use the number 3. If the part doesn't have a known number (*how many gallons*), give it a letter *g*.
- **Create a formula that describes the relationships of the parts.** The following example shows you how easy it is to create a formula to solve a question:

> Paul is eight years older than Sarah. Four years ago, Sarah was half the age Paul is now. How old is Sarah now?

First, determine what you are looking for—you are looking for Sarah's age *now*. So make a rough relationship, using S for Sarah's age now as the unknown for which we will solve. We'll also let P stand for Paul's age now. Now, create a couple of simple equations that state in symbols and numbers what the sentences in the problem say.

"Paul is eight years older than Sarah" becomes: $P = S + 8$.

This can also be written as $P - 8 = S$, since, if Paul is 8 years older than Sarah, Sarah must be 8 years younger than Paul. We'll use the second equation, since it fits better into the scheme of things.

Now look at the second sentence in the problem: "Four years ago, Sarah was half the age Paul is now." Four years ago, Sarah's age was $S - 4$ and that "was" (which means equals) half of Paul's age now. This is: $\frac{1}{2}P$ or $\frac{P}{2}$.

Taken all together, that means: $S - 4 = \frac{P}{2}$.

To get rid of the fraction, multiply this equation through by 2. Note that multiplying both sides of an equation by the same quantity does not change its meaning (value).

$$2\left(S - 4 = \frac{P}{2}\right)$$

$$2S - 8 = P$$

Now you can solve for S by substituting the expression $2S - 8$ for P in the first equation. Remember the first equation? ($P = S + 8$ or $P - 8 = S$).

$P - 8 = S$	
$(2S - 8) - 8 = S$	Substitute $(2S - 8)$ for P.
$2S - 16 = S$	Combine the –8's.
$-16 = -S$	Subtract $2S$ from both sides.
$16 = S$	Multiply by –1
$S = 16$	Flip (for appearances only).

So Sarah's age today is 16 (Paul's is 24, since $P = S + 8$; $P = 16 + 8 = 24$).

Do word problems *still* make you feel like a visitor to a strange land where you don't speak the language? Have no fear. We created a concise English to Math Dictionary to help you translate key phrases.

> The most difficult element of a word problem is trying to translate the relationships into mathematical procedures.

The list includes commonly used words and expressions that appear in many word problems and gives a translation of what they mean in the language of mathematical operations. Try to learn as much of the list as possible. Many of the terms, such as *take away*, are already associated with subtraction, so there actually won't be too many "foreign words" you need to translate.

ENGLISH TO MATH DICTIONARY

Word or Phrase	Mathematical Operation
added to	addition
along with	addition
amounts to	equals
and	addition
by	multiplication
decreased by	subtraction
difference	subtraction
divided by	division
each	multiplication
fewer than	subtraction
fraction	division
greater than	addition
in addition to	addition
increased by	addition
is	equals
is the same as	equals
larger than	addition
less than	subtraction
more than	addition

of	multiplication
part of	division
per	multiplication
piece	division
portion	division
product	multiplication
reduced by	subtraction
smaller than	subtraction
take away	subtraction
times	multiplication
with	addition
without	subtraction

Stepping Stones

Diagrams, especially for geometry problems, are there for a reason. They are filled with clues to the solution. You can usually leap from what you know—the facts you are given—to what you need to know simply by using the parts of the diagram as "stepping stones." Here's an example:

> In the diagram below, $AB = 3$, $AD = 4$, and $BC = 12$. What is the perimeter of the quadrilateral?

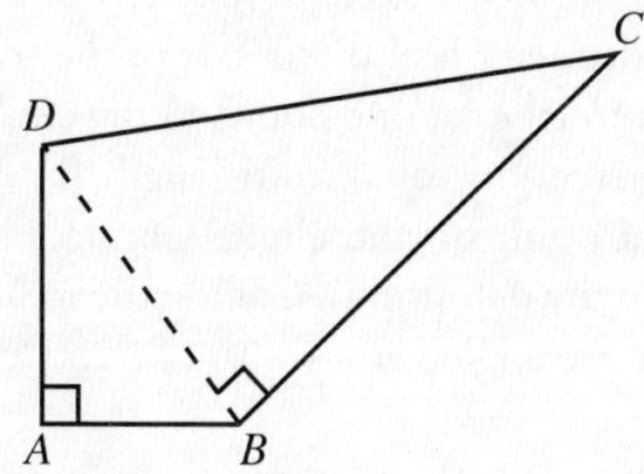

(A) 32
(B) 30
(C) 28
(D) 26

Solving a geometry problem like this one is a matter of working methodically. Just fill in the blank parts of the diagram using what you can deduce from the information you're given. (Use your pencil to mark the new facts right in the question booklet.) You'll eventually work your way to the fact about which you're being asked.

Here's how you'd apply that method to the example. This problem uses two well-known right triangles. We see that, in triangle *ABD*, one leg is 3 and one is 4, which makes *BD* = 5 (the most famous of the "Pythagorean triples," 3 – 4 – 5). This tells us that triangle *BDC* is 5 – 12 – 13 (another famous Pythagorean triple). Thus, *CD* is 13, and the entire perimeter is 3 + 4 + 12 + 13 = 32. So the correct answer is (A).

If you come across a question that does not include a diagram, draw one and create your own stepping stones.

> You don't need to be named Leonardo in order to sketch a diagram that will be clear enough to see the answer right away.

Here's an example:

One side of a rectangle with an area of 18 square inches is the diameter of a circle. The opposite side is tangent to the circle. What is the length of the circle's circumference?

(A) 2π
(B) 6π
(C) 9π
(D) 12π

Without a diagram, this is a difficult problem. With one, it's very easy. Just use the margin of your test booklet to quickly sketch a circle. Put a straight line through the center for the diameter. The diameter is also one side of the rectangle. The opposite side of the rectangle is tangent (or touches at one point) to the circle, so draw that side of the rectangle parallel to the diameter and equal to its length (by definition of being a rectangle) and passing through a point on the circle. Connect the "missing sides" of the rectangle at right angles (again, by definition). Calling the radius of the circle *r*, we see in the following picture that the rectangle has a width of *r* and a length of 2*r*.

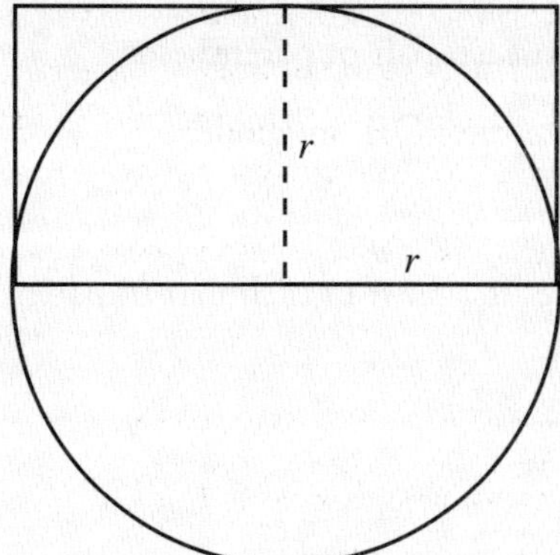

The area of the rectangle is $2r^2 = 18$ (remember the area given by the problem), thus, $r^2 = 9$ and $r = 3$. The circumference of the circle is $2\pi r = 6\pi$. The correct answer is (B).

Word Tricks

Undoubtedly, you have learned many mnemonic (memory) tricks for recalling and/or retaining certain mathematical relationships and facts. Sohcahtoa, of course, is not the name of a native American tribe, but is, rather, the way to remember the basic trigonometric functions of either non-90° angle in a right triangle:

Sine = **o**pposite over **h**ypotenuse, **c**osine = **a**djacent over **h**ypotenuse, and **t**angent = **o**pposite over **a**djacent.

Mrs. Jones, or whoever your eighth grade math teacher was, didn't spend hours drilling that into your head in order to find oil. It was meant to take root for occasions just like this test. The same is true of FOO:

FOO = **F**undamental **O**rder of **O**perations

You may remember FOO as PEMDAS, or **P**lease **E**xcuse **M**y **D**ear **A**unt **S**ally. That stands for:

Parentheses, **E**xponents, **M**ultiplication and **D**ivision, **A**ddition, and **S**ubtraction.

The operations of Parentheses, Exponents, Multiplication, Division, Addition, and Subtraction should be carried out in that order reading from left to right. There will be more on this in Chapter 3.

Another word trick is the FOIL method. No—this was not created by Reynolds Wrap™. It stands for:

First: Multiply the first term in each pair of parentheses.

Outer: Multiply the outer term in each pair of parentheses.

Inner: Multiply the inner term in each pair of parentheses.

Last: Multiply the last term in each pair of parentheses.

Here's an example to illustrate the FOIL method:

$(2 + 6x)(4 + 2x)$

We'll start by multiplying the first term in each pair of parentheses.

$2 \times 4 = 8$

Now multiply the outer terms:

$2 \times 2x = 4x$

And the inners:

$6x \times 4 = 24x$

And finally the last terms:

$6x \times 2x = 12x^2$

Now add them all together:

$8 + 4x + 24x + 12x^2$

The final step is to combine the like terms:

$8 + 28x + 12x^2$

To successfully use the FOIL method, each pair of parentheses must have the same number of terms. And that about wraps up the FOIL method!

Strategy Roundup

Here's a short version of the strategies given in this chapter, along with a few other miscellaneous tips, arranged in a handy list of Do's and Don'ts. After you understand each point and the reasoning behind it, memorizing the boldface sentence should jog your memory—whether you're working on the exercises in the last chapters of this book or the actual exit-level math test itself.

Do's:

- **Read Between the Lines.** Read carefully and make sure you know what's being asked. Also, make sure you know what particular form the answer should take. For example, is the answer supposed to be a number or coordinates for a point on a graph? Is the answer supposed to be a choice that *may be* true, *must be* true, or *may not* be true? Know what's being asked. If, for example, a problem gives you information in terms of square feet but asks for an answer in terms of square yards, it will be easier to solve the problem if you first change all the units into square yards.

Also, be sure to "read" a graph before looking at the questions. Think of this as skimming a reading passage before beginning to work. Look at the structure of the graph (the labels on the axes, the units of measurement, and any information in the key). This is often more important than the data itself.

- **Your Best Estimate.** It's not always necessary to work with exact numbers to solve math problems. Round off and save time. When should you round off? You should round off when the five choices are sufficiently far apart. Answers that are close together require more precise calculation.
- **The Elimination Game.** If you're not sure what to do, and it's a multiple-choice question (which most of them are), choose an answer and plug it into the question. This will often lead you to the right answer more quickly. Which answer should you choose? Start with choice (B) or (C). Answers are in size order, so choices (B) and (C) will always be the middle values. If choice (B) or (C) doesn't work, you might sometimes also be able to tell whether the answer is going to be larger or smaller, given the information in the problem. That will show you which remaining answer to try next.
- **English to Math Translations.** Reduce word problems into more easily understood equations. Let x be that for which you want to solve (time to complete a job, distance traveled, etc.). Then turn every element of the problem into a numerical expression. After you have all the numbers and symbols, it's usually easier to see how you should build the equation that will solve the problem.
- **Stepping Stones.** Diagrams, especially for geometry problems, are filled with clues to the solution. Examine every diagram carefully. It's there for a reason. If there's no diagram, draw one of your own. It can make the solution immediately apparent.

Don'ts:

- **Don't get paralyzed by lengthy calculations.** Most exit-level math questions do not require complicated calculations. If you understand the structure of the problem, the solution is usually evident. So if you're overwhelmed with figuring, stop and move on to the next question.

- **Don't get involved with large numbers.** They're difficult to work with and time-consuming. When very large numbers are given in a problem, don't assume they're part of the needed calculation. Because few problems require a calculator, if you're calculating large numbers, you're probably overlooking the simple principle that will solve the problem.
- **Don't over-rely on your calculator.** Few high stakes math problems require a calculator. Try to limit calculator use to basic arithmetic, percentages, and square roots.
- **Don't bring a new calculator to the test.** Every calculator operates just a bit differently with different keys for different functions. You don't have time during the test to learn how a new calculator works. If you must use a calculator, bring one you're familiar with—and make sure it has fresh batteries.
- **Don't get fooled by trick questions.** Often a question is like a riddle; it prompts an obvious answer, but the obvious answer is wrong. Other times, the answer apparently is impossible to solve, such as the area of an irregular shape. What are you overlooking? In other words, certain questions ask you to "think outside the box."
- **Don't expect trick questions early in the test.** Most tests are usually ordered in complexity from easy to difficult, the first third of the test may have simple questions, with correspondingly simple answers. And besides, there aren't really trick questions on the test since everything you need to know to answer a question will be provided for you right there in the test booklet.
- **Don't assume a guess is right just because it's one of the answers.** Although rounding off and estimating are useful, outright guessing cannot replace calculation. Often, the test choices include the most common student errors, so just because "your" answer is listed doesn't mean it's right. Work it out. Don't guess answers until you're running out of time.

And remember, taking a test that has as much riding on it as your high school diploma can be overwhelming. But you've already taken the first step toward success—you're reading this book. So get some paper and a pen or pencil, turn off the television, and let's get started.

Good luck!

PART II

MATH REVIEW

REVIEWING ARITHMETIC, OR WE'RE COUNTING ON YOU!

The early sections of this review should pass by quickly, but don't be discouraged if you're puzzled by any of the topics. You've learned an incredible amount of math in your long school history; it wouldn't be surprising if you forgot a concept or two over the years.

In the sections below, we're going to use letters to stand for numbers, just as it is done in algebra. That doesn't mean that it is algebra. We are doing it instead of constantly stating and restating "This rule applies to any number, or any group of numbers. Here it is using 2, here it is using 5, here it is using –15." Rather, if you'd like to prove to yourself that it works, you try substituting the 2, 5, –15, or any other number you want. There is only one rule that you must follow:

> Within a single mathematical statement, once the value of *a* is established, *a* must have the same value each time it appears. The same applies to *b, c,* or any letter holding the place of a number.

MATH

Let's Review the Basics

Even though we are starting with basics, there's a good chance that there are a few tips that you may not know about. So try not to read this section too quickly.

You Have an Absolute Value

The *absolute value* of any number N is symbolized by $|N|$ and is simply the number without its sign. Thus, $|8| = 8$, $|-7| = 7$, and $|0| = 0$. It can also be thought of as the distance of the number from zero. The further you get from zero, the larger the absolute value. So numbers far to the left are negative numbers with large absolute values.

When a number line is shown on your exit-level math test, you can safely assume that the line is drawn to scale and that any numbers that fall between the markings are at appropriate locations. Thus, 2.5 is halfway between 2 and 3, and –0.4 is four tenths of the way from 0 to –1. However, always check the scale because the "tick marks" don't have to be at unit intervals. Here's an example:

> On the number line shown below, where is the number that is less than D and half as far from D as D is from G?

```
---+-------+-------+-------+-------+-------+-------+-------+-------+---
   A       B       C       D       E       F       G       H       I
```

To solve this, first note that any number less than D must lie to the left of D.

Get it? Left = less!

The distance from D to G is 3 units. Thus, the point we want must be $1\frac{1}{2}$ units to the left of D—that is, halfway between B and C.

Let's try one more to make sure you understand.

> On the number line shown below, which point corresponds to the number 2.27?

```
---+-----+-----+-----+-----+-----+-----+-----+-----+-----+-----+---
  2.2    A     B     C     D     E     F     G     H     I    2.3
```

Since the labeled end points are 2.2 and 2.3, the ten intervals in between must each be one tenth of the difference. Hence, the tick marks must represent hundredths. That is, A = 2.21, B = 2.22, and so on. Thus, we know that G = 2.27.

FOO on the Laws of Arithmetic

That really should have said "FOO and the laws of arithmetic," but we couldn't let the opportunity for a joke go by. What is FOO? Think back to the math you learned in grammar school. If that's too far in the past to remember, think back to the memory tricks listed in Chapter 2. It is the Fundamental Order of Operations.

In carrying out arithmetic or algebraic operations, you should use this famous memory device to figure out which operation to perform first, next, etc. to recall the correct order of operations: Please Excuse My Dear Aunt Sally. The operations of Parentheses, Exponents, Multiplication, Division, Addition, and Subtraction should be carried out in that order reading from left to right.

Parentheses are used to create one number out of many. Always calculate the number in parentheses first. Thus, $16 - 3 \times 4 = 16 - 12 = 4$, because we normally multiply before adding.

However, if we want the number $16 - 3$ to be multiplied by 4, we must write it this way:

$$(16 - 3) \times 4 = 13 \times 4 = 52.$$

It's the Law

The basic laws of arithmetic were originally defined for whole numbers, but they carry over to all numbers. You should know all of them from past experience, but here's a reminder in case you need it. They are:

- **The commutative law.** It doesn't matter in which order you add or multiply two numbers. That is:

$$a + b = b + a$$

$$ab = ba$$

- **The associative law (or the regrouping law).** It doesn't matter how you group the numbers when you add or multiply more than two numbers. That is:

$$a + (b + c) = (a + b) + c$$

$$a(bc) = (ab)c$$

- **The distributive law.** This is for multiplication over addition. It means you can add first and then multiply, or multiply each term in the sum by the same amount and then add the two products (the answer in a multiplication). Either way, the result is the same. The law can be represented as follows:

$$a(b + c) = ab + ac$$

- **The properties of zero and one.** Zero times any number is zero. Zero added to any number leaves the number unchanged. One times any number leaves the number unchanged.
- **The additive opposite.** For every number n, there is a number $-n$ such that $n + (-n) = 0$. This number is the additive opposite.
- **The multiplicative inverse.** For every number n, except 0, there is a number $\frac{1}{n}$ such that $\left(\frac{1}{n}\right)(n) = 1$. Division by n is the same as multiplication by $\frac{1}{n}$, and division by zero is never allowed.
- **The closure property.** The set of whole numbers is closed for the operations of addition, multiplication, and subtraction. That means if you perform any of those operations on whole numbers, the result will be a whole number. It does not, however, apply to division since one divided by two gives one-half—not a whole number.

> It is very important to know that if the product of several numbers is zero, at least one of the numbers must be zero.

Here's an example of a two-part question:

(a) What is the value of $\frac{3+B}{4\times 3-3B}$ if $B = 3$?

(b) What value is impossible for B?

Here's the answer, broken down for each question. (a) The fraction bar in a fraction acts as a "grouping symbol," like parentheses, meaning we should calculate the numerator and denominator separately. That is, we should read this fraction as $(3 + B) \div (4 \times 3 - 3 \times B)$. When $B = 3$, the numerator is $3 + 3 = 6$, and the denominator is $12 - 3 \times 3 = 12 - 9 = 3$. Therefore, the fraction is $\frac{6}{3} = 2$. (b) Since we cannot divide by zero, we cannot let $4 \times 3 - 3 \times B = 0$. But in order for this expression to equal zero, $4 \times 3 = 3 \times B$. By the commutative law, $B = 4$. The only value that B cannot have is 4.

Divisibility Rules—It Does!

A *factor* or *divisor* of a whole number is a number that divides evenly into the given number, leaving no remainder. For example, the divisors of 24 are 1, 2, 3, 4, 6, 8, 12, and 24 itself.

A *proper divisor* is any divisor except the number itself. Thus, the proper divisors of 24 are 1, 2, 3, 4, 6, 8, and 12. If you want to know whether k is a divisor of n, try to divide k into n and see whether there is any remainder. If the remainder is zero, then n is divisible by k.

There are several useful rules for testing for divisibility by certain small numbers. These are summarized in the table below.

RULES FOR TESTING DIVISIBILITY

Number	Divides into a Number N if. . .
2	N is even; that is, it ends in 2, 4, 6, 8, or 0.
3	The sum of the digits of N is divisible by 3.
4	The last two digits form a number divisible by 4.
5	The number ends in 5 or 0.
6	The number is divisible by 2 and 3.
8	The last three digits form a number divisible by 8.
9	The sum of the digits of N is divisible by 9.
0	The number ends in 0.

Ready to prove that the rules listed above really work? Then try the following example:

> Consider the number 7,380. How many numbers in the table above do not divide evenly into 7,380?

7,380 is divisible by all the numbers in the table except 8. Do you see why? To start with, 7,380 is divisible by 10 and 5 because it ends in 0. It is divisible by 2 because it is even and by 4 because 80 is divisible by 4. However, it is not divisible by 8 because 380 isn't. In addition, the sum of its digits is 18, which is divisible both by 3 and by 9. Since it is divisible by both 2 and 3, it is also divisible by 6.

Let's try another example:

> Which number in the following list is divisible by 3, 4, and 5, but not by 9?
>
> (A) 15,840
> (B) 20,085
> (C) 23,096
> (D) 53,700
> (E) 79,130

The easiest thing to look for is divisibility by 5. Just ask yourself, "Does the number end in 5 or 0?" By inspection, we can eliminate 23,096, which ends in 6. We want the number to be divisible by 4, which means it must be even and its last two digits must form a number divisible by 4. That knocks out the number ending in 5 (which is odd), as well as 79,130, because 30 is not divisible by 4.

This leaves 15,840 and 53,700. The digits of 15,840 add up to 18, while those of 53,700 total 15. Both are divisible by 3, but 15,840 is also divisible by 9. Therefore, only 53,700 meets all the conditions.

It's almost like watching a magician do tricks. This math stuff can really be fun. What's that? You're not convinced? Well, maybe you need to check out a few more things.

Divide and Conquer

Before you divide, er—dive, right into division, you have to know or remember the following terms: The number being divided is called the dividend. The number that you are dividing by is called the divisor. The answer in division is called the quotient. If the quotient is not an integer (the dividend doesn't divide exactly), you have a remainder.

Divisibility follows certain rules with respect to addition, subtraction, and multiplication. If you add or subtract two numbers that are both divisible by some number k, then the new number formed will also be divisible by k. So, 28 and 16 are both divisible by 4. If you take their sum, 44, or their difference, 12, they are also divisible by 4.

If you multiply two numbers together, any number that divides either one also divides the product. Thus, if j divides M and k divides N, then jk divides MN, and both j and k divide MN.

If two numbers being multiplied have a common divisor, then the product is divisible by the square of that number. Thus, $21 \times 15 = 315$ is divisible by 7, because 7 divides 21, and by 5, because 5 divides 15. It is also divisible by $35 = 5 \times 7$, and by 9, because $9 = 3^2$ and 3 divides both 21 and 15.

Let's try an example:

If a and b are whole numbers, and $3a = 2b$, which of the following must be true?

(A) a is divisible by 2, and b is divisible by 3.
(B) a and b are both divisible by 2.
(C) a and b are both divisible by 3.
(D) a is divisible by 3, and b is divisible by 2.

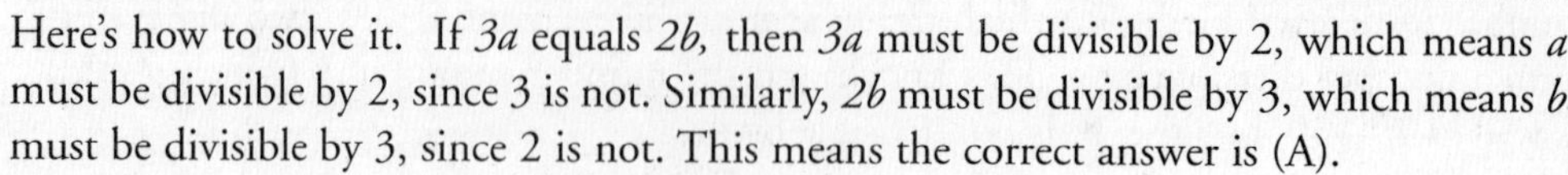

Here's how to solve it. If *3a* equals *2b,* then *3a* must be divisible by 2, which means *a* must be divisible by 2, since 3 is not. Similarly, *2b* must be divisible by 3, which means *b* must be divisible by 3, since 2 is not. This means the correct answer is (A).

Be especially aware of the divisibility properties of even and odd numbers:

Even numbers are those that are divisible by 2: 0, 2, 4, 6, . . .

Odd numbers are not divisible by 2: 1, 3, 5, 7, . . .

Odds and Evens Basics

What can be divided evenly by 2 and have no remainders or decimals? Give up? It's an even integer. Now you are probably wondering what all the other integers are; they are odd numbers.

Here are a few rules for adding, subtracting, and multiplying odd and even numbers:

- If you add or subtract two even numbers, the result is even.

  $4 + 6 = 10$ $\qquad$ $8 - 2 = 6$

- If you add or subtract two odd numbers, the result is even.

  $5 + 3 = 8$ $\qquad$ $7 - 3 = 4$

- Only when you add or subtract an odd and an even number is the result odd.

  $4 + 6 = 10$ (even) $\qquad$ $7 - 3 = 4$ (even)
  But $4 + 3 = 7$ (odd)

- When you multiply any whole number by an even number, the result is even.

  $2 \times 4 = 8$ $\qquad$ $6 \times 5 = 30$

- Only when you multiply two odd numbers will the result be odd.

  $(4)(6) = 24$ (even) $\qquad$ $(4)(7) = 28$ (even)
  But $(3)(7) = 21$ (odd)

You may find it strange, but remember to think of zero as an even number. After all, it comes between two odd numbers, just like every other even number: (–1, 0, 1).

Want to see if these rules really work? Give it a try:

If $3x + 4y$ is an odd number, is x odd or even, or is it impossible to tell?

Ready for the answer? $4y$ must be even, so for the sum of $3x$ and $4y$ to be odd, $3x$ must be odd as well. Since 3 is odd, $3x$ will be odd only if x is odd. Therefore, x is odd.

How about this one?

If $121 - 5k$ is divisible by 3, may k be odd?

Don't rush to read the solution. Think about it first. Done thinking? The fact that a number is divisible by 3 does not make it odd. (Think of 6 or 12) Therefore, $121 - 5k$ could be odd or even. It will be odd when k is even and even when k is odd. (Do you see why?) So, k could be odd or even. For example, if $k = 2$, $121 - 5k = 111$, which is divisible by 3, and if $k = 5$, $121 - 5k = 96$, which is divisible by 3.

Fractions Are Not Beyond Comparison

Two fractions $\frac{a}{b}$ and $\frac{c}{d}$ are defined to be equal if $ad = bc$. For example, $\frac{3}{4} = \frac{9}{12}$ because $(3)(12) = (4)(9)$. This definition uses the process known as *cross-multiplication* and is very useful in solving algebraic equations involving fractions. However, for working with numbers, the most important thing to remember is that multiplying the numerator and denominator of a fraction by the same number (other than zero) results in a fraction equal in value to the original fraction. So, by multiplying the top and the bottom of $\frac{3}{4}$ by 3, we have $\frac{3}{4} = \frac{(3)(3)}{(3)(4)} = \frac{9}{12}$.

Similarly, dividing the numerator and denominator of a fraction by the same number (other than zero) results in a fraction equal in value to the original fraction. It is common to divide through the top and the bottom of the fraction by the greatest common factor of both the numerator and denominator to reduce the fraction to lowest terms. That means that, by dividing the top and the bottom of $\frac{15}{25}$ by 5, we have $\frac{15}{25} = \frac{15 \div 5}{25 \div 5} = \frac{3}{5}$.

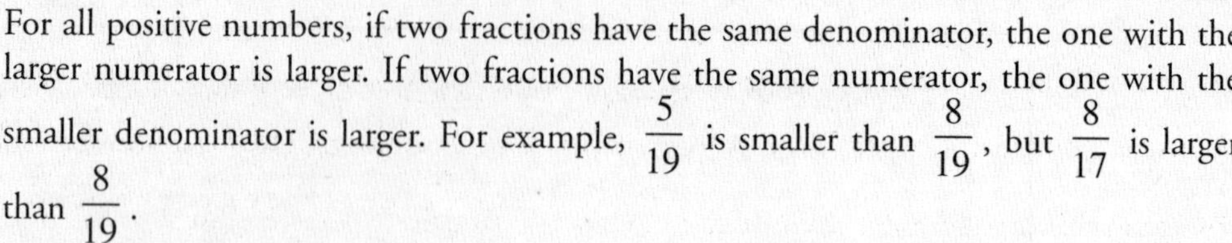

For all positive numbers, if two fractions have the same denominator, the one with the larger numerator is larger. If two fractions have the same numerator, the one with the smaller denominator is larger. For example, $\frac{5}{19}$ is smaller than $\frac{8}{19}$, but $\frac{8}{17}$ is larger than $\frac{8}{19}$.

Now try a few examples:

If b and c are both positive whole numbers greater than 1, and $\frac{5}{c} = \frac{b}{3}$, what are the values of b and c?

This might look like algebra, but it's really not. Using cross-multiplication, $bc = 15$. The only ways 15 can be the product of two positive integers is as (1)(15) or (3)(5). Since both b and c must be greater than 1, one must be 3 and the other 5. Try both cases, and you should see that the only possibility is that $b = 3$ and $c = 5$, making both fractions equal to 1. Remember—we were told that both fractions are equal.

Now check out this one:

Which is larger, $\frac{4}{7}$ or $\frac{3}{5}$?

Take your time. Think about it and try to solve it before looking at the solution.

The first fraction named has a larger numerator, but it also has a larger denominator. To compare the two fractions, rewrite both with the common denominator 35 by multiplying the top and bottom of $\frac{4}{7}$ by 5 and the top and bottom of $\frac{3}{5}$ by 7 to yield $\frac{20}{35}$ and $\frac{21}{35}$, respectively. Suddenly, it has become easy to see that $\frac{3}{5}$ is the larger.

Here's another one:

Which is larger, $\frac{-6}{11}$ or $\frac{13}{-22}$?

First of all, it does not matter where you put the minus sign—top, bottom, or opposite the fraction bar. If there is one minus sign anywhere in a fraction, the fraction is negative.

Next, remember that in comparing negative numbers, the one with the larger absolute value is the smaller number. So start by ignoring the signs and comparing the absolute values of the fractions. If the two fractions had a common denominator or numerator, it would be easy. Let's make it so. Multiply the top and bottom of $\frac{6}{11}$ by 2 to yield $\frac{12}{22}$. Now, it is easy to see that $\frac{13}{22}$ is the larger. That is, $\frac{13}{22}$ has the greater absolute value, meaning that $\frac{-6}{11}$ is the larger number.

Of course, you could have solved either of these last two examples on a calculator. Dividing the numerator by the denominator gives you a decimal equivalent of the fraction. Thus, as a decimal $\frac{4}{7} = 0.571\ldots$ and $\frac{3}{5} = 0.6$. Try $\frac{-6}{11}$ and $\frac{13}{-22}$ this way for yourself.

Were you having trouble remembering how to do arithmetic with fractions? Well, here's your chance to review that, but we won't start in the usual place. Adding and subtracting fractions is not as easy as multiplying them.

Fractions: Multiply and Divide

Multiplication of fractions is easy. You just multiply across (multiply the numerators together, then multiply the denominators together). It would make things easier if you reduce or simplify the fractions first so you don't end up with a large number.

> In multiplication, answers are called products.

In symbols, $\frac{a}{b} \times \frac{c}{d} = \frac{ac}{bd}$. Prefer numbers? Here you go: $\frac{3}{5} \times \frac{10}{9} = \frac{30}{45} = \frac{2}{3}$. Notice that the product was simplified by factoring 15 out of both the numerator and the denominator.

Now it's time for some examples.

> Jasmine earns $\frac{3}{4}$ of what Sidney earns, and Sidney earns $\frac{2}{3}$ of what Paul earns. What fraction of Paul's salary does Jasmine earn?

> Here's a tip: When working with any numbers, <u>of</u> can usually be interpreted to mean <u>times</u>.

Using *J*, *S*, and *P* to stand for the people's earnings respectively, we have:

$$S = \frac{2}{3}P, J = \frac{3}{4}S$$

Therefore, $J = \frac{3}{4} \times \frac{2}{3}P$, which works out as $\frac{3}{4} \times \frac{2}{3}P = \frac{6}{12}P = \frac{1}{2}P$.

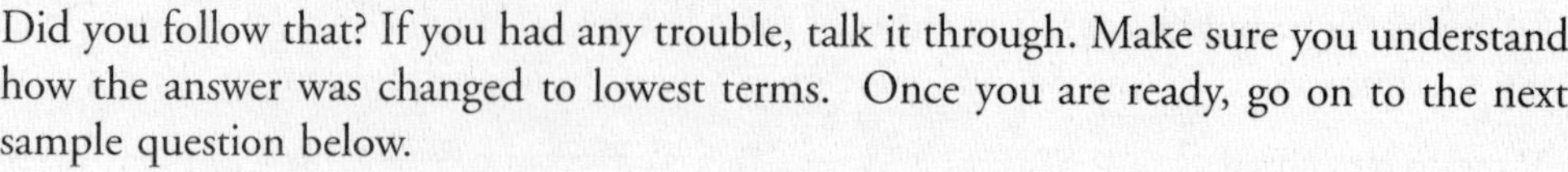
Did you follow that? If you had any trouble, talk it through. Make sure you understand how the answer was changed to lowest terms. Once you are ready, go on to the next sample question below.

> Pedro has half as many CDs as Andrea has, and Marcia has $\frac{3}{5}$ as many CDs as Andrea. What fraction of Marcia's number of CDs does Pedro have?

Using P, A, and M to stand for the number of CDs each owns respectively, we have:

$$P = \frac{1}{2}A \text{ and } M = \frac{3}{5}A$$

The question asks what *fraction* of Marcia's number of CDs Pedro has. That looks like this:

$$\frac{P}{M} = \frac{\frac{1}{2}A}{\frac{3}{5}A}$$

That's one fraction being divided by another fraction (also known as a complex fraction). $\frac{A}{A} = 1$, since anything divided by itself = 1. That leaves the pure number division: $\frac{1}{2} \div \frac{3}{5}$.

Now here comes the good part. Division, you may recall, is the reciprocal operation of multiplication. A reciprocal, in case you've forgotten, is the number you multiply another number by to make 1. The reciprocal of 2, for example, is one half. The reciprocal of $n = \frac{1}{n}$.

To divide a number by 2, you can multiply it by one half. Go ahead and try it; I'll wait. In fact, instead of dividing any number by another, multiply it by its reciprocal. And that's exactly how you divide fractions. You multiply the first fraction by the reciprocal of the divisor (the one it's being divided by):

$$\frac{1}{2} \div \frac{3}{5} = \frac{1}{2} \times \frac{5}{3} = \frac{5}{6}$$

So, Pedro has $\frac{5}{6}$ as many CDs as Marcia.

Just for the record: $\frac{a}{b} \div \frac{c}{d} = \frac{a}{b} \times \frac{d}{c}$.

Addition and Subtraction

To add or subtract fractions with the same denominator, simply add or subtract the numerators. For example, $\frac{5}{17}+\frac{3}{17}=\frac{8}{17}$, and $\frac{5}{17}-\frac{3}{17}=\frac{2}{17}$.

However, if the denominators are different, you must first rewrite the fractions so they will have the same denominator. That is, you must find *a common denominator.*

> Most books and teachers stress that you should use the least common denominator (LCD), which is the least common multiple (LCM) of the original denominators. This will keep the numbers smaller. However, any common denominator will do!

If you are rushed, you can always find a common denominator by just taking the product of the two denominators. For example, to add $\frac{5}{12}+\frac{3}{8}$, you can multiply the denominators 12 and 8 to find the common denominator 96. Thus:

$$\frac{5}{12}+\frac{3}{8}=\frac{5\times 8}{12\times 8}+\frac{3\times 12}{8\times 12}=\frac{40}{96}+\frac{36}{96}=\frac{76}{96}$$

Now you can divide both the numerator and the denominator by 4 to express the fraction in its lowest terms; that is: $\frac{76}{96}=\frac{19}{24}$.

To find the least common denominator, you must first understand what a least common multiple is. Given two numbers M and N, any number that is divisible by both is called a *common multiple* of M and N. The *least common multiple (LCM)* of the two numbers is the smallest number that is divisible by both. For example, 9 and 12 both divide into 108, so 108 is a common multiple; but the LCM is 36.

For small numbers, the easiest way to find the LCM is simply to list the multiples of each number (in writing or in your head) until you find the first common multiple. For example, for 9 and 12 we have the following multiples:

For 9: 9 18 27 <u>36</u> 45. . .

For 12: 12 24 <u>36</u> 48 60. . .

The first number that appears in both lists is 36.

The traditional method for finding the LCM, which is the method that translates most readily into algebra, requires that you find the *prime factorization* of the numbers.

> A whole number is either prime or composite. A prime is a whole number greater than 1 for which the only factors (divisors) are 1 and the number itself. Any whole number that is not prime is composite.

All composite numbers can be factored into primes in an essentially unique way. To find an LCM, you must find the smallest number that contains all the factors of both numbers. Thus, 9 factors to (3)(3), and 12 factors to (2)(2)(3). The LCM, then, is the smallest number that has all the same factors, that is, two 3s and two 2s. Since (3)(3)(2)(2) = 36, the LCM is 36. If that's not clear to you, reread this paragraph and think about each step. It should make sense.

This definition also extends to sets of more than two numbers. Thus, the LCM of 12, 15, and 20 must contain all the prime factors of all three numbers: (2)(2)(3); (3)(5); (2)(2)(5). So, the LCM is (2)(2)(3)(5) = 60.

Now, to add $\frac{5}{12}+\frac{3}{8}$ using the smallest possible numbers, we find the LCM of 12 and 8, which is 24. Then, we write $\frac{5}{12}=\frac{10}{24}$ and $\frac{3}{8}=\frac{9}{24}$.

Therefore:

$$\frac{5}{12}+\frac{3}{8}=\frac{10}{24}+\frac{9}{24}=\frac{19}{24}$$

Ready for an example? Here you go:

Find the LCM for 18 and 30.

Really do it. Don't look at the solution yet. Got it? Now go ahead.

Using prime factorization, 18 = (2)(3)(3), and 30 = (2)(3)(5). Since the factors 2 and 3 are common to both numbers, we need only multiply in one extra 3 to get the factors of 18 and 5 to get the factors of 30. Thus, the LCM = (2)(3)(3)(5) = 90. Did you get that?

Now try another one:

> Mario figures that he can finish a certain task in 20 days. Angelo figures that he can finish the same task in 25 days. What fraction of the task can they get done working together for seven days?

Think this through and try to solve it before you look at the answer below.

Done thinking? OK. In seven days, Mario would do $\frac{7}{20}$ of the entire task. In the same week, Angelo would do $\frac{7}{25}$ of the entire task. Therefore, working together they do $\frac{7}{20}+\frac{7}{25}$ of the whole job.

Now we have to add two fractions that have the same numerator. Can we add them directly by finding the sum of the denominators? We sure hope you didn't fall for that. It's the denominators that must be the same—not just either/or. The LCD here is 100:

$$\frac{7}{25}+\frac{7}{20}=\frac{28}{100}+\frac{35}{100}=\frac{63}{100}$$

$\frac{63}{100}$ may also be expressed as 0.63 or 63%. Do you know why? What a sneaky way to lead into the next section!

Fractions, Decimals, and Percents—The Little Guys (Sometimes)

Every fraction can be expressed as a *decimal,* which can be found by division. Those fractions for which the prime factorization of the denominator involves only 2s and 5s will have terminating decimal expansions. Others will have repeating decimal expansions. For example, $\frac{3}{20}=.15$, while $\frac{3}{11}=0.272727\ldots$

To convert a number given as a decimal into a fraction, you must know what the decimal means. In general, a decimal represents a fraction with a denominator of 10, or 100, or 1,000, etc., where the number of zeros is equal to the number of digits to the right of the decimal point. So, for example, 0.4 means $\frac{4}{10}$; 0.52 means $\frac{52}{100}$; and $0.103=\frac{103}{1000}$.

Decimals of the form 3.25 are equivalent to *mixed numbers;* $3.25 = 3 + \frac{25}{100}$. For purposes of addition and subtraction, mixed numbers may be useful, but for purposes of multiplication or division, it is usually better to convert a mixed number into a fraction greater than 1, like this:

$$3\frac{1}{4}=\frac{13}{4}$$

How did we do that? Formally, we realize that $3 = \frac{3}{1}$, and we add the two fractions $\frac{3}{1}$ and $\frac{1}{4}$, using the common denominator 4. In informal terms, we multiply the whole number, 3, by the denominator of the fraction, 4, and add the numerator of the fraction to get the numerator of the resulting *improper fraction.*

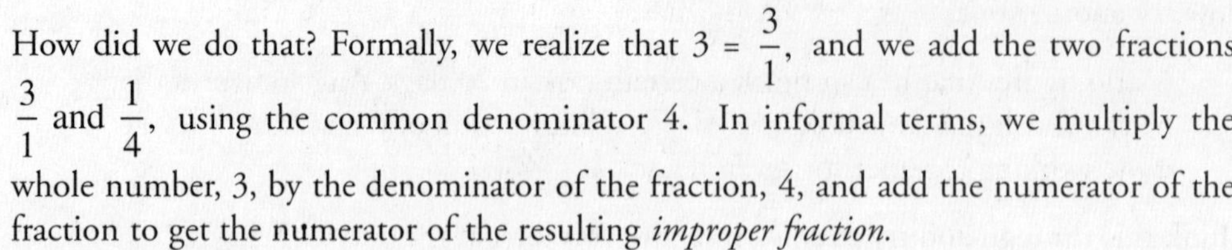

And that's how we get the numerator (3)(4) + 1 = 13. If a fraction stayed out late and did not call home to explain, we'd consider *that* an *improper* fraction.

Time for an example:

> If $\frac{0.56}{1.26}$ reduced to lowest terms is $\frac{a}{b}$, and a and b are whole numbers, what is b?

Think about this really carefully. You already know how to do it. You just might not realize that you do.

Rewriting both numerator and denominator as their fractional equivalents, we get $\frac{\frac{56}{100}}{\frac{126}{100}}$, which means $\frac{56}{100} \div \frac{126}{100}$. We now accomplish the division by inverting the denominator of the second fraction and multiplying. Thus:

$$\frac{56}{100} \times \frac{100}{126} = \frac{56}{126}.$$

Now divide top and bottom by the greatest common factor, 14:

$$\frac{56 \div 14}{126 \div 14} = \frac{4}{9}$$

As you can see, $b = 9$. That was not the only way that problem could have been solved, so if you used a different way and got the same answer, well, good for you. You should be proud!

Per<u>cent</u> means per <u>hundred</u> (from the Latin word *centum*, meaning hundred). That is, percents are fractions based on 100 being one whole. In other words, 100% = one. So, for example, 30% means 30 per hundred, or as a fraction $\frac{30}{100}$, or as a decimal 0.30.

To convert a number given as a percent to a decimal, simply move the decimal point two places to the left and remove the "%" sign. To convert a decimal to a percent, go the opposite way. Move the decimal two places to the right, and add the "%" sign.

Remember that when written as a percent the number should look bigger, therefore, the "large" 45% becomes the "small" 0.45, and the "small" 0.73 becomes the "large" 73%. Remember too that 9% = 0.09, and *not* 0.9, which is 90%.

Let's try the following example:

> In a group of 20 English majors and 30 history majors, 50% of the English majors and 20% of the history majors have not taken a college math course. What percent of the entire group has taken a college math course?

To solve this, start with the English majors. Since 50% = 0.50, 50% of 20 = (0.50)(20) = 10. For the history majors, 20% = 0.20; 20% of 30 = (0.20)(30) = 6. Hence, a total of 16 out of 50 people in the group have not taken math, which means that 34 people have. As a fraction, 34 out of 50 is $\frac{34}{50} = 0.68 = 68\%$.

Try these two common problems:

> Arthur had $500 in a bank account at 5% annual interest. How much money was in the account at the end of one year?
>
> Mary bought a camcorder for $300. Sales tax was 6%. How much did she have to pay the clerk?

Interest is calculated as Principal × Rate × Time, or $I = prt$.

So, to find out how much money Arthur had after a year, multiply $500 × .05, which is 5% as a decimal. Since the period is 1 year, you don't need to multiply by that.

$500 × .05 = $25.00

Of course, that amount of interest must be added to the principal to get the total:

$500 + $25 = $525

There are two ways to find Mary's total cost. You could find 6% of $300 and then add it on, as we did with Arthur, or you could multiply $300 by 1.06, since your cost is 1 times the price and another .06 times the price. Look!

.06 × $300 = $18.00 $300 + $18 = $318

or

1.06 × $300 = $318

Pretty cool, huh?

Just Average

There are three common measurements used to define the typical value of a collection of numbers. However, when you see the word *average* with no other explanation, it is assumed that what is meant is the *arithmetic mean.* The average in this sense is the sum of the numbers divided by the number of numbers in the collection. In symbols, $A = \frac{T}{n}$.

So, for example, if on four math exams you scored 82, 76, 87, and 89, your average at this point is (82 + 76 + 87 + 89) ÷ 4 = 334 ÷ 4 = 83.5.

OK. Now you try.

> At an art show, Eleanor sold six of her paintings at an average price of $70. At the next show, she sold four paintings at an average price of $100. What was the overall average price of the 10 paintings?

Did you really work that out? You wouldn't kid us, would you? All right—we believe you. Then you must have figured that you can't just say the answer is 85, the average of 70 and 100, because we do not have the same number of paintings in each group. We need to know the overall total. Since the first six average $70, the total received for the six was $420. Do you see why? $70 = \frac{T}{6}$; therefore, $T = (6)(70) = 420$. In the same way, the next four paintings must have brought in $400 in order to average $100 a piece. Therefore, we have a total of 10 paintings selling for $420 + $400 = $820, and the average is $\frac{820}{10} = \$82$.

Now you are getting it. Try another one:

> Erica averaged 76 on her first four French exams. To get a B in the course, she must have an 80 average on her exams. What grade must she get on the next exam to bring her average to 80?

If her average is 76 on four exams, she must have a total of (4)(76) = 304. In order to average 80 on five exams, her total must be (5)(80) = 400. Therefore, she must score 400 – 304 = 96 on her last exam. Erica had better study extra hard!

> The other measurements used to define the typical value of a set of numbers are the <u>median</u>, which is the middle number when the numbers are arranged in increasing order, and the <u>mode</u>, which is the most common number (the number appearing most often).

Here's one more for the road:

> Which is greater for the set of nine integers {1, 2, 2, 2, 3, 5, 6, 7, 8}, the mean minus the median or the median minus the mode?

Did you get it? The median (middle number) is 3, the mode is 2, and the mean is (1 + 2 + 2 + 2 + 3 + 5 + 6 + 7 + 8) ÷ 9 = 4. Thus, the mean minus the median is 4 – 3 = 1, and the median minus the mode is 3 – 2 = 1. The two quantities are equal. And that's the law of averages. (Don't take that last sentence seriously.)

Deviation and Variance

The most elementary measure of variation is the spread, also known as the *range*. In the last problem with the 9 numbers, the spread was from 1 to 8. We find the range by subtracting the smallest from the largest:

> 8 – 1 = 7, so the range of integers is 7.

The *variance* is defined as the sum of the squared *deviation* (difference) of all the members of the set of n numbers from the mean divided by one less than n. For the set [1, 2, 2, 2, 3, 5, 6, 7, 8}, with a mean which we've found to be 4, n is 8, $n - 1 = 7$, and the deviations from the mean are 3, 2, 2, 2, 1, 2, 3, 4

The squared deviations from the mean are therefore

> 9, 4, 4, 4, 1, 4, 9, 16

The sum of those squared deviations from the mean are 51. Dividing by $n - 1$, or 7, we get $\frac{51}{7} = 7\frac{2}{7}$ as the variance. Since the fractional part is really not useful to this discussion of whole numbers, disregard it and call the variance 7.

Standard deviation is defined as the square root of the variance, so the standard deviation for this group of numbers from the mean is $\sqrt{7}$. We'll study square roots more closely in the next chapter.

In My Estimate . . .

Often you need an exact answer to a question; sometimes you don't. In those cases, it is a time-saver if you can **estimate** your answer. Suppose you were told that Bill sold 321 tickets to the fund-raising benefit, Charlotte sold 180, and Frank sold 92. About how many tickets were sold?

Well, say the answer choices were (A) 400, (B) 600, (C) 800, (D) 1,000. There is no need to actually add the numbers. 180 is close to 200, 321 is close to 300, and 92 is close to 100. $200 + 300 + 100 = 600$. By rounding each number to the nearest hundred, we came up with an answer in a shorter time than it would have taken to actually add the numbers.

How do you know when to estimate and when to do the arithmetic? First of all it depends on how close together the answer choices are. If they are four consecutive numbers, then you had better do the arithmetic. The same is true if they are fractions or decimals that are close to one another. If the answers are hundreds or thousands apart, estimating will usually do the trick. Another signal that estimating is okay is if the question says *about* how much or how many. That's an indication that the question isn't looking for an exact number.

Richard had 275 jellybeans; Rosalita had 620 jellybeans. About how many more jellybeans than Richard did Rosalita have. The hardest part here is figuring out that you're going to need to subtract. After that, 620 is about 600 and 275 is about 300. $600 - 300 = 300$. That's mental arithmetic. She had about 300 more jellybeans than he had.

Permutations

If one event can occur in p different ways, and a second event can occur in q different ways, then there are exactly $p \times q$, or pq ways that the two events can occur together. How many different ways can a woman coordinate an outfit if she has four pairs of slacks and six different blouses?

For openers, she can select a pair of slacks in four different ways. The next thing she must do is to select one of 6 different blouses. By **the multiplication principle for events,** stated above, there are $(4)(6) = 24$ different ways to select an outfit, or 24 different outfits she can wear.

In how many ways can five CDs be arranged on a shelf of a CD rack that has room for exactly five CDs? The first space can be filled with any one of the five CDs, the second space with any of the four remaining CDs, the third space with any of the remaining three CDs, and so on. Therefore, there are $(5)(4)(3)(2)(1) = 120$ ways to arrange five CDs on a single shelf with room for only five CDs.

Now, consider a set of nine CDs. There is room for only three more on a certain shelf. In how many ways can 3 out of the 9 be arranged in the available space? Well, the first space can be filled with any of the nine CDs, the second space with any of eight, and the third with any of 7. Therefore, there are (9)(8)(7) = 504 ways that three out of nine books could be arranged in the available space.

An ordered arrangement of some or all the objects in a set is called a **permutation**. The number of ways to arrange nine things taken three at a time is written as ${}_9P_3$ or as $P(9, 3)$. The general form of a permutation is ${}_nP_r$ or $P(n, r)$ and is read "the permutation of n things taken r at a time."

$$ {}_nP_r = P(n, r) = \frac{n!}{(n-r)!} $$

$n!$ is read as "n factorial" and means $(n)(n-1)(n-2)(n-3)\ldots(1)$.

If any of the objects in a permutation are repeats, then we use a different formula. The number of permutations of n objects that contains p alike and q alike is:

$$ \frac{n!}{p!q!} $$

How many ways can the letters of the word "Mississippi" be arranged? Try to do it.

There are eleven letters in "Mississippi," four of which are "i," four of which are "s," and two of which are "p." That means we need to use the formula for repeated elements:

$$ \frac{n!}{p!q!} \rightarrow \frac{11!}{4!4!2!} = 34{,}650 $$

That means there are 34,650 ways to arrange the letters in the word "Mississippi." Do you want to see how many of them you can find? Just kidding!

Combinations

When it doesn't matter to you in which order the objects are selected, use a **combination** rather than a permutation. The combination of n things taken r at a time is written ${}_nC_r$ or $C(n, r)$. The formula for finding n objects taken r at a time is

$$ {}_nC_r = C(n, r) = \frac{n!}{r!(n-r)!} $$

A class contains 20 students. How many groups containing five students can be formed? Since the order in which the students are chosen for the group is not relevant, this is a combinations problem, with $n = 20$ and $r = 5$.

$$C(20,5) = \frac{20!}{5!(20-5)!}$$

$$= \frac{(20)(19)(18)(17)(16)(15!)}{(5)(4)(3)(2)(1)(15!)}$$

Do you see how to simplify this?

$$= (19)(6)(17)(16)$$

$$= 11{,}628$$

There are 11,628 different groups that can be formed.

A Picture Is Worth . . .

I'm sure you know the completion of that line, but on the off chance that you don't, it goes, "A picture is worth a thousand words." That's what makes graphs so important for displaying and analyzing data.

A graph is a picture of mathematical data, usually referring to a single subject or a set of related subjects. There are several types of graphs, ranging from pictographs to bar, line, and circle graphs. Every graph contains a **legend** or **key**, which may be a small inset or along the axes. The legend tells you what the graph means. Always read the legend before attempting to interpret a graph's meaning. Let's start with a pictograph.

Small Farms in Mercer County (1995–2000)

(house icon) = 200 farms

Year

2000

1999

1998

1997

1996

1995

How many fewer small farms were there in Mercer County in 2000 than in 1997? Well, first of all, there are 8 more houses in 1997 than in 2000. Since each house stands for 200 farms (You read the legend, didn't you?), there were 8 × 200, or 1600 more small farms in 1997.

1. How many small farms were there in Mercer County in 1999? Go ahead; figure it out. I'll wait for you. Nine houses at 200 farms per means there were 1800 small farms in 1999.
2. Answer this True or False: The loss of small farms in Mercer County was probably due to consolidations into large factory farms and conversion of farmland to housing developments.

Well, did you give that plenty of thought? It sounds plausible, right? Well sounding plausible is no reason to draw a conclusion on a test of mathematical skill. The graph gives no reasons for the loss of small farms, so the best answer to the question is "How the heck should I know?"

No Holds Barred

The bar graph is a logical extension of the picture graph. It looks as if a rectangle were drawn around each row of pictures and then the pictures themselves were erased. Markings along the axis are used to tell number, since there are no longer pictures to count. Bar graphs may be vertical as well as horizontal, and, unlike picture graphs, they can be used to compare two or more things.

1. How many more women than men teach part-time in Lindaville?

To answer the question, we need first to examine the legend. There, we find that shaded bars are for females and unshaded for males. We also learn that the numbers written along the horizontal axis need to be multiplied by 100. Put a straight edge at the right end of the shaded "Teach" bar, and look down at the marking on the axis. It's 18. That's 1800 female part-time teachers. Do the same thing with the unshaded "Teach" bar and you'll find 1400 male part-time teachers. 1800 –1400 = 400 more female teachers.

2. At which job are there as many women as there are men who write?

To answer this question we need to compare the end of the unshaded "Write" bar with the ends of the shaded bars to find one that ends in the same place. Again, a straight edge would be helpful. It turns out that the answer is editing.

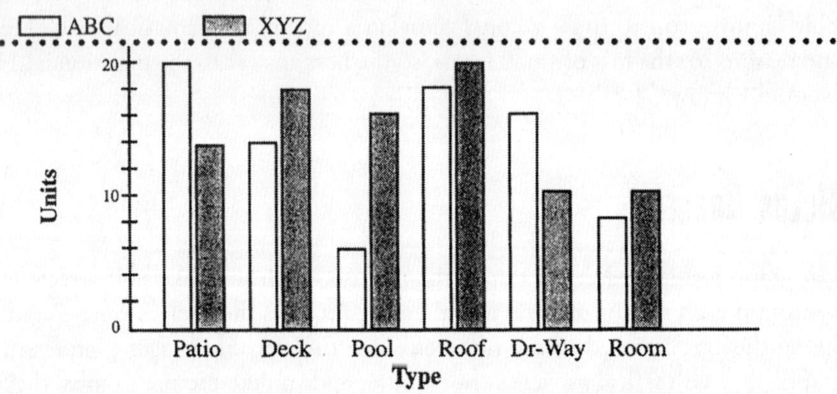

3. How many more patios did ABC contractors install last year compared to XYZ?

ABC installed 20 patios as compared to XYZ's 14. That's a difference of 6.

4. How many more roofs would you expect ABC to install this year compared to XYZ?

I don't see any information about this year; do you? The answer is "Not enough information."

5. How many roofs were installed by both companies last year?

Did you notice that each tick on the vertical axes stands for 2? So 20 and 18 add up to 38 roofs installed by both companies.

The Line Up

You may think of a line graph as being formed by connecting the topmost points of the vertical bars on a bar graph and then erasing the bars themselves. Line graphs can be used to display the same information as bar graphs, but they are better suited than bar graphs for displaying continuous information, such as the range of temperatures over a period of time or stock-price variations. It is easier to visualize the peaks and valleys on a line graph than on a bar graph, especially if more than one item is being considered. Check this out:

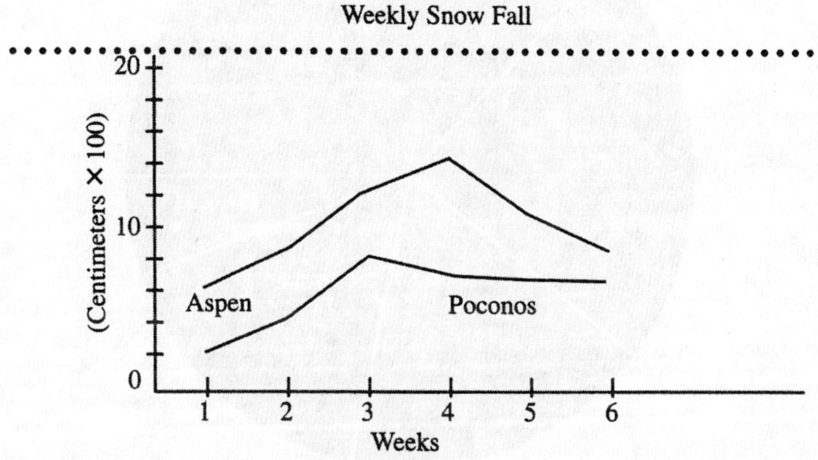

1. What is the difference in the amount of snowfall in the Poconos and in Aspen in Week 3?

A line graph is best read with the aid of two straight edges—one parallel to each of the axes on the graph. Notice that each vertical tick means 2 × 100 cm of snow. The third week saw 1200 cm in Aspen and 800 in the Poconos. That's a difference of 400 cm.

2. For which week(s) is the snowfall in the Poconos greater than the first week's snowfall in Aspen?

Bring your straight edge down, keeping it square with the axes and against the vertical one until it reaches Aspen's snowfall for Week 1. The edge is now covering the Poconos line for 3, 4, and 5. Therefore, in those weeks the Poconos' snowfall was greater.

Circle the Wagons

Circle graphs are also known as pie charts (one look should tell you why). They differ from other types of graphs in that they tell you how various parts of a whole are portioned out. Every pie chart in its entirety represents one whole thing. It may be a dollar, the total income of a company, the population of the world, or a person's income for a specific period of time. Each sector of the circle (slice of the pie) represents how a part of that whole is made up. When working with circle graphs, always keep in mind that the whole is 100 percent.

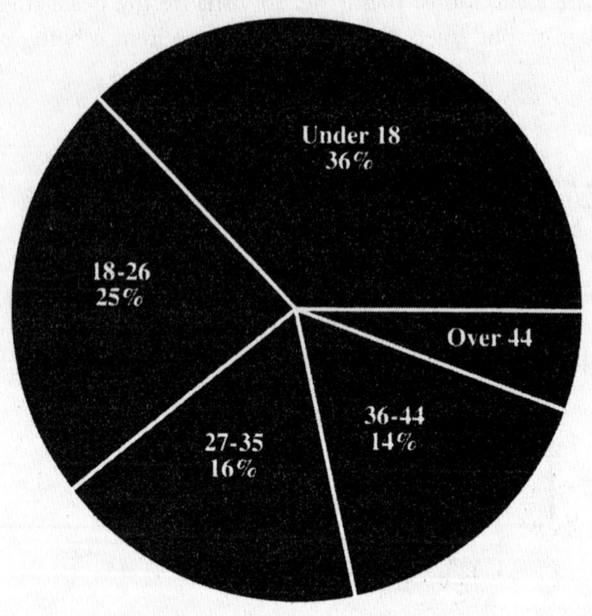

The following questions refer to the graph above.

1. What percent of Rockin' Records' customers are under 27 years of age?

36% is shown as being under 18, and another 25% are aged 18 to 26. Add those two percentages together, and you'll get 61% under 27 years old.

2. What percent of Rockin' Records' customers are over age 44?

To find this answer, we have to add up all the percentages that are shown on the chart, and then subtract that number from 100%—the amount the whole chart represents:

$$36 + 25 + 16 + 14 = 91$$

That 91% is the group we're *not* interested in. 100 – 91 = 9, so nine percent are over age 44.

3. How many of Rockin' Records customers are aged 27 to 35?

The graph gives percentages, not numbers. If we knew how many total clients the company had, we could find 16% of that, which would answer the question, but with the information that we have, the question is unanswerable.

Now it's time for your first pop quiz. Don't worry; with everything you just read, this should be a breeze.

Pop Quiz

1. What is the value of $2x - (y + 3z)$, when $x = 4$, $y = 5$, and $z = 2$?
   (A) −3
   (B) 3
   (C) 9
   (D) 12

2. Which of the following equations demonstrates the associative property of multiplication?
   (A) $a + b = b + a$
   (B) $a \times b = b \times a$
   (C) $a \times (b + c) = (b + c) \times a$
   (D) $(a \times b) \times c = a \times (b \times c)$

3. Two fifths of the faculty members at Boyleston Community College drive to work each day. Which of the following is NOT true?
   (A) 40% of the faculty members drive to work.
   (B) $\frac{3}{5}$ of the faculty members do not drive to work.
   (C) More than half of the faculty members drive to work.
   (D) 60% of the faculty members do not drive to work.

4. As part of Angelo's strict diet, he is restricted to taking in no more than 4,000 calories per day. If he calculated that his breakfast accounted for 960 calories, what percent of this maximum daily calorie allowance does he have left?
   (A) 24
   (B) 48
   (C) 52
   (D) 76

5. After four tests, Richard's average test score is 85. If Richard scores 100 on his fifth test, what will his new average score be?
   (A) 82
   (B) 85
   (C) 86
   (D) 88

Answers and Explanations

1. **The correct answer is (A).** Substitute the numbers like this: 2(4) – [5 + 3(2)] Remember the "Please Excuse My Dear Aunt Sally" rule—Parentheses, Exponents, Multiplication and Division, Addition and Subtraction—when evaluating this problem:

   $2(4) - [5 + 3(2)] =$

   $8 - [5 + 6] =$

   $8 - 11 = -3.$

2. **The correct answer is (D).** Time for the Elimination Game. You can eliminate choice (A) right away, because it deals with only addition, and the question asks for the associative property of multiplication. This rule states that if three numbers are multiplied, it doesn't matter in which order they are multiplied. For example:

   $(2 \times 3) \times 5 = 6 \times 5 = 30$

   $2 \times (3 \times 5) = 2 \times 15 = 30$

3. **The correct answer is (C).** You can find the decimal version of two fifths by dividing 2 by 5; the answer is 0.4. Since one half is the same as 0.5, it must be true that two fifths is less than one half. Therefore, it is not true that more than half of the faculty members drive to work.

4. **The correct answer is (D).** "Per cent" means "out of 100." You know the part and the whole regarding Angelo's diet, so set up a proportion that equals the first fraction ($\frac{960}{4000}$ equal to $\frac{x}{100}$) and cross-multiply:

$$\frac{960}{4000} = \frac{x}{100}$$
$$4000 \times x = 960 \times 100$$
$$4000x = 96{,}000$$
$$\frac{4000x}{4000} = \frac{96{,}000}{4000}$$
$$x = 24$$

   Since he has already eaten 24% of his daily caloric allowance, he has 100 – 24, or 76%, remaining for the rest of the day.

5. **The correct answer is (D).** There are three important values when determining the average of a series of numbers: the number of elements you are averaging, the average value of those elements, and the total value of those elements. To find the total value, multiply the number of elements (in this case, the four tests) by the average value (85). Since $4 \times 85 = 340$, Richard scored a total of 340 points on his first four tests. If he scores a perfect 100 on the fifth test, he has a new total of 340 + 100, or 440 points scored on *five* tests. To find the new average, divide 440 by 5: $400 \div 5 = 88$.

CHAPTER 4

REVIEWING ALGEBRA, OR DON'T CALL ME AL

So much for arithmetic. Now comes the good stuff. Algebra is a way of solving problems that relies upon the arithmetic that we've already reviewed and know perfectly—er, at least, pretty well. In reviewing algebra, we'll start off with baby steps, walking before we begin to run.

Just for Autograph Collectors: Adding and Subtracting Signed Numbers

To add two numbers of the same sign, just add their absolute values and attach their common sign. So 7 + 9 = 16, and (–7) + (–9) = –16. You could drop the parentheses and instead of (–7) + (–9), write –7 – 9, which means the same thing.

> Adding a negative number is the same thing as subtracting a positive number. Think about that.

When adding numbers of opposite signs, temporarily ignore the signs, subtract the smaller from the larger, and attach to the result the sign of the number with the larger absolute value. That means, 9 + (–3) = 6, but (–9) + 3 = –6 Again, we could have written 9 + (–3) = 9 – 3 = 6 and (–9) + 3 : –9 + 3 = –6.

When subtracting, change the sign of the second number (known as the *subtrahend)* and then use the rules for addition. That means that 7 – (–3) = 7 + 3 = 10 and –7 – 3 = –7 + (–3) = –10.

Alternatively, you can work with the letters first: $-A - (-B) = -A + B$ = –(–5) + (–6) = 5 – 6 = –1.

The Times They Are a Changin'

If you multiply two numbers with the same sign, the result is positive. If you multiply two numbers with opposite signs, the result is negative. The exact same rule holds for division. Thus, (–4)(–3) = +12, and (–4)(3) = –12. For division, it doesn't matter which is negative and which is positive; thus, (–6) ÷ (2) = –3; and (6) ÷ (–2) = –3, but

(–6) ÷ (–2) = +3.

If you have a string of multiplications and divisions to do and the number of negative factors is even, the result will be positive. If the number of negative factors is odd, the result will be negative. Of course, if even one factor is zero, the result is zero, and if even one factor in the denominator (divisor) is zero, the result is undefined. To demonstrate this, try the following example:

> If A = (234,906 – 457,219)(35)(–618) and B =(–2,356)(–89,021)(–3,125), which is larger, A or B?

MATH

Whatever you do, don't do the arithmetic! You don't need to do it to find the answer. 457,219 is greater than 234,906, so the difference is a negative number. Now, A is the product of two negative numbers and a positive number, which makes the result positive. *B* is the product of three negative numbers and must be negative. Every positive number is greater than any negative number, so *A* is greater than *B*.

Let's try another one:

If $\frac{AB}{MN}$ is a positive number and *N* is negative, which of the following is possible?

(A) *A* is positive, and *B* and *M* are negative.

(B) *A, B,* and *M* are negative.

(C) *A, B,* and *M* are positive.

(D) *B* is positive, and *A* and *M* are negative.

To determine the sign of the fraction, we can just think of *A, B, M,* and *N* as four factors. Knowing that *N* is negative, the product of the other three must also be negative in order for the result to be positive. The only possibilities are that all are negative, or one is negative and the other two are positive. This works only for choice (B); therefore, the correct answer is (B).

Getting Very Power-ful!

In an expression of the form b^n, b is called the base and n is called the *exponent* or *power.* We say, "b is raised to the power n."

Note that $b^1 = b$, so the power 1 is usually omitted.

If n is any positive integer, then b^n is the product of n b's. For example, 4^3 is the product of three 4's, that is, $4^3 = 4 \times 4 \times 4 = 64$.

As a result of this, certain rules for operations with exponents are forced upon us.

$b^m \times b^n = b^{m+n}$. That is, when multiplying powers of the same base, keep the base and add the exponents. Thus, $3^3 \times 3^2 = 3^{2+3} = 3^5 = 243$.

$(ab)^n = a^n b^n$ and $\left(\frac{a}{b}\right)^n = \frac{a^n}{b^n}$. That is, to raise a product or quotient to a power, raise each factor to that power, whether that factor is in the top or bottom. Thus, $(2x)^3 = 2^3x^3 = 8x^3$, and $\left(\frac{2}{x}\right)^3 = \frac{2^3}{x^3} = \frac{8}{x^3}$.

$(b^m)^n = b^{mn}$. That is, to raise a power to a power, retain the base and multiply exponents. Thus, $(2^3)^2 = 2^6 = 64$.

$\frac{b^n}{b^m} = b^{n-m}$ if $n > m$, and $\frac{b^n}{b^m} = \frac{1}{b^{m-n}}$ if $n < m$. That is, to divide powers of the same base, subtract exponents. For example, $\frac{4^5}{4^2} = 4^3 = 64$ and $\frac{4^2}{4^5} = \frac{1}{4^3} = \frac{1}{64}$.

For various technical reasons with which you needn't be troubled, $x^0 = 1$ for all x except $x = 0$, in which case it is undefined. Taking advantage of this definition, one can define b^n in such a way that all the laws of exponents given above still work even for negative powers. This definition is $b^{-n} = \frac{1}{b^n}$.

Now you have the choice of writing $\frac{x^3}{x^5}$ as $\frac{1}{x^2}$ or as x^{-2}.

Ready for some sample questions?

If $x = 2$, which is larger, 1.10 or $x^0 + x^{-4}$?

Are you sure that you've worked that out? Okay, then here comes the answer:

If $x = 2$, $x^0 = 2^0 = 1$, and $x^{-4} = 2^{-4} = \frac{1}{2^4} = \frac{1}{16} = 0.0625$. That means, $x^0 + x^{-4} = 1.0625$, which is less than 1.10.

Which of the following expressions is equivalent to $\frac{(2x)^3}{x^7}$?

(A) $\frac{1}{8x^4}$

(B) $\frac{8}{x^{-4}}$

(C) $(8x)^{-4}$

(D) $8x^{-4}$

Cubing the numerator, we cube each factor. Since $2^3 = 8$, we have $\frac{(2x)^3}{x^7} = \frac{8x^3}{x^7}$. We now divide x^3 by x^7 by subtracting the exponents: $3 - 7 = -4$.

Notice that we could have written $8x^4$ as $\frac{8}{x^{-4}}$. The correct answer is (D).

Be alert to the properties of even and odd powers. Even powers of real numbers cannot be negative. This rule applies to both positive and negative integer powers. Thus, the numerical value of x^2 is positive as is that of x^{-2}—except for $x = 0$, when x^2 is zero and x^{-2} is undefined (because you cannot divide by zero).

Odd powers are positive or negative depending upon whether the base is positive or negative. Thus, $2^3 = 8$, but $(-2)^3 = -8$. Zero to any power is zero, except zero to the zero, which is undefined.

> Note that -3^2 means $-(3^2) - -7$. If you want the square of (3), which equals +9, you must write it $(-3)^2$.

Let's try a couple more:

If $x < 0$ and $y > 0$, what is the sign of $-4x^4y^3$?

Did you determine that x^4 is positive, because it has an even power? y^3 is positive because y is, and -4 is obviously negative. The product of two positives and a negative is negative. Therefore, $-4x^4y^3$ is negative.

Now, this next one is a little tricky, but you just might learn something from it.

If $x^4 + 3y^2 = 0$, what is the sign of $2x - 6y + 1$?

Did you get it? Since neither x^4 nor $3y^2$ can be negative, the only way their sum can be zero is if both x and y are zero. Therefore, $2x - 6y + 1 = +1$, which is positive. Hopefully, you just learned that a problem does not always mean what the problem looks like it means.

> One more tip before we move on: Commit to memory small powers of the numbers that come up frequently. Be especially sure to know the powers of 2: 2, 4, 8, 16, 32, . . . and the powers of 3: 3, 9, 27, 81, . . .

Blowing Things Out of Proportion

A fractional relationship between two quantities is frequently expressed as a *ratio.* A ratio can be written as a fraction, $\frac{b}{a}$, or in the form *b:a* (read "*b* is to *a*"). A *proportion* is a statement in which two ratios are equal. To say, for example, that the ratio of passing to failing students in a class is 5:2 means that if we set up the fraction $\frac{p}{f}$ representing the relationship between the number of passing and failing students, it should simplify to $\frac{5}{2}$. If we write this statement as *p:f* :: 5:2, we read it "*p* is to *f* as 5 is to 2," and it means $\frac{p}{f} = \frac{5}{2}$.

When you are told that one quantity, say *y*, *varies directly* with (or as) *x*, that means simply that $y = kx$, where *k* is some constant.

> Often, a good way to work with information given in ratio form is to represent the numbers as multiples of the same number.

Now try the following example:

> The ratio of Democrats to Republicans in a certain state legislature is 5:7. If the legislature has 156 members, all of whom are either Democrats or Republicans (but not both), what is the difference between the number of Republicans and the number of Democrats?
>
> (A) 14
> (B) 26
> (C) 35
> (D) 37

To solve this, let the number of Democrats be $5m$ and the number of Republicans be $7m$, so that $D: R :: 5m : 7m = 5:7$. The total number of legislators is $5m + 7m = 12m$, which must be 156. Therefore, $12m = 156$, and $m = 13$. Thus, the difference is:

$7m - 5m = 2m = 2(13) = 26.$

The correct answer is (B).

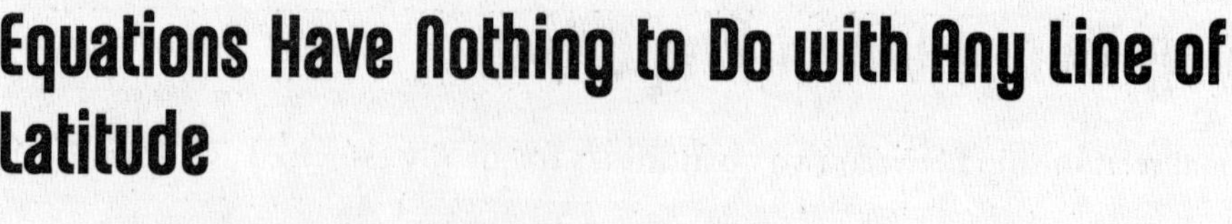

Equations Have Nothing to Do with Any Line of Latitude

To solve a linear equation, remember these rules:

- If you add or subtract the same quantity from both sides of an equation, the equation will still be true and will still have the same roots (solutions).
- If you multiply or divide both sides of an equation by any number except zero, the equation will still be true and will still have the same roots.

Use these two properties to isolate the unknown quantity on one side of the equation, leaving only known quantities on the other side. This is known as *solving for the unknown.*

If $14 = 3x - 1$ and $B = 6x + 4$, what is the value of B?

From the first equation, $3x - 1 = 14$. Add 1 to both sides:

$$\begin{array}{r} 3x - 1 = 14 \\ 1 = \ \ 1 \\ \hline 3x = 15 \end{array}$$

Divide both sides by 3:

$$\frac{3x}{3} = \frac{15}{3};\ x = 5$$

Of course, the question asked for B, not x. So we substitute $x = 5$ into $B = 6x + 4$ and get:

$B = 6(5) + 4 = 34.$

Ready for another?

If $\frac{2x}{3} + 2 = a$ and $y = 2x + 6$, what is the value of y in terms of a?

How do we do this? First, realize that if we knew what x was in terms of a, then we could substitute that expression for x into $y = 2x + 6$ and have y in terms of a. In other words, we want to solve $\frac{2x}{3} + 2 = a$ for x.

> As a general rule, if an equation involves one or more fractional coefficients, it pays to multiply both sides by the common denominator in order to make the fractions disappear. So, multiply through by 3 to clear the fractions. Be careful: use the distributive law and multiply every term on both sides by 3.

You should now have: $2x + 6 = 3a$. Now add –6 to both sides of the equation:

$$\begin{aligned} 2x + 6 &= 3a \\ -6 &= -6 \\ \hline 2x &= 3a - 6 \end{aligned}$$

Now divide by 2:

$$\frac{2x}{2} = \frac{3a-6}{2}; x = \frac{3a-6}{2}$$

Substituting:

$$y = 2\left(\frac{3a-6}{2}\right) + 6$$

$$y = 3a - 6 + 6 = 3a$$

Now for a Little Variety

To say that y *varies directly* with x^2 or x^3 or any given power means that $y = kx^2$ or kx^3. If you are told that y varies inversely with x, it means that $y = \frac{k}{x}$. Similarly, if y varies inversely with x^n, it means that $y = \frac{k}{x^n}$.

In each of these equations, k stands for the *constant of proportionality*. Usually, the problem is to first determine k, and then solve further. Try the example below to see if you understand this.

> The time it takes to run a computer sorting program varies directly with the square of the number of items to be sorted. If it takes 7 microseconds to sort a list of 12 items, how long will it take to sort 40 items?

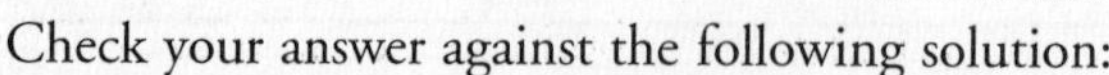

Check your answer against the following solution:

Letting t = time in microseconds and x = the number of items to be sorted, the relationship must be $t = kx^2$. When $x = 12$, $k = 7$. Therefore, $7 = k(12)^2 = 144k$. Hence, $k = \frac{7}{144}$. Therefore, $t = \frac{7}{144}x^2$. When $x = 40$, $t = \frac{7}{144}(40)^2 = \frac{7(1600)}{144}$ = about 77.8.

Let's try one more to make sure you can tackle this type of question:

The time it takes to paint a wall is directly proportional to the area of the wall and inversely proportional to the number of painters. If 3 painters can paint 1000 square feet of wall in 6 hours, how many square feet can 8 painters paint in 15 hours?

Here's how we solved it:

Let t = time, A = area, and p = number of painters. The relationship must be $t = k\left(\frac{A}{p}\right)$. Now, when $A = 1000$ and $p = 3$, $6 = k\left(\frac{1000}{8}\right)$. That is, $6 = 125k$ and $k = \frac{6}{125}$. Now we substitute $p = 8$ and $t = 15$ into $t = \left(\frac{6}{125}\right)\left(\frac{A}{p}\right)$, yielding $15 = \left(\frac{6}{125}\right)\left(\frac{A}{8}\right) = \frac{3A}{500}$. Multiplying by 500 and dividing by 3, we have $A = 1500$.

The Inequalities of Linear Algebra

The statement that a number M is less than another number N means that $N - M$ is positive. In other words, when you subtract a smaller number from a larger number, the result is positive. In symbols, this can be expressed: $M < N$ or $N > M$. Remember, the arrow *always points to the smaller* number.

On the number line, if $M < N$, we can infer that M lies to the left of N. This means, in particular, that any negative number is less than any positive number. It also implies that, for negative numbers, the one with the larger absolute value is the smaller number.

Inequalities can be solved in the same way as equations. When working with inequalities, remember these rules:

- If you add or subtract the same quantity from both sides of an inequality, it will still be true in the same sense. Thus, $14 > 7$ and $14 - 5 > 7 - 5$.
- If you multiply or divide both sides of an inequality by the same positive number, the inequality will still be true in the same sense. Thus, $3 < 8$ and $(6)(3) < (6)(8)$.
- If you multiply or divide both sides of an inequality by the same negative number, the inequality will still be true, but with the sense *reversed.* Thus, $4 < 9$; but if you multiply by (-2), you get $-8 > -18$. Notice that the "<" has become a ">."

Remember, for negative numbers, the one with the larger absolute value is the smaller number.

Notice that these rules hold whether you are working with < (is less than) and > (is greater than) or ≤ (is less than or equal to) and ≥ (is greater than or equal to). Use them to isolate the unknown quantity on one side of the inequality, leaving only known quantities on the other side. This is called *solving for the unknown.* Solutions to inequalities can be given in algebraic form or displayed on the number line.

Let's try an example:

For what values of x is $12 - x \geq 3x + 8$?

We solve this just like an equation. Start by adding the like quantity $(x - 8)$ to both sides in order to group the x terms on one side and the constants on the other; thus:

$$12 - x \geq 3x + 8$$
$$x - 8 = x - 8$$
$$4 \geq 4x$$

Now divide both sides by 4, which does not change the sense of the inequality, yielding:

$$1 \geq x$$

The inequality is true for any number less than or equal to 1 and false for any number greater than 1. For example, if $x = 3$, $12 - x = 9$ and $3x + 8 = 17$, and the inequality is not satisfied. Graphically, this can be shown as in the figure below:

Notice that the darkened section is the set of solution values, and the solid dot at $x = 1$ indicates that the value 1 is included in the solution set. By contrast, see the following figure. It shows the solution set for $x < 2$, where the open circle shows that $x = 2$ is not included.

Ready to try another question?

If $A < 2 - 4B$, can you tell how large B is in terms of A? Can you tell how small B is?

What we are really being asked is to solve the inequality for B. To start, add –2 to both sides, like this:

$$\begin{aligned} A &< 2 - 4B \\ -2 &= -2 \\ \hline A - 2 &< -4B \end{aligned}$$

Next divide by –4, remembering to reverse the inequality, like so:

$$\frac{A-2}{-4} > B; \ \frac{2-A}{4} > B$$

Notice two things here. When we changed the denominator on the left-hand side from –4 to +4, we also changed the sign of the numerator by changing $(A - 2)$ to $(2 - A)$. Of course, this is the equivalent of multiplying the numerator and the denominator by –1.

Also, this tells us what B is less than, but nothing about what B is greater than. For example, if A were 6, then $B < -1$, but B could be –100 or –1000 or anything else "more negative" than –1.

Logical, Very Logical

The fundamental ideas of logic are applied throughout algebra and geometry, and they don't suddenly stop there. Any statement must be true or false, but can never be both.

The statement "12 – 4 = 8" is true.

The statement "7 > –15" is false.

Two statements can be combined into a single statement using the word **and** (mathematical symbol, $\wedge$). Statements combined by using **and** are called **conjunctions.** Call the first statement above, **P**, and the second one **Q**. Then their conjunction is **P $\wedge$ Q.**

A **conjunction P $\wedge$ Q** is **true** when **P** and **Q** are **both true.**

A **conjunction P $\wedge$ Q** is **false** when either **P** or **Q** or both are **false.**

The conjunction 12 – 4 = 8 and 7 > –15 is **false** because **one** of the statements is false. That means that in this case, **P $\wedge$ Q** is **false.**

The conjunction "carrots are edible **and** red is a color" is **true**, because **both** parts are **true.**

For the two statements **P and Q**, there are four possible combinations of truth values: They are displayed in the following truth table:

P	Q	$P \wedge Q$	
T	T	T	Both Statements are true.
T	F	F	Only one statement is true.
F	T	F	Only one statement is true.
F	F	F	Both Statements are false.

Are these conjunctions true or false?

1. $(-7 \times -3 + 6 = 27) \wedge (4 + 9 \times 5 = 49)$ 2. $(19 - 4 \times 3 = 7) \wedge (15 - 8 < 7)$

In problem 1, the first statement is true and the second statement is true, so the conjunction is true. In conjunction 2, the first statement is true, but the second is false. That makes the conjunction false.

Two statements may also be combined by the word **or**. In everyday usage, a mother might tell her son, "You may have a hamburger or a hot dog for lunch today." What she means is **either** you have a hamburger **or** you have a hot dog. Only one of the two choices, not both, may take place. In mathematics, however, both taking place is considered as a possibility. In other words, if one **or** the other **or** both statements are true, then the entire statement is true. This is called a **disjunction**, and the mathematical symbol for it is $\vee$.

Statement **p**: Pigs can fly. Statement **q**: $15 - 27 = -12$

Disjunction: Pigs can fly **or** $15 - 27 = -12$

This disjunction is true, since one of the two statements is true.

A disjunction **p** $\vee$ **q** is **true** when at least **one** of the statements is **true.**

A disjunction **p** $\vee$ **q** is **false** when **both** statements are **false.**

A disjunction's truth table looks like this:

P	Q	$P \vee Q$	
T	T	T	Both Statements are true.
T	F	T	At least one statement is true.
F	T	T	At least one statement is true.
F	F	F	Both Statements are false.

DeMorgan's Law

DeMorgan's Law is a rule of inference about the NOT, AND, and OR operators. It is used to distribute a negative to a conjunction or disjunction. Let's look at the statement, "It is not true that he ate both Cereal and Pancakes."

Formally, that would be written: $\sim(C \wedge P)$, read "It is not true that he ate both Cereal and Pancakes." In the formal expression, C refers to the phrase "He ate Cereal" and P means "He ate Pancakes."

DeMorgan's Law states that the expression can be converted into another expression that is completely equivalent to the original one: $\sim C \vee \sim P$, meaning "He did not eat Cereal or he did not eat Pancakes."

To appreciate why this is equivalent, let's see what the original statement means. There are three possibilities:

1. He ate Cereal, but not Pancakes. Then C is true and P is false, or ~P is true.
2. He ate Pancakes, but not Cereal. Then P is true and C is false, or ~C is true.
3. He did not eat either Cereal or Pancakes. Then C and P are both false, or ~C and ~P are true.

Look closely at the three conclusions and you'll see in all of them that either ~C is true or ~P is true, or both ~C and ~P are true. This is an example of a disjunction. Formally we can write the following, together with the original statement:

$\sim(C \wedge P)$: It is not true that he ate both Cereal and Pancakes.

$\sim C \vee \sim P$: He did not eat Cereal or he did not eat Pancakes.

That is exactly what DeMorgan's Law means. Above the line of dashes is the given expression; below the line is the new expression formed by applying DeMorgan's Law. While in our example, it turned a conjunction into a disjunction, negating each member of the expression, it can also do the opposite and turn a disjunction into a conjunction:

$\sim(N \vee M)$: It is not true that the Newspaper is boring or the Magazine is interesting.

$\sim N \wedge \sim M$: The Newspaper is not boring and the Magazine is not interesting.

DeMorgan's Law can work both ways. Either of the examples above can be changed back into the original one by applying the same law.

Double Your Pleasure, Double Your Fun. . .

Many word problems lead to equations in two unknowns. Usually, you need as many equations as there are unknowns to solve for all or some of the unknowns. In other words, to solve for two unknowns, two independent equations are needed; to solve for three unknowns, three equations are needed, and so on. However, there are exceptions.

You should know the following two methods for solving two equations with two unknowns.

1. Method of substitution
2. Method of elimination by addition and subtraction

We'll show you examples of both methods. The first example uses the method of substitution:

> Mrs. Green and her three children went to the local movie. The total cost of their admission tickets was $14. Mr. and Mrs. Arkwright and their five children went to the same movie, and they had to pay $25. What was the cost of an adult ticket, and what was the cost of a child's ticket?

Expressing all amounts in dollars, let x = cost of an adult ticket, and let y = cost of a child's ticket.

For the Greens: $x + 3y = 14$

For the Arkwrights: $2x + 5y = 25$

The idea of the method of substitution is to solve one equation for one variable in terms of the other and then substitute that solution into the second equation. Here, we solve the first equation for x, because that is the simplest one to isolate:

$$x = 14 - 3y$$

Next, we substitute what we found for x in the second equation:

$$2(14 - 3y) + 5y = 25$$

This gives us one equation with one unknown that we can solve:

$$\begin{aligned} 28 - 6y + 5y &= 25 \\ -y &= -3 \\ y &= 3 \end{aligned}$$

Now that we know $y = 3$, we put this into $x = 14 - 3y$ to get:

$$x = 14 - 3(3) = 5$$

Thus, the adult tickets were $5.00 each and the children's tickets were $3.00 each.

Here is an example using the method of elimination (remember the Elimination Game we discussed in Chapter 1?):

> Paula and Dennis went to the bakery. Paula bought 3 rolls and 5 muffins for a total cost of \$3.55. Dennis bought 6 rolls and 2 muffins for a total cost of \$3.10. What was the price of one roll?

To solve this, keep in mind that, when there are dollars and cents, it's easiest to express all prices in terms of cents. Let r = the cost of a roll; let m = the cost of a muffin.

Paula paid $3r + 5m = 355$.

Dennis paid $6r + 2m = 310$.

The idea of the method of elimination is that adding equal quantities to equal quantities gives a true result. So we want to add some multiple of one equation to the other equation such that when the two equations are added together, one variable will be eliminated. In this case, it is not hard to see that if we multiply the first equation by –2, the coefficient of r will become –6. Then, if we add the two equations, r will drop out. Here's how it works:

–2 times the first equation is	$-6r - 10m =$	-710
The second equation is:	$6r + 2m =$	310
Adding:	$-8m =$	-400

Dividing by –8, $m = 50$. We now substitute this into either of the two equations. Let's use the second:

$6r + (2)(50) = 310$

$6r = 210$

$r = 35$

So, muffins are 50 cents each and rolls are 35 cents a piece.

The Word's Out, and It's a Problem

There are word problems of many different types. Many, like age or coin problems, involve only common sense. For others, there are specific formulas or pieces of factual knowledge that can be helpful.

For example, for *consecutive integer problems,* you need to know that consecutive integers differ by 1; therefore, a string of such numbers can be represented by $n, n + 1, n + 2, \ldots$ Consecutive even or odd integers differ by 2, so a string of such numbers can be represented as $n, n + 2, n + 4, \ldots$ That's right, in algebraic notation, *consecutive odd and consecutive even numbers are represented the same way*. After all, aren't both types exactly 2 apart?

Travel problems usually require you to use the formula d = rt, distance equals rate × time.

Here's the first example to try:

> Sarah is 6 years older than Myles. Three years ago, Sarah was twice as old as Myles. How old is Sarah today?

If you have trouble setting up the equations, try plugging in possible numbers. Suppose that Sarah is 20 today. If Sarah is 6 years older than Myles, how old is Myles? He is 14. You get from 14 to 20 by adding 6. So if S is Sarah's age and M is Myles', $S = M + 6$

Three years ago, Sarah was $S - 3$, and Myles was $M - 3$. So, from the second sentence, we know that $S - 3 = 2(M - 3)$, or $S - 3 = 2M - 6$. Thus, $S = 2M - 3$. Now, substituting $S = M + 6$, into the second equation:

$$M + 6 = 2M - 3$$

$$M = 9$$

Therefore, Sarah is 9 + 6 = 15.

Here's another example to help build your confidence when solving word problems:

> Three consecutive odd integers are written in increasing order. If the sum of the first and second and twice the third is 46, what is the second number?

Go ahead, you really ought to try to work this one out before checking the solution.

Calling the smallest number x, the second is $x + 2$, and the third is $x + 4$. Therefore, $x + (x + 2) + 2(x + 4) = 46$.

$$x + x + 2 + 2x + 8 = 46$$

$$4x + 10 = 46$$

$$4x = 36$$

$$x = 9$$

Hence, the second number is 9 + 2 = 11. Let's try one more word problem:

> It took Andrew $1\frac{1}{2}$ hours to drive from Aurora to Zalesville at an average speed of 50 miles per hour. How fast did he have to drive back in order to reach Aurora in 80 minutes?

Here's the solution: The distance from Aurora to Zalesville must be given by $d = rt = (50)(1.5) = 75$ miles. Since 80 minutes is 1 hour and 20 minutes, or $1\frac{1}{3} = \frac{4}{3}$ hours, we must solve the equation $75 = \frac{4}{3}r$. Multiplying by 3, we have $225 = 4r$; then, dividing by 4, $r = 56.25$ mph.

Wasn't that a lot of fun? You didn't think so? Oh, well! You're sure to enjoy the next section.

Coming to Terms with Algebra

In any group of algebraic and arithmetic expressions, each expression is called a *term. Monomial* describes a single term; for example, we might say that $2x + 3y^2 + 7$ is the sum of three terms or three monomials.

Technically, if we enclose an algebraic expression in parentheses, it becomes one term, so that we could say that $(x + 2y) + (3x - 5y^2)$ is the sum of two monomials. But usually, when we talk about a monomial, we mean a term that is a single product of certain given constants and variables, possibly raised to various powers. Examples might be 7, $2x$, $-3y^2$, $4x^2z^5$. Each of these is a monomial.

In a monomial, the constant factor is called the *coefficient of the variable.* Thus, in $-3y^2$, -3 is the coefficient of y^2. If we restrict our attention to monomials of the form $A \times n$ (that is to say numerical coefficients and variables multiplied together), the sums of such terms are called *polynomials* ("poly-" means many). *Polynomials with two terms* are called *binomials,* and those with three terms are called *trinomials* ("bi-" means two, and "tri-" means three). Expressions like $3x + 5$, $2x^2 - 5x + 8$, and $x^4 - 7x^5 - 11$ are all examples of polynomials.

The three examples just given are of degree 1, 2, and 5, respectively.

> In a polynomial, the highest power of the variable that appears is called the degree of the polynomial.

Try to solve the following example on your own:

Find the value of $3x - x^3 - x^2$ when $x = -2$.

We hope you didn't peek at this solution. Substitute -2 every place you see an x:

$$3(-2) - (-2)^3 - (-2)^2 = -6 - (-8) - (+4) = -6 + 8 - 4 = -2$$

Monomials with identical variable factors can be added or subtracted by adding or subtracting their coefficients: $3x^2 + 4x^2 = 7x^2$, and $3x^4 - 9x^4 = -6x^4$. To multiply monomials, take the product of their coefficients and take the product of the variable parts by adding exponents of factors with like bases: $(-4xy^2)(3x^2y^3) = -12x^3y^5$.

Monomial fractions can be simplified to be expressed in lowest terms by dividing out any common factors of the coefficients and then using the usual rules for subtraction of exponents in division. For example:

$$\frac{6x^3y^5}{2x^4y^3} = \frac{3y^2}{x}$$

Here's one more example to try:

Combine $9y - \frac{6y^3}{2y^2}$ into a single monomial.

This was simple, right? The fraction simplifies to $3y$, and $9y - 3y = 6y$.

I'll Have the Combo—To Go

Polynomials are added or subtracted simply by combining like monomial terms in the appropriate manner. Thus, $(2x^2 + 5x - 3) + (3x^2 + 5x - 12)$ is summed by removing the parentheses and combining like terms to yield $5x^2 + 10x - 15$. You can check this out by solving the following example:

What is the sum of $(3a^2b^3 - 6ab^2 + 2a^3b^2)$ and $(5a^2b^3 - 2a^3b^2)$?

First, remove the parentheses to combine the terms with identical letter parts by adding their coefficients:

$(3a^2b^3 - 6ab^2 + 2a^3b^2) + (5a^2b^3 - 2a^3b^2)$

$3a^2b^3 - 6ab^2 + 2a^3b^2 + 5a^2b^3 - 2a^3b^2$

$8a^2b^3 - 6ab^2$

Notice that the $2a^3b^2$ and $-2a^3b^2$ terms exactly cancelled out.

To multiply a polynomial by a monomial, use the distributive law to multiply each term in the polynomial by the monomial factor. For example, $2x(2x^2 + 5x - 11) = 4x^3 + 10x^2 - 22x$. When multiplying a polynomial by a polynomial, repeatedly apply the distributive law to form all possible products of the terms in the first polynomial with the terms in the second.

HIGH STAKES

The most common use of this is in multiplying two binomials, such as $(x + 3)(x - 5)$. In this case, there are four terms in the result: $x \cdot x = x^2$; $x(-5) = -5x$; $3 \cdot x = 3x$; and $3(-5) = -15$. But the two middle terms are added together to give $-2x$. Thus, the product is $x^2 - 2x - 15$.

Remember—a dot (·) means multiply.

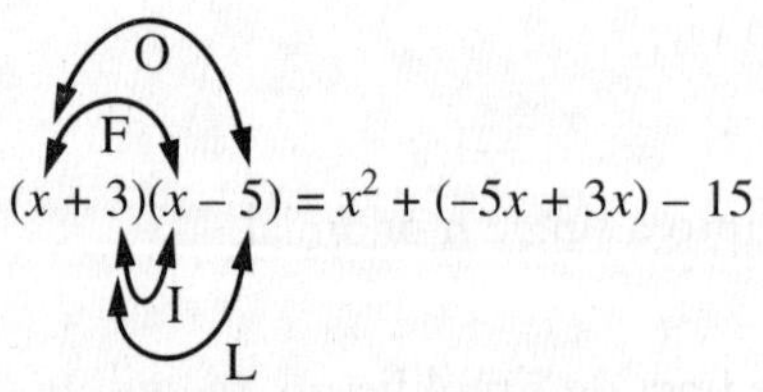

$$(x + 3)(x - 5) = x^2 + (-5x + 3x) - 15$$

$$= x^2 - 2x - 15$$

Be sure to remember these special cases:

- $(x + a)^2 = (x + a)(x + a) = x^2 + 2ax + a^2$
- $(x - a)^2 = (x - a)(x - a) = x^2 - 2ax + a^2$

OK. Let's try another one:

If m is an integer, and $(x - 6)(x - m) = x^2 + rx + 18$, what is the value of $m + r$?

The product of the last terms, $6m$, must be 18. If you don't see that, think about where the "18" came from on the right side of the equation. Therefore, $m = 3$. If $m = 3$, then the sum of the outer and inner products becomes $-6x - 3x = -9x$, which equals rx. Hence, $r = -9$, and $m + r = 3 + (-9) = -6$.

The Monomial Factor

Factoring a monomial from a polynomial simply involves reversing the distributive law. Sound hard? It's really not. For instance, if you are looking at $3x^2 - 6xy$, you should see that $3x$ is a factor of both terms. That means that you could just as well write this expression as $3x(x - 2y)$. Multiplication using the distributive law will restore the original expression.

Now try this example:

If $x - 5y = 12$, which is greater, $15y - 3x$ or -35?

Since we were told that $x - 5y = 12$, we can see that $15y - 3x$ factors to $-3(x - 5y)$. Therefore, it must equal $-3(12)$, which $= -36$, which is less than -35.

The Difference of Two Squares

Diane may be kind of geeky and Henry may wear a plastic shirt-pocket protector, but they're not the kinds of squares this section is about!

When you multiply $(a - b)(a + b)$ using the FOIL method (remember this from Chapter 2?), the middle terms exactly cancel out, leaving just $a^2 - b^2$. Thus, the difference of two squares, $a^2 - b^2 = (a - b)(a + b)$.

For example, $x^2 - 16 = (x - 4)(x + 4)$, and $x^2 - 36 = (x - 6)(x + 6)$. Do you think $x^2 - 100 = (x - 10)(x + 10)$? You're darned right it does.

However, the sum of two squares—$b^2 + 16$, for example—cannot be factored. That's right, not at all.

Think you've got it? Good. Try the example below.

If x and y are positive integers, and $x - 2y = 5$, which of the following is the value of $x^2 - 4y^2$?

(A) 0
(B) 16
(C) 45

Since $x^2 - 4y^2 = (x - 2y)(x + 2y) = 5(x + 2y)$, from the equation above, $x^2 - 4y^2$ must be divisible by 5. Therefore, 16 is not possible. If the result is to be zero, $x + 2y = 0$, which means that $x = -2y$, so that both numbers cannot be positive. That means the expression must equal 45, which you get if $x = 7$ and $y = 1$. The correct answer is (C).

Here's another one to solve:

If x and y are positive integers, and $y^2 = x^2 + 7$, what is the value of y?

No peeking. OK—are you finished?

If we rewrite the equation as $y^2 - x^2 = 7$ and factor, we have $(y - x)(y + x) = 7$. Thus, 7 must be the product of the two whole numbers $(y - x)$ and $(y + x)$. But 7 is a prime number that can only be factored as 7 times 1. Of course, $(y + x)$ must be the larger of the two; that means that $y + x = 7$, and $y - x = 1$. Adding the two equations gives us $2y = 8$; $y = 4$. Of course, $x = 3$, but nobody asked us that.

Square Roots Do not Imply Square Trees

The square root of a number *N*, written $\sqrt{N}$, is a number that when squared produces *N*. Therefore, $\sqrt{4} = 2$, $\sqrt{9} = 3$, $\sqrt{16} = 4$, and so on.

The symbol $\sqrt{\ }$ is called the *radical* sign, and many people refer to $\sqrt{N}$ as *radical N*. When we write $\sqrt{N}$, it is understood to be a positive number. So when faced with an algebraic equation like $x^2 = 4$, where you must allow for both positive and negative solutions, write $x = \pm\sqrt{4} = \pm 2$ (where ± is read *as plus or minus).*

You should be aware that $\sqrt{0} = 0$ and $\sqrt{1} = 1$. Square roots of negative numbers are not real numbers.

All positive numbers have square roots, but most are irrational numbers. Only perfect squares like 4, 9, 16, 25, 36, . . . have integer square roots.

If you assume that you are working with nonnegative numbers, you can use certain properties of the square root to simplify radical expressions. The most important of these rules is: $\sqrt{AB} = \sqrt{A} \times \sqrt{B}$. This can be used to advantage in either direction. Reading it from right to left, we may write:

$$\sqrt{3} \times \sqrt{12} = \sqrt{36} = 6\cdot$$

But you should also know how to use this rule to simplify radicals by extracting perfect squares from "under" the radical. That is to say, $\sqrt{18} = \sqrt{9 \times 2} = 3\sqrt{2}$.

The key to using this technique is to recognize the perfect squares in order to factor in a sensible manner. It would do you little to no good to factor 18 as 3 × 6 in the preceding example, since neither 3 nor 6 is a perfect square.

Take a shot at the following example:

If $\sqrt{5} \times \sqrt{x} = 10$, which is larger, $\sqrt{x}$ or $2\sqrt{5}$?

Pretty easy, right? Since $10 = \sqrt{100}$ and $\sqrt{5} \times \sqrt{x} = \sqrt{5x}$, we know that $5x = 100$ and $x = 20$. But $20 = 4 \times 5$, so $\sqrt{20} = 2\sqrt{5}$. That means that the two quantities are equal.

The Trinomial Factor

When you multiply two binomials $(x + r)(x + s)$ using the FOIL method, the result is a trinomial of the form $ax^2 + bx + c$, where b, the coefficient of x, is the sum of the constants r and s, and the constant term c is their product. We won't worry about a for the time being.

Trinomial factoring is the process of reversing this multiplication. For example, to find the binomial factors of $x^2 - 2x - 8$, we need to find two numbers whose product is –8 and whose sum is –2. Since the product is negative, one of the numbers must be negative and the other positive. The possible factors of 8 are 1 and 8 and 2 and 4. In order for the sum to be –2, we must choose –4 and +2. So, $x^2 - 2x - 8 = (x - 4)(x + 2)$.

Always look at the sign of the last term in a trinomial first. Suppose it's positive. Then look at the sign of the middle term. If that's also positive, both terms are positive. If the middle term is negative and the last term positive, there's only one explanation. This means that both factors of the last term are negative. So, $x^2 - 6x + 8 = (x - 4)(x - 2)$.

This technique can sometimes be used to solve quadratic equations (more on these in Chapter 6). If you have an equation like $x^2 - 7x + 6 = 0$, you can factor the trinomial. To do this, you need two numbers whose product is +6 and whose sum is –7. Since the product is positive, both must be of the same sign, and since the sum is negative they must both be negative. It is not hard to see that –6 and –1 are the only correct options.

Once the trinomial is factored, the equation becomes $(x - 1)(x - 6) = 0$. Of course, the only way a product of two or more numbers can be zero is if one of the numbers is zero. Thus, either:

$$x - 1 = 0 \text{ or } x - 6 = 0$$

$$x = 1 \text{ or } x = 6$$

Try the following example and see for yourself:

> The area of a rectangle is 60 and its perimeter is 32. What are its dimensions?

To solve this, you must recognize that the area of a rectangle is determined by the formula $A = LW$, and its perimeter is determined by the formula $P = 2L + 2W$ (where A stands for area, P for perimeter, L for length, and W for width). In this case, we have $LW = 60$ and $2L + 2W = 32$. Dividing by 2, $L + W = 16$. Therefore, $L = 16 - W$. We substitute what we just found into the equation $LW = 60$, giving:

$$(16 - W)W = 60$$

$$16W - W^2 = 60$$

Grouping everything on the right-hand side, we have

$$0 = W^2 - 16W + 60$$

We did that to get rid of the negative second degree term. Notice that you can move a term from one side of the equal sign to the other by simply changing its sign. Next, we'll move the "= 0" to the right, simply because we can without changing the meaning of anything, and most people are used to working from left to right.

$$W^2 - 16W + 60 = 0$$

Now, factoring:

$$(W - 10)(W - 6) = 0$$

This yields $W = 10$ or $W = 6$. Of course, if $W = 6$, $L = 10$, and if $W = 10$, $L = 6$. Either way, the dimensions are 6×10.

The Quadratic Formula Has Nothing to Do with Baby Formula

Some quadratic equations are not solvable by factoring using rational numbers. For example, because $x^2 + x + 1$ has no factors using whole numbers, $x^2 + x + 1 = 0$ has no rational roots (solutions).

In other cases, rational roots exist, but they are difficult to find. For example, $12x^2 + x - 6 = 0$ can be solved by factoring, but the solution is not easy to see:

$$12x^2 + x - 6 = (3x - 2)(4x + 3)$$

Setting each factor equal to zero, $3x - 2 = 0$ or $4x + 3 = 0$ yields $x = \frac{2}{3}$, or $x = \frac{3}{4}$.

What can you do when faced with such a situation? You use the *Quadratic Formula*, which states that for any equation of the form $ax^2 + bx + c = 0$, the roots are:

$$x = \frac{-b \pm \sqrt{b^2 - 4ac}}{2a}$$

> The Quadratic Formula always works. That is, there are some quadratics (most of them, actually) that do not factor, so you can't solve them by factoring. The Quadratic Formula will always find the solution, whether the quadratic was factorable or not.

If you have not committed this formula to memory yet, do it now. The *a, b,* and *c* represent the three numerical parts of the equation in the order that they appear. Memorize this mantra: "*x = minus b plus or minus the square root of b squared minus 4ac all over 2a.*" The "*all over*" is probably the most important part.

Once you've got the formula down, try your hand at the following question.

If $6x^2 - x - 12 = 0$, what is the smallest integer greater than x?

Use the quadratic formula to solve for x. First identify a, b, and c as $a = 6$, $b = -1$, and $c = -12$. We substitute into the formula, to get:

$$x = \frac{-(-1) \pm \sqrt{-1^2 - 4(6)(-12)}}{2(6)} = \frac{1 \pm \sqrt{1+288}}{12} = \frac{1 \pm \sqrt{289}}{12} = \frac{1 \pm 17}{12}$$

Using the plus sign:

$$x = \frac{1+17}{12} = \frac{18}{12} = \frac{6}{4} = 1\frac{1}{2}$$

Using the minus sign:

$$x = \frac{1-17}{12} = \frac{-16}{12} = -\frac{4}{3} = -1\frac{1}{3}$$

Both possible values of x are less than 2, so the correct answer is 2.

The Sky's the Limit

Later, in Chapter 6, we're going to review graphing quadratic equations. You should be aware that some such graphs have no limit and go on up (or down) infinitely. Others can get very close to a certain value but can never actually reach that value. Imagine, if you will, a graph in which a curve is approaching $x = 2$ from the left. The graph gets closer and closer to the line $x = 2$, but no matter how far up the line is extended, it never actually reaches it. We say that $x = 2$ is the **limit** for the x value of that curve. You're familiar with limits in real life. As a child, you were told to go no farther away than such and such a landmark. As a teenager you're told to be home by such and such a time, and no later. Isn't it reassuring to know that graphs can have limits too?

Complex Numbers Don't Refer to Vitamins B_6 or B_{12}

Sometimes when applying the quadratic formula, the *discriminant*, $d = b^2 - 4ac$, will be a negative number. In such a case, you have to deal with the square root of a negative number. This negative number is called *imaginary.* In general, if N is any positive number, then $\sqrt{-N}$ is written as $i\sqrt{N}$, where i is the square root of –1.

Numbers of the form bi, where b is a real number, are called *pure imaginary numbers.* For example, $\sqrt{-4} = i\sqrt{4} = 2i$ and $\sqrt{-3} = i\sqrt{3}$ are both pure imaginary numbers.

Numbers of the form $a + bi$, where a and b are both real numbers, are called *complex numbers.* Thus, complex numbers have both a real and an imaginary part.

> When doing arithmetic with complex numbers, just think of i as an unknown, like x, except whenever you get an i^2 in a computation, replace it with –1.

Here's an example:

If $z = 4 + 3i$ and $w = 3 - 4i$, $zw - \dfrac{z}{w} = ?$

(A) $14 - i$
(B) $7 - 25i$
(C) $24 - 6i$
(D) $24 - 8i$

The correct answer is (D). Multiplying $(4 + 3i)(3 - 4i)$ by the FOIL method yields $12 - 7i - 12i^2$. Replacing i^2 with –1, we have $12 - 7i - 12(-1) = 12 - 7i + 12 = 24 - 7i$.

To find $\dfrac{z}{w}$ in the form $a + bi$ so that we can subtract it from zw, we need to rationalize the denominator of the fraction by multiplying the numerator and denominator of the fraction by the *conjugate* of w. (The conjugate of $a + bi = a - bi$.) When you multiply these two, the term involving i drops out, and you end up with just $a^2 + b^2$. Like this:

$$\frac{z}{w} = \left(\frac{4+3i}{3-4i}\right) \times \frac{3+4i}{3+4i} = \frac{12+25i+12i^2}{3^2+4^2} = \frac{25i}{25} = i$$

Hence, $zw = \frac{z}{w} = (24 - 7i) - i = 24 - 8i$. The correct answer is (D).

> The conjugate of a complex number is often referred to as the complex conjugate for, hopefully, obvious reasons.

Let's try another example:

Which of the following is one root of $x^2 - 4x + 5 = 0$?

(A) $4 - i$

(B) $2 - i$

(C) $2 + 2i$

(D) $3i$

This one's a bit more complicated, but you can do it. Using the quadratic formula with $a = 1$, $b = -4$, and $c = 5$, we have:

$$x = \frac{-(-4) \pm \sqrt{4^2 - 4(1)(5)}}{2(1)} = \frac{4 \pm \sqrt{16 - 20}}{2} = \frac{4 \pm \sqrt{-4}}{2} = \frac{4 \pm 2i}{2}$$

Dividing each term in the numerator by the denominator 2 gives us $x = 2 \pm i$. Since we can choose either + or –, we see that $2 - i$ is one root. This means that the correct answer is (B).

Raising the Roots and Fractional Exponents

The symbol $\sqrt[n]{x}$ is used to represent the nth root of the number x. The nth root of x is that number which, when raised to the nth power, gives x as a result. For example, $\sqrt[3]{8} = 2$ because $2^3 = 8$.

Roots can also be represented by using fractional exponents. To be precise, we define $x^{\frac{1}{n}} = \sqrt[n]{x}$. In particular, the $\frac{1}{2}$ power of a number is its square root. So, for example:

$$16^{\frac{1}{2}} = \sqrt[2]{16} = \sqrt{16} = 4$$

and

$$125^{\frac{1}{3}} = \sqrt[3]{125} = 5$$

In addition, other fractional powers can be defined by using the laws of exponents. That is, one can interpret an expression like $x^{\frac{3}{5}}$ to mean $\left(x^{\frac{1}{5}}\right)^3$ because $\frac{3}{5} = \left(\frac{1}{5}\right)^3$. So we get:

$$32^{\frac{3}{5}} = \left(\sqrt[5]{32}\right)^3 = 2^3 = 8$$

Negative fractional powers can be similarly calculated by remembering that $x^{-n} = \frac{1}{x^n}$.

For example, to calculate $8^{\frac{-2}{3}}$, we first find $8^{\frac{-2}{3}} = \frac{1}{\left(\sqrt[3]{8}\right)^2} = \frac{1}{(2)^2} = \frac{1}{4}$.

Find the value of $\dfrac{3x^0 + x^{\frac{1}{2}}}{2 + x^{\frac{3}{4}}}$ if $x = 16$.

Are you finished yet? Let's work through the solution. First, let's calculate the numerator and denominator separately. In the numerator, $x^0 = 1$ for any x and $x^{\frac{1}{2}} = \sqrt{x}$. So, $3(16^0) + 16^{\frac{1}{2}} = 3(1) + \sqrt{16} = 3 + 4 = 7$.

In the denominator, $16^{-\frac{3}{4}} = (16^{-\frac{1}{4}})^3$, which means that the denominator is $\frac{16}{8} + \frac{1}{8} = \frac{17}{8}$. The original expression is equal to $16^{-\frac{3}{4}} = \frac{1}{\left(\sqrt[4]{16}\right)^3} = \frac{1}{2^3} = \frac{1}{8}$, which means that the denominator is $\frac{16}{8} + \frac{1}{8} = \frac{17}{8}$. So, the original expression is equal to $\dfrac{7}{\frac{17}{8}} = 7\left(\frac{8}{17}\right) = \frac{56}{17}$.

Just in case that last solution confused you, remember— when dividing by a fraction, the divisor is inverted (turned upside-down) and then you multiply.

Learning to Function Properly

Two variables, let's say x and y, may be related in a number of ways. In a *function* or *functional relationship,* one variable, usually x, is called the *independent variable.* The other, usually y, is the *dependent variable.* For every choice of x, precisely one y is defined. As x varies, y varies in an exactly predictable fashion.

In this situation, we say that "y is a function of x," meaning that the value of y is determined by the value of x. The function itself is denoted by f (or g, or h,...). The collection of possible values of the independent variable is called the *domain* of f. The y-value associated with a given x-value is denoted by $f(x)$ (read "f of x"). The collection of possible values of the dependent variable is called the range of f.

If an expression $f(x)$ defines a function, then the y value corresponding to any specific x can be found by simply substituting the value for x in the expression $y = f(x)$.

Ready to try an example? Here you go:

> Suppose that the relation between x and y is given by $y = f(x)$, where $f(x) = x^2 + 3x - 4$. Find $f(1)$ and $f(2 + a)$.

To find the value of the function for any number, substitute that number for x in the expression for $f(x)$. In essence, we think of this function as $f(\ ) = (\ )^2 + 3(\ ) - 4$, and then we fill in the blanks. To find $f(1)$, we substitute 1 for x wherever it appears, like this:

$$f(1) = (1)^2 + 3(1) - 4 = 1 + 3 - 4 = 0$$

So $f(1) = 0$. In the same manner:

$$f(2+ a) = (2+ a)^2 + 3(2 + a) - 4$$

$$= 4 + 4a + a^2 + 6 + 3a - 4$$

$$= a^2 + 7a + 6$$

Let's try another one:

> Letting $f(x) = x^2$ and $g(x) = x + 3$, find each of the following:
>
> (A) $g(2)f(5)$
>
> (B) $f(g(1))$
>
> (C) $g(f(x))$

(A) $g(2) = 2 + 3 = 5$; $f(5) = 5^2 = 25$; $g(2)f(5) = 5(25) = 125$.

(B) To find $f(g(l))$, first find $g(l) = 1 + 3 = 4$. Now $f(g(1)) = f(4) = 4^2 = 16$.

(C) To find $g(f(x))$, substitute $f(x)$ every place you see an x in $g(x) = x + 3$. In other words, $g(f(x)) = f(x) + 3$. But, since $f(x) = x^2$, $g(f(x)) = x^2 + 3$.

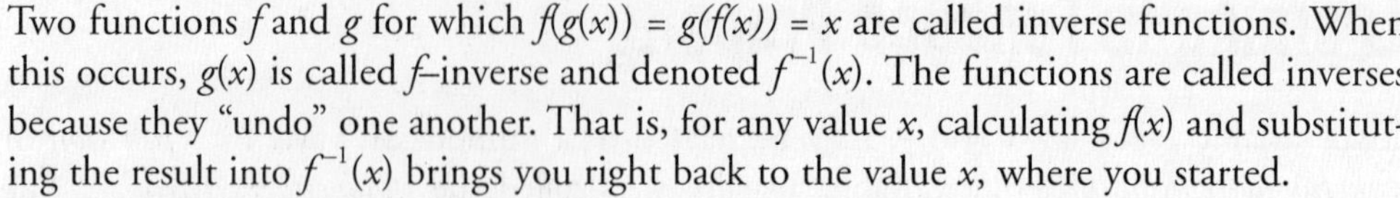
Two functions f and g for which $f(g(x)) = g(f(x)) = x$ are called inverse functions. When this occurs, $g(x)$ is called f–inverse and denoted $f^{-1}(x)$. The functions are called inverses because they "undo" one another. That is, for any value x, calculating $f(x)$ and substituting the result into $f^{-1}(x)$ brings you right back to the value x, where you started.

Of course, you might rightly say, "Then why bother in the first place?" Well, we hope you understand why after the next section.

These Opposites Are Very Attractive

Among the most important examples of inverse functions are the *exponential* and *logarithmic functions.* For any constant $b > 0$ and $b \neq 1$, the exponential functions $f(x) = b^x$ and $g(x) = \log_b x$ are inverse functions. That is, $\log_b b^x = x$ and $b^{\log_b x} = x$. That is, the logarithm is the exponent. b is called the base of the logarithm.

The two most frequently encountered bases are 10, the base for *common logarithms,* and e, the base for *natural logarithms.* You should know that the symbol $\log x$ with no base shown is assumed to be the logarithm to the base 10. The symbol $\ln x$ is used as short hand for the natural logarithm. That is, $\ln x = \log_e x$. Thus, $\log 10^x = x$; $10^{\log x} = x$; $\ln e^x = x$; and $e^{\ln x} = x$.

The main properties of the exponential function are determined by the laws of exponents.

It is important to recognize that the relationships $b^k = N$ and $\log_b N = K$ are equivalent. That is, any relationship between the variables written in logarithmic form may be rewritten in exponential form, and vice versa.

Here's a quick example:

If $\log_x 125 = 3$, what is x?

This statement is equivalent to $x^3 = 125$, for which we can see by inspection that $x = 5$.

There are certain properties of the logarithm that you should know that also follow from the laws of exponents.

- $\log_b M + \log_b N = \log_b MN$
- $\log_b M - \log_b N = \log_b \frac{M}{N}$

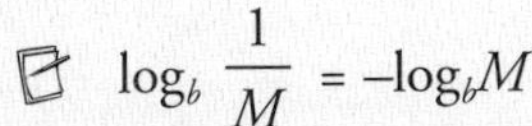

- $\log_b \frac{1}{M} = -\log_b M$
- $k\log_b M = \log_b M^k$

You should also know that $\log_b 1 = 0$, and that the $\log_b M$ is only defined for positive values of M; that is, the log is undefined for zero or negative values.

Ready for another example?

> If $f(x) = 6^x$ and $g(x) = \log_6 x$, what expression is equal to $f(2g(M))$?
> (A) 2^M
> (B) 6^M
> (C) M^6
> (D) M^2

Here's the solution: $2g(M) = 2\log_6 M = \log_6 M^2$. Therefore, $f(2g(M)) = M^2$. The correct answer is (D).

Pop Quiz

Ready for another Pop Quiz?

1. What is the result when (36×10^{-3}) is multiplied by (5×10^{-4})?
   (A) 18×10^{1}
   (B) 18×10^{-1}
   (C) 18×10^{-6}
   (D) 18×10^{-7}

2. Forty high school students were asked who they wanted to speak at graduation, and 12 students answered Kelly Clarkson, winner of *American Idol.* Based on the results of this survey, how many students in a class of 200 would likely indicate that they want Kelly Clarkson to speak at graduation?
   (A) 24
   (B) 36
   (C) 60
   (D) 120

3. Solve for b: $2b > 40$
   (A) $b = 20$
   (B) $b > 20$
   (C) $b < 20$
   (D) $b \geq 20$

4. What are the roots of the equation $2x^2 + 7x + 5 = 0$?

5. Irving is using chicken wire to build a rectangular chicken coop that will enclose 400 square feet of space. If Irving wants to spend as little money as possible, which of the following dimensions for the coop will cost him the least amount of money?
   (A) 10×40
   (B) 20×20
   (C) 16×25
   (D) 12.5×32

6. At Dodgeville Dairies, the formula for the production of cottage cheese is $f(x) = x^2 - 12x + 27$, in which x represents the number of gallons of milk used. For what value of x will the production of cottage cheese be the greatest?
   (A) 1
   (B) 3
   (C) 9
   (D) 10

Answers and Explanations

1. **The correct answer is (C).** Scientific (exponential) notation is a type of shorthand used when a number is either very big or very small. In this case, $5 \times 10^{-4} = 0.0005$ (to determine this, write a 5 on your paper and move the decimal point four spaces to the left). Whenever you multiply two numbers in exponential notation, multiply the numbers first ($36 \times 5 = 180$), and multiply the exponential terms by adding the exponents ($10^{-3} \times 10^{-4} = 10^{-7}$). The result is 180×10^{-7}. At this point, choice (D) might be tempting, but you're not done yet. $180 \times 10^{-7} = (18 \times 10) \times 10^{-7}$; by the associative property of multiplication, this is the same as $18 \times (10 \times 10^{-7})$, which equals $18 \times (10^1 \times 10^{-7})$, or 18×10^{-6}.

2. **The correct answer is (C).** This problem calls for a proportion to compare the smaller sampling of students to the larger group. Line up the relationships between the parts and the wholes to set up the proportion:

   $$\frac{12}{40} = \frac{x}{200}$$

   Whenever two fractions are equal to each other, you can cross multiply:

   $$40 \times x = 12 \times 200$$

   $$40x = 2{,}400$$

   $$\frac{40x}{40} = \frac{2{,}400}{40}$$

   $$x = 60$$

3. **The correct answer is (B).** Inequalities can be solved just like equalities as long as you don't multiply or divide by a negative number. You don't have to do that here, so just divide both sides of the inequality by 2:

$$2b > 40$$
$$\frac{2b}{2} > \frac{40}{2}$$
$$b > 20$$

4. When you're asked to solve a quadratic equation, it always pays to see if you can save a little time (and avoid the quadratic formula) by factoring. After a little trial and error, you can determine that $2x^2 + 7x + 5 = 0$ is factorable:

   $2x^2 + 7x + 5 = (2x + 5)(x + 1)$.

   Set each factor equal to zero to find the roots:

$$2x + 5 = 0 \qquad x + 1 = 0$$
$$x = -\frac{5}{2}. \qquad x = -1.$$

5. **The correct answer is (B).** For this problem, you need to know how to calculate the perimeter of a rectangle; the formula is $2l + 2w$, in which l is the length and w is the width. Calculate each of the perimeters among the answer choices:

   (A) $2(10) + 2(40) = 20 + 80 = 100$

   (B) $2(20) + 2(20) = 40 + 40 = 80$

   (C) $2(16) + 2(25) = 32 + 50 = 82$

   (D) $2(12.5) + 2(32) = 25 + 64 = 89$

   Since Irving wants to save money, he will pick the rectangle with the smallest perimeter (and that will thus require the least amount of chicken wire).

6. **The correct answer is (A).** Plug in the four answer choices and see which one gives you the greatest answer. Be careful of the trick, though: The test writers want you to pick choice (D), because 10 is the greatest number among the choices. As we'll see, looks can be deceiving:

   (A) $f(1) = (1)^2 - 12(1) + 27 = 16$

   (B) $f(x) = (3)^2 - 12(3) + 27 = 0$

   (C) $f(x) = (9)^2 - 12(9) + 27 = 0$

   (D) $f(x) = (10)^2 - 12(10) + 27 = 7$

CHAPTER 5

REVIEWING GEOMETRY—IT'S NOT JUST FOR SQUARES

There are certain things you need to remember from geometry for your math exit-level exam, and some things that you don't. For example, you need to know that π (pi) is a constant that has a lot to do with a circle, and which can only be approximated. Unless specifically told to use a different value, such as $\frac{22}{7}$, go with $\pi = 3.14$. You will need to remember how to solve a geometric proof. You'll also need to remember some basic terms, like congruent, similar, rhombus, trapezoid, and parallel lines. Don't forget right angles or wrong angles. (We just made up that last one to see whether you were paying attention.) We cover all of the above in this chapter and more.

First, let's start with a few essential definitions:

- A *point* is a location in a *plane* (flat surface) that has no dimension—in other words, it does not take up space.

MATH

- A *ray* is an infinite series of points. Infinite means "continuing forever without end." A ray has a single endpoint and has a direction, which never changes.
- A *line* is an infinite series of points having no endpoint or is two opposite rays with the same endpoint.
- A *line segment* is a portion of a line with two definite endpoints. A line segment is the shortest distance between two points.

Learning All the Angles

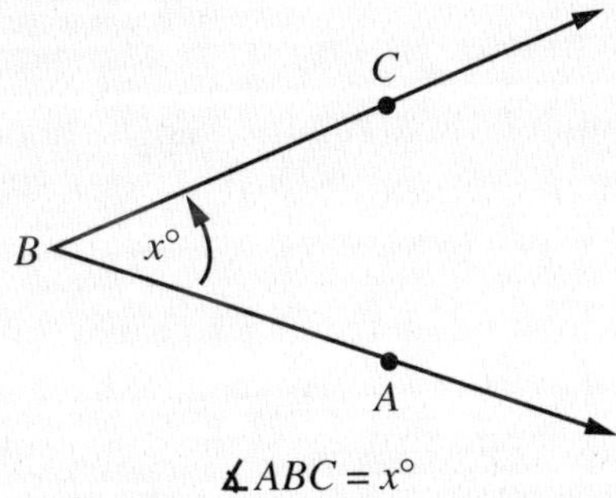

$\measuredangle ABC = x°$

Before we plunge right into sample angle problems, you need to know some of the basics. So here are some points to remember:

- An *angle* is formed when two *rays* going in different directions originate from the same point.
- Angles are usually measured in *degrees* or *radians.*
- A *radian* is the length of arc on a circle equal in length to the radius of that circle.
- 2π radians make a full circle.

From that information, and the fact that there are 360° of central angle (an angle formed by 2 *radii* when one stays still and the other is rotated through one entire arc of the circle), you should be able to compute equivalent angles, degrees to radians. Of course, the previous sentence assumes that you know that radii are the plural of *radius,* which is a line from the center of a circle to the circle itself. So, $180° = \pi$ radians, $90° = \frac{\pi}{2}$ radians, and so forth.

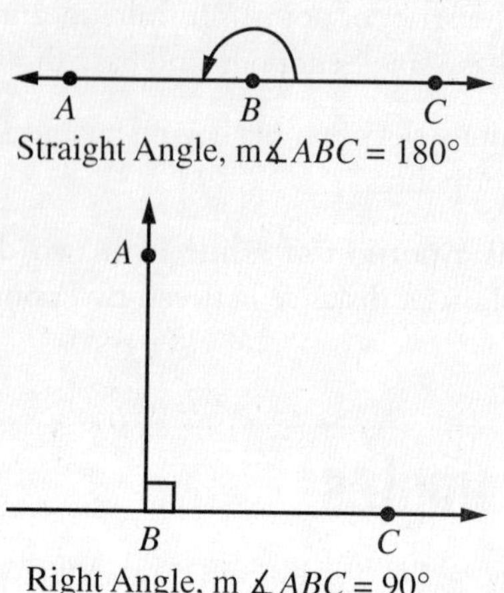

Straight Angle, m∡ABC = 180°

Right Angle, m ∡ABC = 90°

A *straight angle* has a measure of 180°. Any two angles adding up to 180° are called *supplementary angles.* For example, two angles that measure 80° and 100° are supplementary.

With the above information in mind, note that two equal supplementary angles are 90° each, and a 90° angle is called a *right angle.* Two angles that add up to 90° (a right angle) are called *complementary.* This means that 25° is the complement of 65°.

Based upon the amount of rotation, angles may be classified. Angles less than 90° are called *acute,* and angles between 90° and 180° are called *obtuse.* The sum of all the angles around a given point must total 360°. Two lines, rays, or segments that meet at right angles are called *perpendicular.*

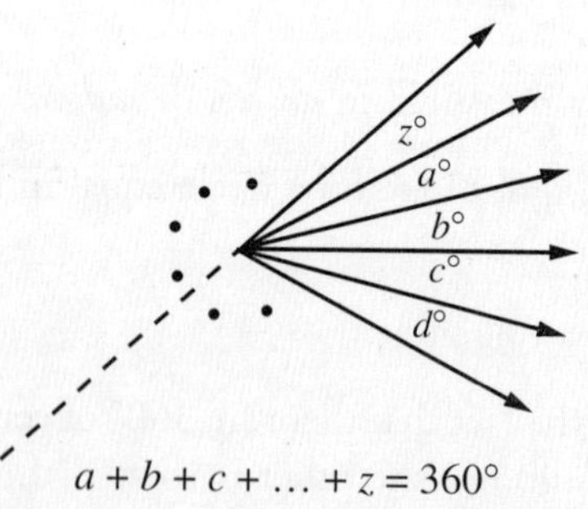

$a + b + c + \ldots + z = 360°$

Now let's get to some sample questions to put your new knowledge of angles to the test.

Find x in the diagram below.

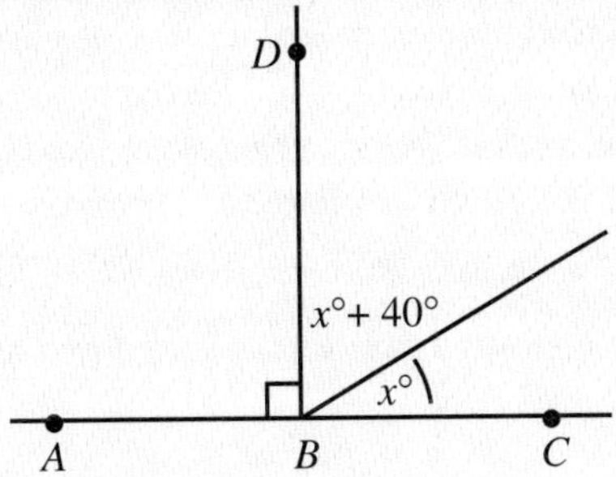

Since $\angle ABD$ is a right angle, so is $\angle DBC$. Thus, $x + (x + 40) = 90$. Removing parentheses: $x + x + 40 = 90$, $2x = 50$, $x = 25$.

Here's another chance to find that x again. Check out the diagram below.

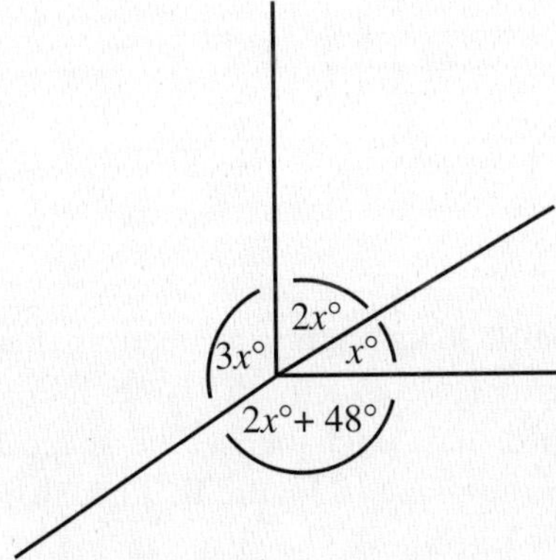

Did you find it? If you did, you would have come to the following solution:

$8x + 48 = 360$, $8x = 312$, $x = 39$.

Symmetry

Symmetry is a sameness. Have you ever folded a piece of paper in half and then cut out half a heart-shape? Most people have. Unfold the paper and there's your heart. If you turn the unfolded heart over onto its back so that what was the back is now in front, the figure looks the same. That is known as **bilateral symmetry**. Bilateral means **two sides.** When a figure has bilateral symmetry, both sides are the same.

A second type of symmetry is **point symmetry**, also known as **rotational symmetry**.

Point Symmetry?

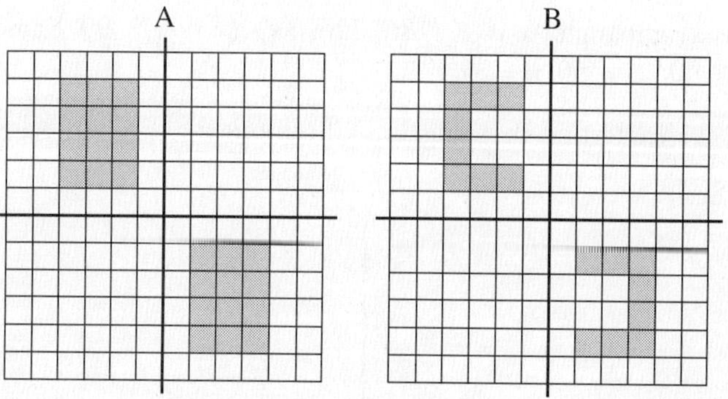

Look at Figure A. The geometric shape in the first quadrant has been rotated 180° around the origin. The resulting figure looks exactly the same. It could just as easily have been slid diagonally across the grid. It is unchanged. The shape in A is said to have point symmetry. Compare that to the shape in Figure B. That shape has clearly been turned, and now opens in the other direction. The shape in Figure B does NOT have point symmetry.

Transformations

There are many ways to change (transform) a figure without changing its shape or size. If you have ever seen a house next to a lake, looking into the lake, if it is calm enough, you will see the reflection of the house. The house appears to be in a different position, and with a different orientation (upside down), but the reflection has not changed in shape or size from the original house. The house is said to have been **transformed** by **reflection**. The diagram below shows two such transformations.

Reflections

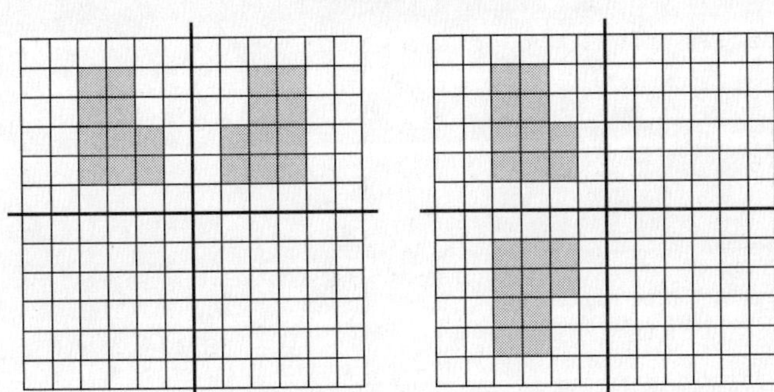

The shape on the left has been reflected across the *y*-axis. It is as if the *y*-axis were the mirror. In the right-hand diagram, the shape has been reflected across the *x*-axis. It is as if the *x*-axis were the mirror. Reflections may also be thought of as **flips.**

A second type of transformation is known as **translation**. That's a fancy name for a **slide.**

Translations

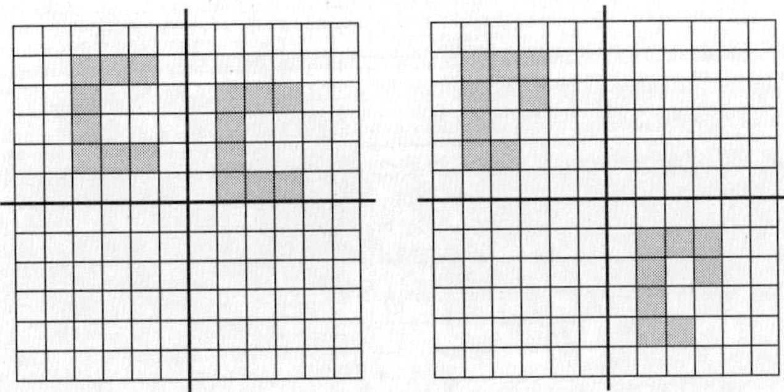

Look at both diagrams above. In each case, the figure's orientation has not changed as it has been moved. Their shapes and sizes also have not changed. These are both examples of transformation by translation, or sliding. Hey, I've got a million of 'em—well, two more, anyway.

You are already familiar with rotation of 180° to test for symmetry; well, rotation about a point is also a form of transformation.

Rotations

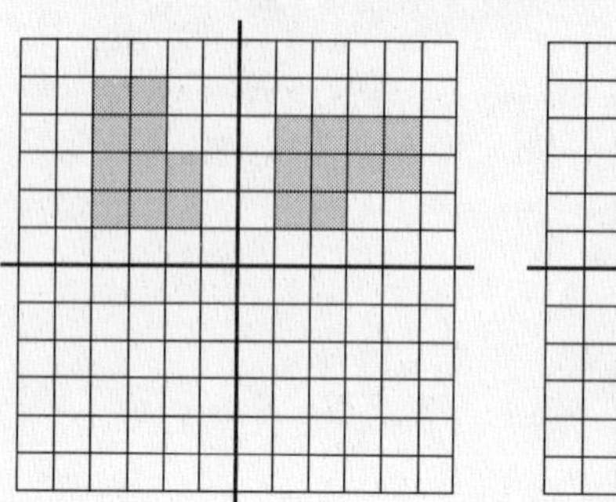

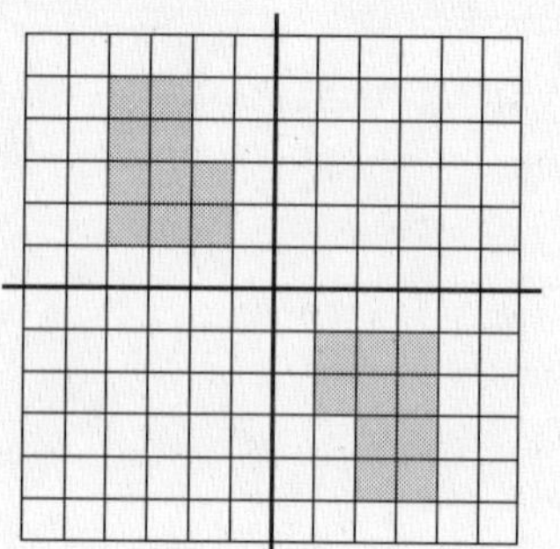

The shape on the left has been rotated 90° about the origin, while the one on the right has been rotated 180°. Notice that neither rotation displays any form of point symmetry. Also notice that neither the size nor the shape has been altered—a situation that will change in our fourth and final transformation.

Dilation

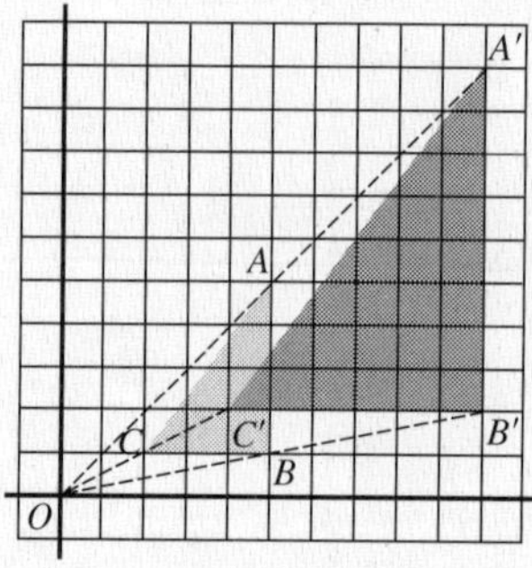

Dilation is the last of the transformations we'll look at. Triangle *ABC* has been dilated centered on point *O* to form triangle *A'B'C'*. Notice that the new triangle has the same shape as the original one, but is a different size. It was dilated with a scale factor of 2—which means the sides of the new triangle are twice as large as those of the original. Follow the dotted lines from Point *O* through the vertices of the original triangle, *ABC*, and you'll see how triangle *A'B'C'* was formed.

Triangles—The Original Three-Pointers

Closed figures made up of line segments are known as polygons. The word polygon means "many sides." The simplest of the polygons is the triangle—a closed figure with three sides. We'll cover polygons in general later in this chapter. In this section, let's focus on triangles.

There are two ways to classify triangles—by angles or by sides. Here are the three types of triangles that are classified by sides:

- **Equilateral triangle:** a triangle that has three sides of equal length
- **Isosceles triangle:** a triangle that has two sides of equal length (the sides are known as the legs and the non-equal side is known as the base)
- **Scalene triangle:** a triangle that has no two sides equal in length

There are three types of triangles that are classified according to their angles:

- **Acute triangle:** contains only acute angles (reminder: acute means containing fewer than 90°)
- **Right triangle:** contains exactly one right angle
- **Obtuse triangle:** contains exactly one obtuse angle (reminder: obtuse means that an angle is greater than 90° but less than 180°)

Add up the measures of the three angles in any triangle and you'll get 180°, which is the same as the measure of a straight angle. This fact is usually combined with other properties in the solution of geometric problems.

And speaking of problems, try the following example:

> In triangle *ABC,* the degree measure of $\angle B$ is 30° more than twice the degree measure of $\angle A$, and the measure of $\angle C$ is equal to the sum of the other two angles. How many degrees are there in the smallest angle of the triangle?

Did you work it through? Here's a breakdown of the solution:

Calling the measure of $\angle A$ in degrees x, we have the following:

x = number of degrees in $\angle A$

$2x + 30$ = number of degrees in $\angle B$

$x + (2x + 30) = 3x + 30$ = number of degrees in $\angle C$

Add this up and we have $x + 2x + 30 + 3x + 30 = 180$. Combining like terms:

$6x + 60 = 180;\ 6x = 120;\ x = 20.$

Clearly, $2x + 30$ and $3x + 30$ are larger than x, so the smallest angle is 20°.

In a triangle, the sum of the lengths of any two sides must exceed the length of the third. Therefore, you cannot draw a triangle with sides of lengths 3, –6, –10, because $3 + 6 < 10$. Therefore, in comparing any two sides, the longer side will be opposite the larger angle.

Now try the following example:

> A triangle has sides with lengths of 5, 12, and x. If x is an integer, what is the minimum possible perimeter of the triangle?

To solve this, you need to note that, in any triangle, the sum of the lengths of any two sides must exceed the length of the third. Therefore, $x + 5 > 12$, which means that $x > 7$. The smallest integer greater than 7 is 8. Hence, the minimum possible perimeter is $5 + 12 + 8 = 25$.

Can you see why the maximum perimeter of this triangle is 33? $5 + 12 = 17$, so the third side cannot be larger than 16.

Isosceles Triangles Are Not Three-Cornered Popsicles

As you now know, a triangle with two sides of equal length is called an *isosceles triangle.* If all three sides are equal, or congruent, it is called an *equilateral triangle.* The angles opposite the equal sides in an isosceles triangle (as shown in the diagram below) are equal in measure; therefore, if two angles in a triangle are congruent, the triangle is isosceles.

If all three angles are equal, the triangle is equilateral. This tells us that for an equilateral triangle, each angle has a degree measure of 60°. For those of you who are faint of heart, turn away, while I tell the rest that an equilateral triangle is also *equiangular.* That means if the sides are equal, so are the angles.

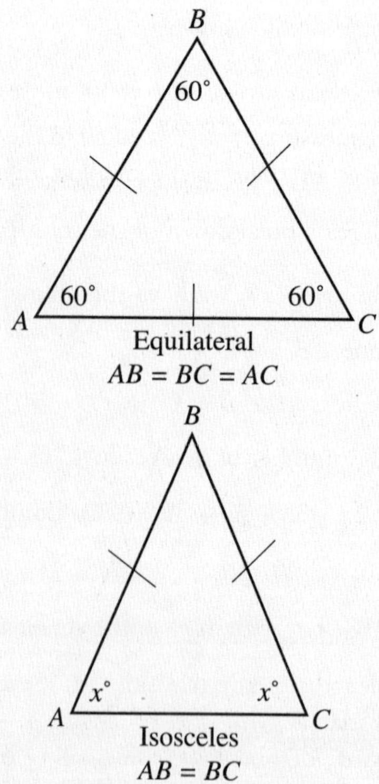

Here is a good example of how this fact can be used in a problem:

If in triangle *ABC*, as shown in the figure below, $AC = BC$ and $x \leq 50$, what is the smallest possible value of y?

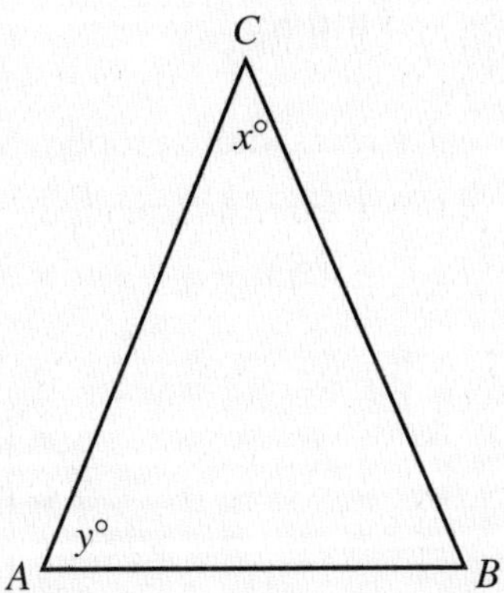

Since sides *AC* and *BC* are of equal length, the two base angles, $\angle A$ and $\angle B$, must be equal. As always, the three angles must total 180°. Hence, $x + 2y = 180$, which means that

$$y = \frac{180 - x}{2} = 90 - \frac{1}{2}x.$$

Now, the smallest possible value for y is achieved when x is as large as possible; that is, when

$x = 50$, for which $y = 65$.

Here's another example, just to make sure you *really* understand it:

In the triangle shown below, $AB = BC$. Which is longer, *AC* or *AB*?

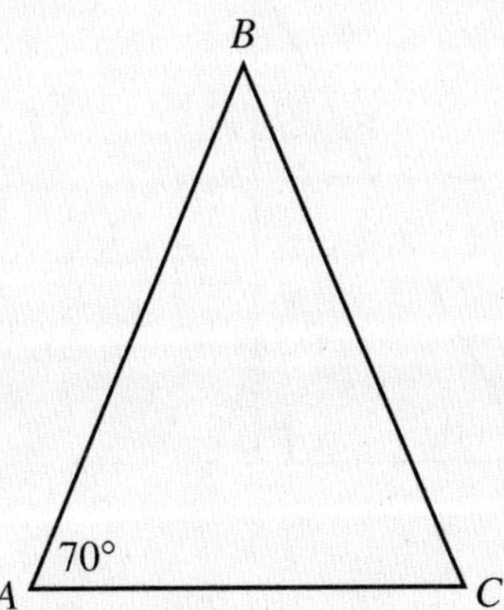

Note: Diagram not drawn to scale.

Since the triangle is isosceles, the base angles are equal. Thus, m$\angle A$ = m$\angle C$ = 70°. This implies that $\angle B$ = 40° (in order to reach the full 180° in the triangle). But that means that $AB > AC$, because it is the side opposite the larger angle.

You're So Special? Right, Triangles!

There are two special right triangles with whose properties you should be familiar. The first is the *isosceles right triangle,* also referred to as the *45°-45°-90° triangle.* By definition, its legs are of equal length, and its hypotenuse is $\sqrt{2}$ times as long as either leg.

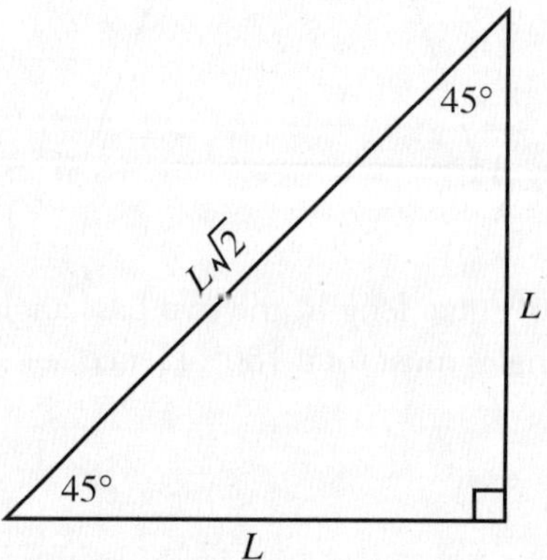

The other important right triangle is the *30°-60°-90° triangle.* You can see by reflecting it across its altitude that this is half of an equilateral triangle. So, the shorter leg is half the hypotenuse, and the longer leg (the one opposite either right triangle's 60° angle) is $\sqrt{3}$ times the shorter leg.

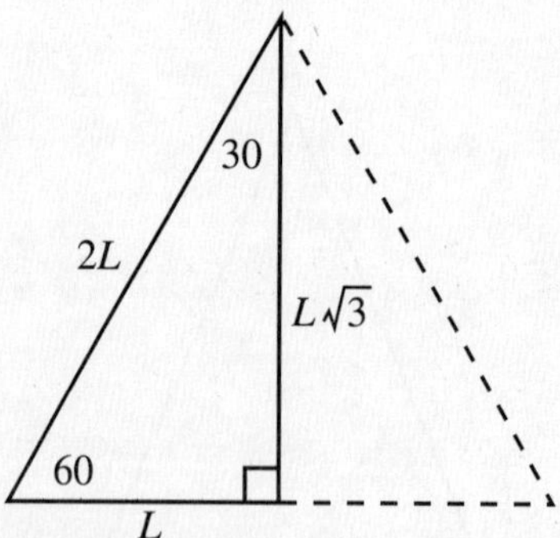

Remember these two triangles, as well as the Pythagorean Triples (if you are not sure of these, see the next section that covers the Pythagorean Theorem), because they always come up, and it'll save you a lot of grief.

OK. Let's try an example:

Find the area of the region shown in the diagram below.

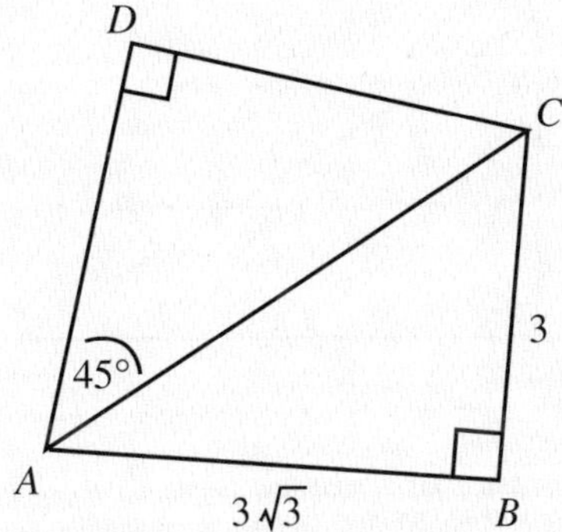

Here's a breakdown of the solution. Since $BC = 3$ and $AB = 3\sqrt{3}$, we know that triangle ABC is a 30°-60°-90° right triangle. That means that we know that $AC = 6$, and taking one-half the product of the legs, the triangle has an area of $\frac{1}{2}(3)(3\sqrt{3}) = \frac{9}{2}\sqrt{3}$.

Since triangle ADC is an isosceles right triangle with a hypotenuse of 6, and we know that the hypotenuse is the length of a leg times $\sqrt{2}$, each leg must be the hypotenuse divided by $\sqrt{2}$ (work it out as an equation if you need to), or $\frac{6}{\sqrt{2}}$.

Again, taking one-half the product of the legs, the triangle has an area of $\frac{1}{2}\left(\frac{6}{\sqrt{2}}\right)\left(\frac{6}{\sqrt{2}}\right) = \frac{1}{2}\left(\frac{36}{2}\right) = \frac{36}{4} = 9$. Finally, by adding the two areas, we have $9 + \frac{9}{2}\sqrt{3}$.

In the figure above, if side BC were equal to CD and side AB were equal to AD it would be known as a kite. Picture it on a string and with a rag tail.

The Pythagorean Theorem Is Just Right—er, Triangles

As we already mentioned, when one angle in a triangle is a right angle, the triangle is called a *right triangle.* The longest side of a right triangle, which is opposite the right angle, is called the *hypotenuse.*

The *Pythagorean Theorem* tells us that the square formed on the hypotenuse of a right triangle is equal to the sum of the squares on the other two sides (or *legs).* In symbols, we usually remember this as shown in the figure below.

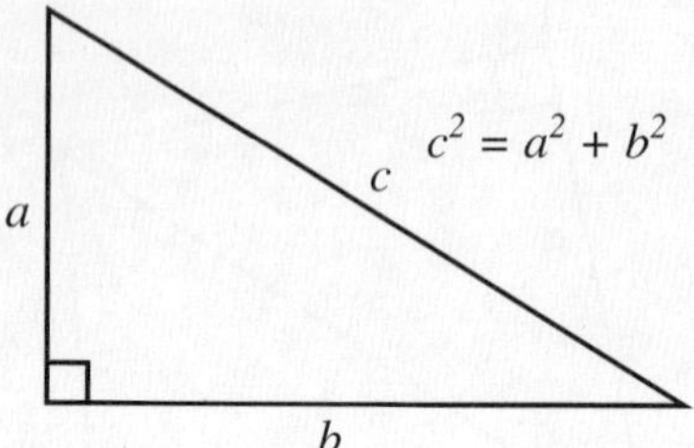

In the interest of making life easier on yourself, you should remember some well-known *Pythagorean triples,* that is, sets of whole numbers such as *3-4-5* for which $a^2 + b^2 = c^2$. Right triangles whose sides correspond to the numbers that make up a Pythagorean triple appear commonly on exit exams. Other less easily recognized Pythagorean triples are 5-12-13, 8-15-17, and 7-24-25. In addition, look for multiples of the triples, such as 6-8-10 or 15-20-25.

There are other important cases that yield non-integer solutions for the lengths of the sides of a right triangle. For example, the hypotenuse of a triangle with one leg of length 1 and the other of length 2 can be found by writing $c^2 = 1^2 + 2^2$. Thus, $c^2 = 5$ and $c = \sqrt{5}$.

Time to try to find the *x* again in another example.

Find *x* in the diagram below.

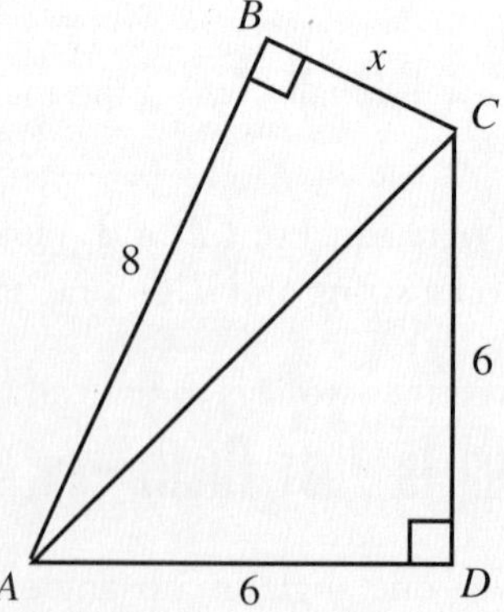

Did you find it? Using the Pythagorean Theorem in triangle *ACD,* the theorem tells us that, if c = side *AC,* then $6^2 + 6^2 = c^2$. So, $c^2 = 72$. In triangle ABC, letting x represent the length of *BC,*

$$72 = c^2 = x^2 + 8^2. \text{ That is, } x^2 = 72 - 64 = 8. \text{ Thus } x = \sqrt{8} = 2\sqrt{2}.$$

See Any Triangles in the Area?

In any triangle, you can construct a line from one *vertex* (intersection) perpendicular to the opposite side. (Sometimes that side may have to be extended outside the triangle, as shown in the second case below.) This line is called the *altitude* or *height.* The area of a triangle is given by the formula $A = \frac{1}{2}bh$, where b = the length of the base and h = the height (length of the altitude).

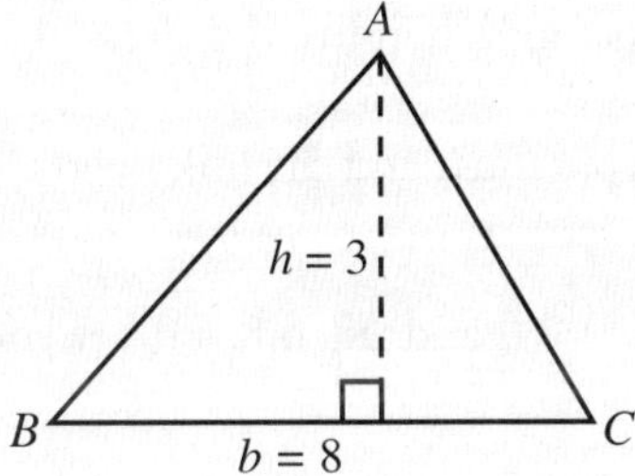

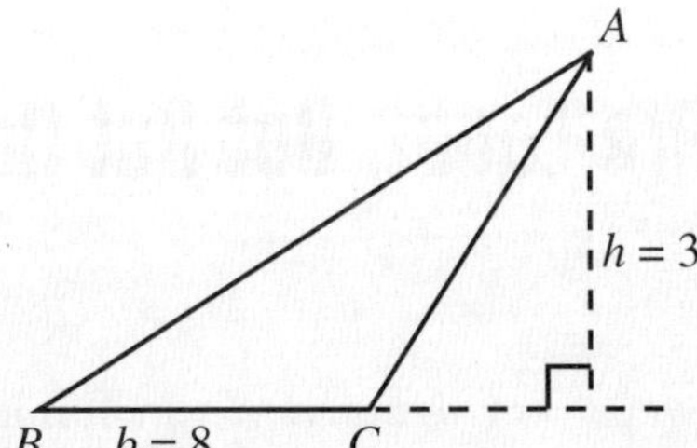

Both triangles shown in the diagram above have the same area:

$$A = \frac{1}{2}(8)(3) = 12$$

For a right triangle, you can use the two legs as base and altitude since they are always perpendicular to one another. For example, in a 5-12-13 right triangle, the area is $\frac{1}{2}(5)(12) = 30$.

Here's an example:

> In triangle *ABC*, *AB* = 6, *BC*= 8, and *AC* = 10. Find the altitude from vertex *B* to side *AC*.

Since the sides are 6-8-10, the triangle is a disguised 3-4-5 right triangle (didn't you notice the funny moustache?) with AC being the hypotenuse. Drawing the triangle as described produces the diagram below.

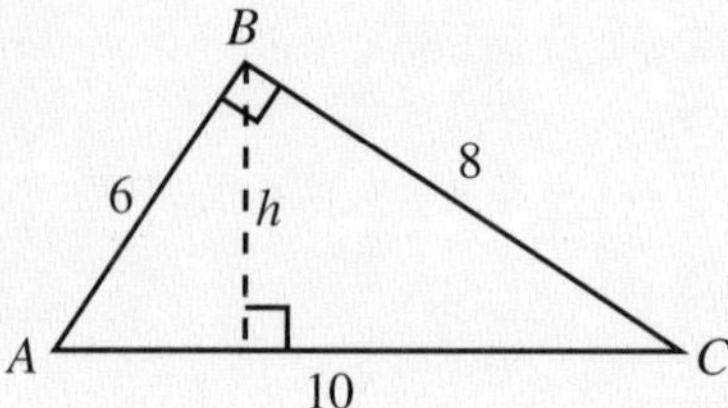

By using the two legs as base and height, the area of the triangle must be $A = \frac{1}{2}(6)(8) = 24$. By using the hypotenuse and the unknown altitude, the area must be $A = \frac{1}{2}(10)(h) = 5h$. Therefore, $5h = 24$, and $h = 4.8$. I'll bet you enjoyed that one. I know I did.

Vertical Angles Are Equal, But Not Necessarily Vertical

When two lines intersect, two pairs of *vertical angles* are formed (as shown in the following diagram). The "facing" pairs are equal and, of course, the two angles that form a pair on one side of either line add up to 180°. Notice that vertical angles are angles on two sides of a vertex, formed by a pair of intersecting lines; they do not have to go up and down, like the traditional meaning of the word "vertical." As a matter of fact, the two vertical angles marked $x°$ are horizontal. How about that!

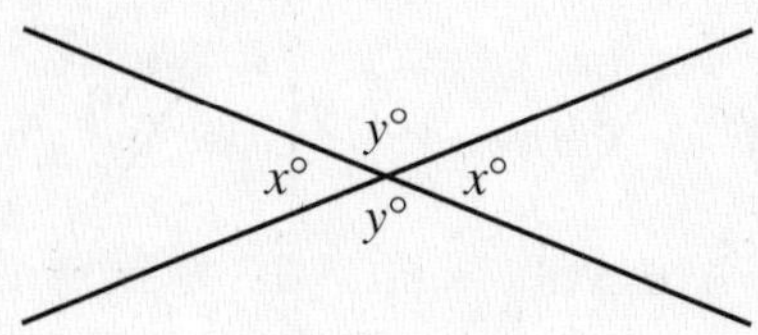

Try the following example:

In the diagram below, which is larger, $x + y$ or $w + z$?

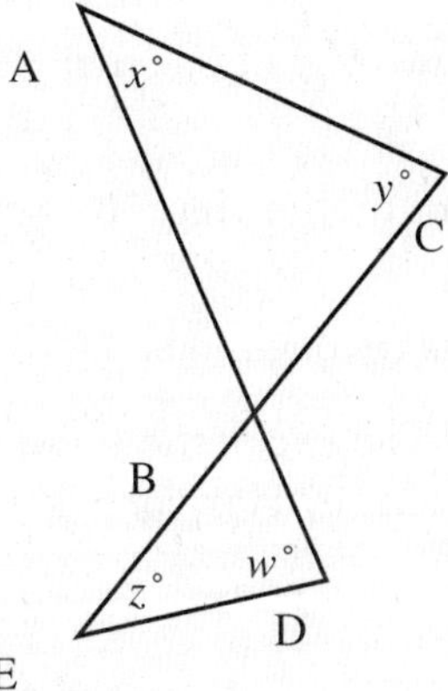

OK. We know that the sum of the angles in any triangle is 180°. Letting the measure of the vertical angles in either triangle be m, we have, in the upper triangle, $x + y = 180 - m$.

Looking at the smaller triangle, we know that $w + z = 180 - m$. Therefore, $x + y = w + z$. The quantities named are equal.

Hmm, There's Something Similar about Those Triangles.

Two triangles with two corresponding angles of equal angle measure are known as **similar triangles.**

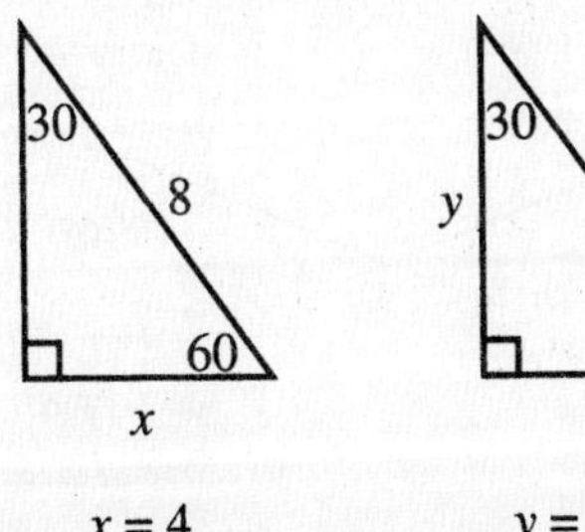

$x = 4$ $\qquad$ $y = 5\sqrt{3}$

The fact of the matter is, if two angles of one triangle are equal in degree measure with two angles of another triangle, then their third angles must also be of equal degree measure. Similar triangles are similar in shape, but their sides are not necessarily equal in length. Should their sides be equal in length they would be known as **congruent** triangles. What is true of the sides of similar triangles is that they are in proportion. With that in mind, find x in the triangle above.

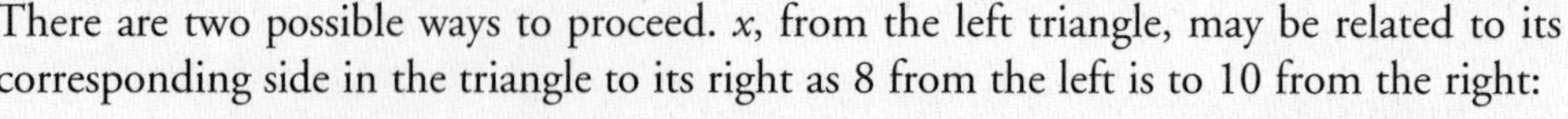

There are two possible ways to proceed. x, from the left triangle, may be related to its corresponding side in the triangle to its right as 8 from the left is to 10 from the right:

$$\frac{x}{5} = \frac{8}{10}; \text{ then } 10x = 40; x = 4$$

Or, you could have related the two legs of one triangle to those of the other, like this:

$$\frac{x}{8} = \frac{5}{10}; \text{ cross multiplying, } 10x = 40; \text{ then } x = 4$$

How did you like that one? Let's try one more.

> Study the diagram below. The two vertical lines are parallel. Can you prove that the two triangles are similar? How long is side Y?

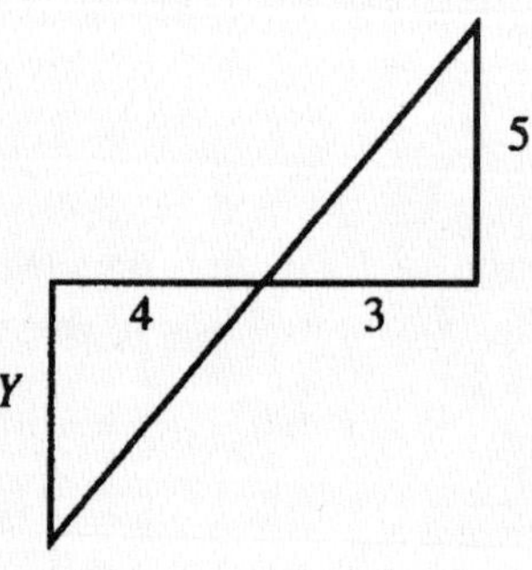

There is a form for a geometric proof, and it consists of having two columns, one for statements, and one for reasons.

Statement	Reason
1. *The vertical lines are parallel.*	1. *Given*
2. *The two angles formed at the intersection of the parallel lines and the transversal are equal.*	2. *Corresponding angles of parallel lines are equal.*
3. *The two angles formed in the triangle where the transversal and the horizontal intersect are equal.*	3. *Vertical angles are equal.*
4. *The triangles are similar.*	4. *If two angles of a triangle are Equal to two angles of another triangle, they are similar ... triangles.*

The last reason might have been abbreviated, simply Angle, Angle, or AA.

Now that the triangles have been proven to be similar, all that is needed is a proportion to find the value of *Y*.

$$\frac{Y}{4} = \frac{5}{3}\text{; cross multiplying, } 3Y = 20; Y = 6\frac{2}{3}$$

There you go.

Working for Scale

Scale drawings are very much like similar triangles, in that their parts are in proportion. The scale names what that proportion (or multiplier) is. Suppose a scale drawing of a parking lot is in the shape of a rectangle, and is 7 cm wide and 13 cm long. The scale is 1 cm = 20 meters. What are the actual dimensions of the parking lot?

Well, if 1 cm stands for 20 meters (m) then 7 cm stands for 7 × 20 = 140 m. That's the width. Next, the length must be 13 × 20 = 260 m. So the actual dimensions are: w = 140 m; l = 260 m.

Let's try another type of scale drawing problem. Marcia is building a scale model of an automobile. The actual car is 18 feet long. The scale is $\frac{11}{32}$ in. = 1 ft. How long will the model be?

To solve, multiply $\frac{11}{32} \times 18$. $\quad \frac{11}{32} \times \frac{18}{1} = \frac{198}{32} = 6\frac{3}{16}$ in.

Let's try one more. A model-railroader is building a layout with a scale of $\frac{1}{2}$ in. = 5 ft. The tallest tree on his layout is $6\frac{1}{2}$ inches tall. How tall must the real tree be? Do you see how to solve it? How about like this?

$$6\frac{1}{2} = \frac{13}{2}$$

$$\frac{13}{2} \times \frac{5}{1} = \frac{65}{2}$$

$$= 32\frac{1}{2}\text{ ft.}$$

Transversals Are Not from Transylvania

Parallel lines are two or more lines in the same plane that, no matter how far extended, will *never* meet. If you start with two lines parallel to one another and draw a line that crosses them, the crossing line is called a *transversal.* The intersection of the transversal with the parallel lines creates several sets of related angles. In particular, the *corresponding angles* (labeled *C* in the following diagram) and the *alternate interior angles* (labeled *A* in the following diagram) are always equal. You should notice that there is a second pair of alternate interior angles on the opposite sides of the transversal from the pair marked. There are three other pairs of corresponding angles in addition to the ones marked.

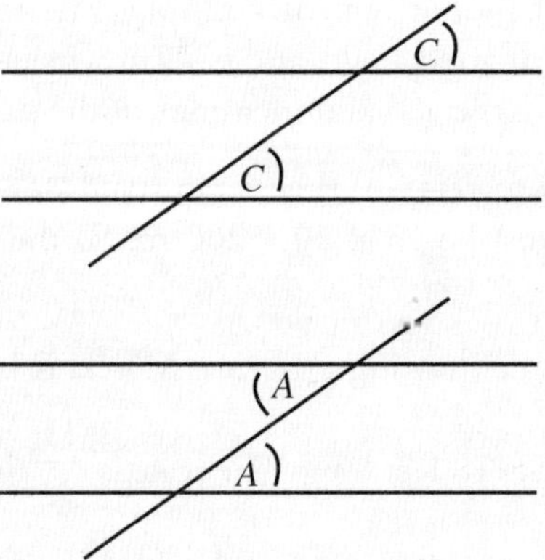

Combining these properties with your knowledge about vertical angles and the angles in a triangle can lead to some interesting examples.

In the diagram below, ℓ_1 is parallel to ℓ_2. Find x.

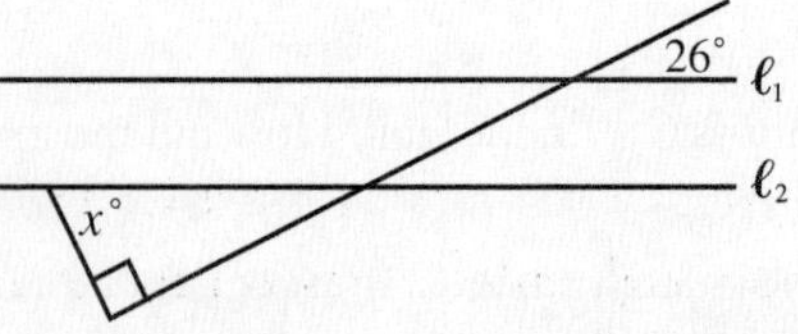

Here's an illustrated version of the solution with the diagram labeled below.

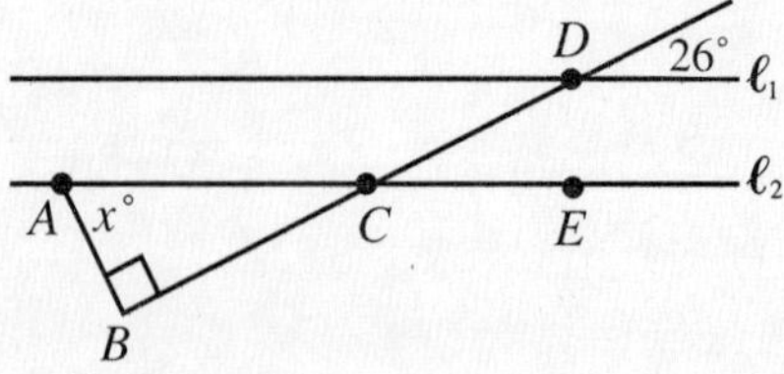

We see that m$\angle DCE = 26°$, which makes m$\angle ACB = 26°$. Since triangle ABC is a right triangle, x is the complement of 26°, or 64°.

You're going to really enjoy this next one:

In the diagram below, lines ℓ_1 and ℓ_2 are parallel. Find x.

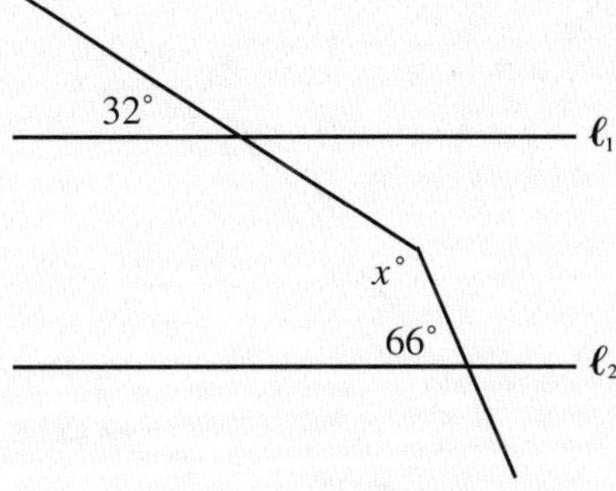

Sometimes, you have to improvise. A crooked transversal is of no help, so let's do something about that. Extend the line AB, as shown in the diagram below.

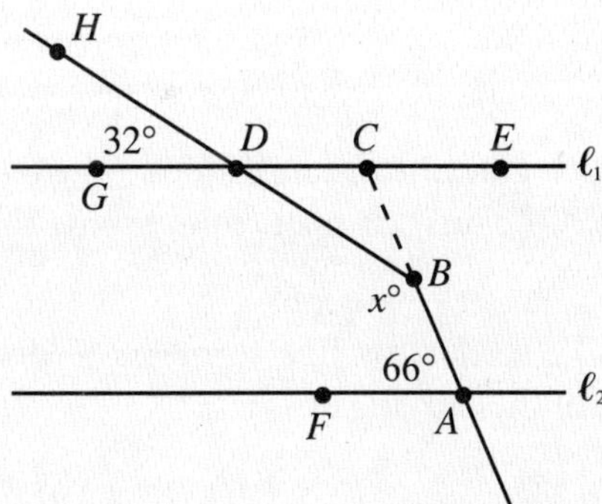

Look at the angles in triangle BCD. As alternate interior angles, m$\angle BCE$ = m$\angle BAF$ = 66°, so its supplement in the triangle, m$\angle C$, must equal 114°. As vertical angles, m$\angle CDB$ = m$\angle HDG$ = 32°. Therefore, in the triangle, m$\angle CDB$ = 32°. Since the three angles in the triangle must sum to 180°, m$\angle CBD$ = 34°. So x is the supplement to 34°—that is, 146°.

Polygon Does Not Necessarily Mean the Parrot's Missing

Any geometric figure with straight line segments for sides is called a *polygon.* It is possible to draw a polygon with one or more interior angles greater than 180°, as illustrated in the figure below.

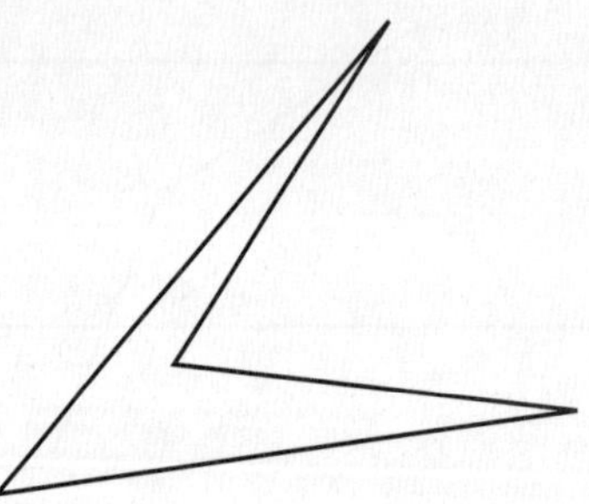

However, if each of the interior angles in the polygon is less than 180°, we have a *convex polygon.* The sum of the angle measurements in any convex polygon is $180(n - 2)$, where n is the number of sides. Thus, for a triangle, $n = 3$, so the sum is $180(3 - 2) = 180°$. For a *quadrilateral* (a four-sided figure), $n = 4$, and the sum is 360°. For a *pentagon* (a five-sided figure), $n = 5$, and the angle sum is 540, and so on.

To find th*e perimeter* of a polygon (the distance around the figure), simply add together the lengths of all the sides. Of course, it may require some thinking to determine each length.

To find its area, connect the vertices by line segments to divide the polygon into triangles; then sum the areas of these triangles.

Now for the example to solve:

Find the area of figure *ABCDE* shown below.

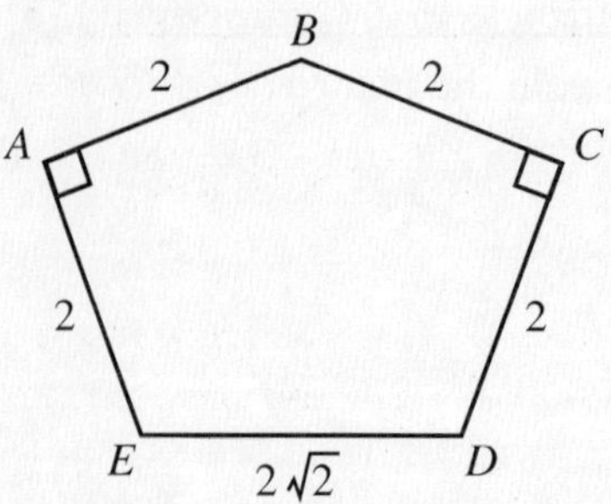

Ready for the solution?

By drawing the line segments *BE* and *BD,* we divide the region into three triangles as shown. Triangles *ABE* and *BCD* are both 45°-45°-90° right triangles, making $BE = BD = 2\sqrt{2}$.

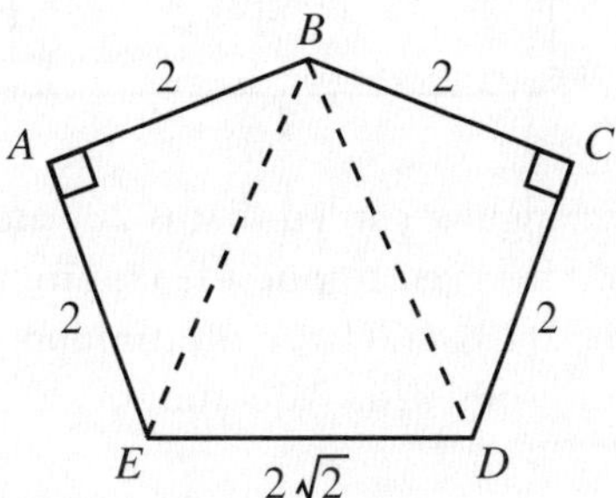

This makes the central triangle an equilateral triangle, even though it may not look like it. Remember, don't assume that a figure is drawn to scale, unless it says so. The area of each of the two outer triangles is $\frac{1}{2}(2)(2) = 2$, so the two together have an area of 4. The center triangle has a base whose length is $2\sqrt{2}$. If you draw the altitude, you get a 30°-60°-90° right triangle with a shorter leg whose length is $\sqrt{2}$. This makes the height $\sqrt{3}$ times that, or $\sqrt{6}$. This gives an area of $\frac{1}{2}\left(2\sqrt{2}\right)\left(\sqrt{6}\right) = \sqrt{12} = 2\sqrt{3}$. Finally, the total area of the polygon is $4 + 2\sqrt{3}$.

A *parallelogram* is a quadrilateral in which the pairs of opposite sides are parallel. The opposite angles and the opposite sides in a parallelogram are equal (see the figure below).

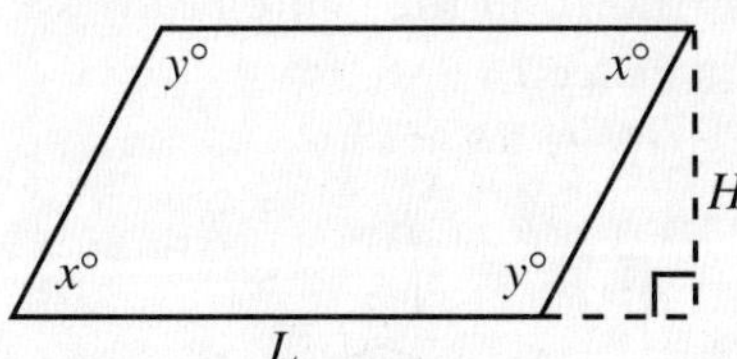

The area of a parallelogram is determined by its length times its height; that is, $A = LH$, as labeled in the diagram.

If the angles in the parallelogram are right angles, we have a *rectangle.* For a rectangle of length L and width W, the area is $A = LW$, and the perimeter is $P = 2L + 2W$.

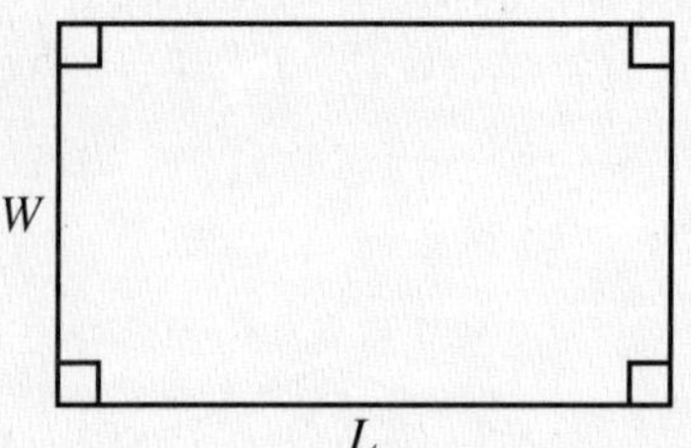

For example, the area of a rectangular garden that is 20 yards long and 10 yards deep is (20)(10) = 200 square yards. However, to put a fence around the same garden (that is, around its perimeter) requires 2(20) + 2(10) = 60 running yards of fencing. These relatively easy formulas can lead to some tricky questions.

Time for another example:

> If sod comes in 4 × 4 foot squares costing $3.50 per square, how much will it cost to sod the lawn shown below (all distances indicated in feet)? You may assume that all angles that appear to be right angles are right angles.

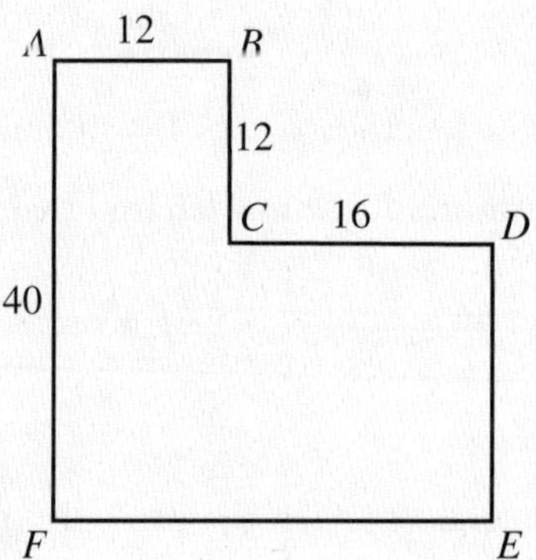

Completing the rectangle, as shown in the figure below, we see that the large rectangle *AGEF* is 40 × 28 = 1,120 square feet.

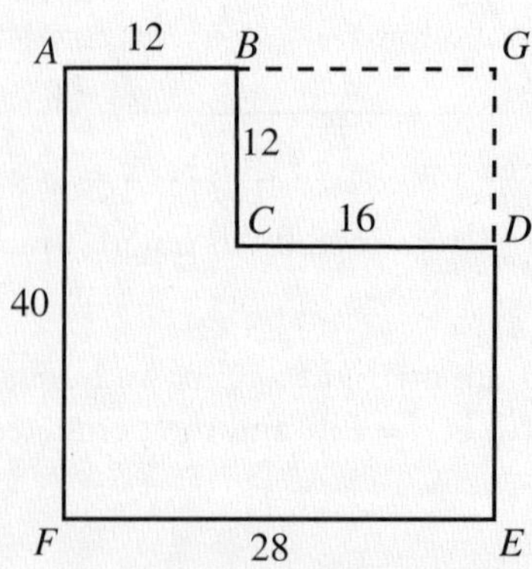

The smaller rectangle *BGDC* is 12 • 16 = 192 square feet. (Yes, "•" is a multiplication sign.) Hence, the area that must be sodded is 1,120 – 192 = 928 square feet. Now, each 4 × 4-foot piece of sod is 16 square feet. Therefore, we need 928 ÷ 16 = 58 squares of sod at \$3.50 each. The total cost is (58)(3.50) = \$203.

Here's one more example (you should be good at this by now!):

> A rectangle has one side whose length is 6 and a diagonal whose length is 10. What is its perimeter?

And here's the solution:

> Notice that the diagonal of a rectangle divides the rectangle into two identical right triangles. Hence, the other side of this rectangle can be calculated by using the Pythagorean Theorem. We recognize that side 6 and diagonal 10 implies that we have a 6-8-10 right triangle [(3-4-5)(2)], so the unknown side is 8. The perimeter is, therefore, 2(6) + 2(8) = 28.

Hey, that was easy, right? If you had any problems, look over the info on polygons again.

Congruent Triangles

Congruent triangles differ from similar triangles in that they are the same shape and **size**. If you placed one congruent triangle on top of another, with both oriented the same way, you would see only one triangle. Triangles can be shown to be congruent if any of the following conditions exist (A is used to stand for angle, and S for side):

1. All sides of one triangle (Δ) are congruent to all sides of another (SSS).
2. Two sides and their included angle of one Δ are congruent to the same on the other (SAS).
3. Two angles and their included side of one Δ are congruent to the same on the other (ASA).
4. One side and two angles of one Δ are congruent to the same on the other (AAS or SAA).
5. The hypotenuse and one leg of a right Δ are congruent to the same on the other (HL).

By the way, the symbol ≅ means "is congruent to."

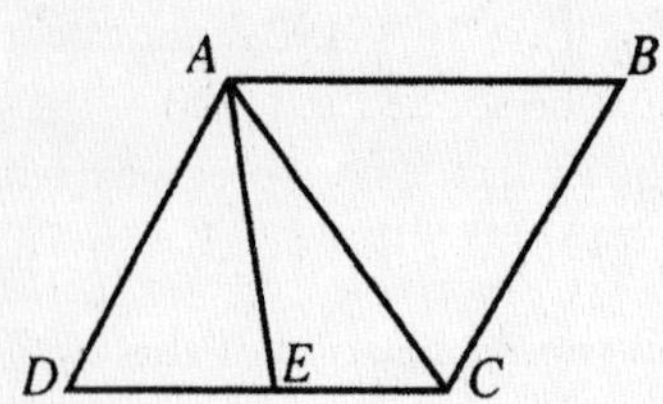

Given: *ABCD* is a parallelogram.

Prove: $\Delta ADC \cong \Delta ABC$.

Statement	Reason
1. *ABCD* is a parallelogram	1. Given
2. $AD \cong BC$, and $AB \cong DC$	2. Opposite sides of a parallelogram are ≅.
3. $\angle B \cong \angle D$	3. Opposite angles in a parallelogram are ≅.
4. $\Delta ADC \cong \Delta ABC$	4. SAS ≅ SAS.

How did you like that little exercise? Let's try one more.

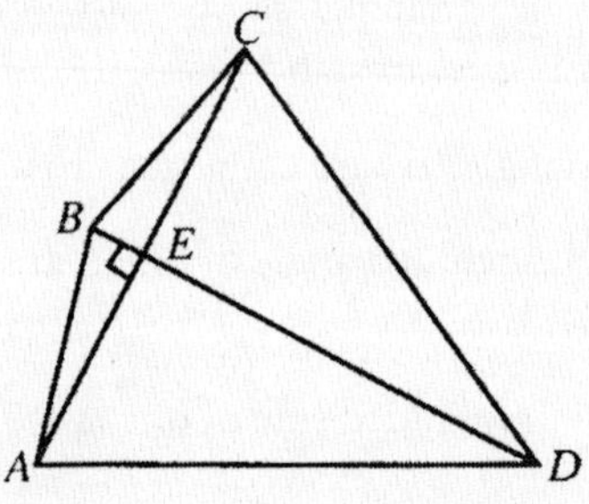

Given: $BD \perp AC$, $\angle CAD \cong \angle ACD$.

Prove: $\angle ADE \cong \angle CDE$.

Statement	Reason
1. $BD \perp AC$, $\angle CAD \cong \angle ACD$.	1. Given
2. $\angle CED$ and $\angle AED$ are right angles.	2. Definition of perpendicular lines.
3. $CD \cong AD$	3. Sides of ΔCDA, opposite ≅∠s are ≅.*
4. $DE \cong DE$	4. Reflexive or identical or common.
5. $\Delta ADE \cong \Delta CDE$.	5. HL ≅ HL.

*By definition, ΔCDA is isosceles.

Study all of the different reasons for being able to state that triangles are congruent. You'll be amazed how many times that will come in handy, along with the dictum that corresponding parts of congruent triangles are congruent (CPCTC).

Going around in Better Circles

A line segment from the center of a circle to any point on the circle is called a *radius* (plural *radii).* We know, you remembered, but why take chances? All radii of the same circle are equal in length. A line segment that passes through the center of the circle and cuts completely across the circle is called a *diameter.* A diameter is, of course, twice as long as any radius. Thus, $d = 2r$.

Any line cutting across a circle from one point on it to another is called a *chord,* and no chord can be longer than the diameter. A portion of a circle is called an *arc.* Any arc has a degree measure that equals the measure of the *central angle* (an angle whose vertex is the center of the circle) subtended by it, as shown in the figure below.

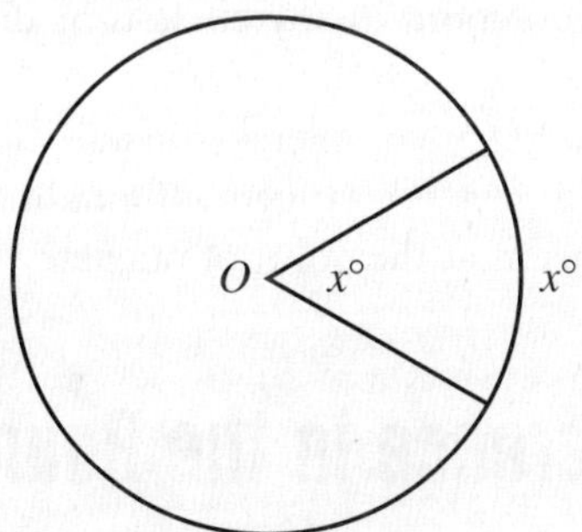

The smaller part of the circle bounded by the two radii and their intercepted arc (in the diagram above) is called a **sector** of the circle.

Try the following example:

> If the arc *PS* in the diagram below has a degree measure of 62°, is the chord *PS* longer or shorter than the radius of the circle?

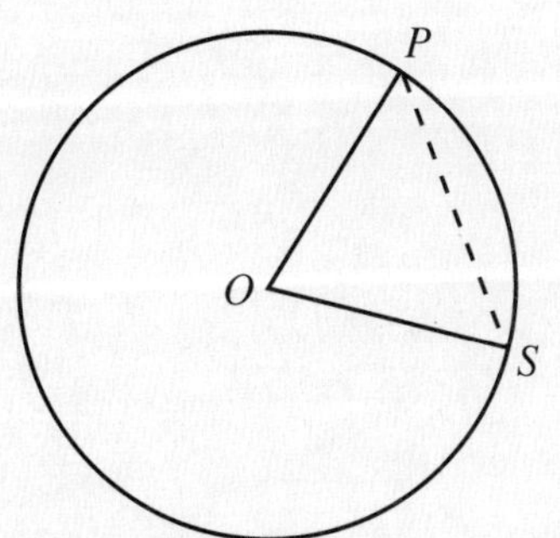

Since all radii are equal, triangle *OPS* is isosceles, and the angles at *P* and *S* must be equal. Suppose each is x. Now, $2x + 62 = 180$. (Remember: there are 180° in a triangle.) Hence, $x = 59$. Therefore, *PS* is opposite the largest angle in the triangle and must be the longest side. That is, *PS* is longer than a radius.

Some Other Lines and Segments Associated with Circles.

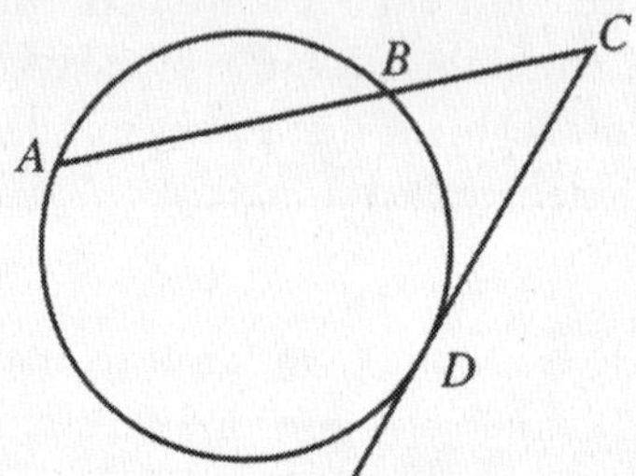

Segment *AB* stretches between two points on the circle's circumference. Such a segment is known as a **chord.** The largest chord in any circle is its **diameter.** In this circle, chord *AB* extends to *C*, a point outside the circle. A segment such as *AC* is known as a **secant.** The final line in this diagram, *CD*, is completely outside the circle, but touches it at one point only, *D*. Such a line is known as a **tangent**. If a radius were to be drawn from the center of the circle to that tangent at the point of tangency, it would form a right angle.

Area and Circumference in the Round

The distance around a circle (analogous to the perimeter of a polygon) is its *circumference.* For any circle of radius r, the circumference is given by the formula $C = 2\pi r$; that is, the circumference equals twice the radius times π (a constant, designated by the Greek letter pi, whose value is approximately 3.1415).

The area of the same circle is given by the formula $A = \pi r^2$; that is, the area equals pi times the radius squared.

Try this one on for size:

Find the area of the shaded region shown in the diagram below. (The curved side is a *semicircle;* that is, an arc equal to half a complete circle.)

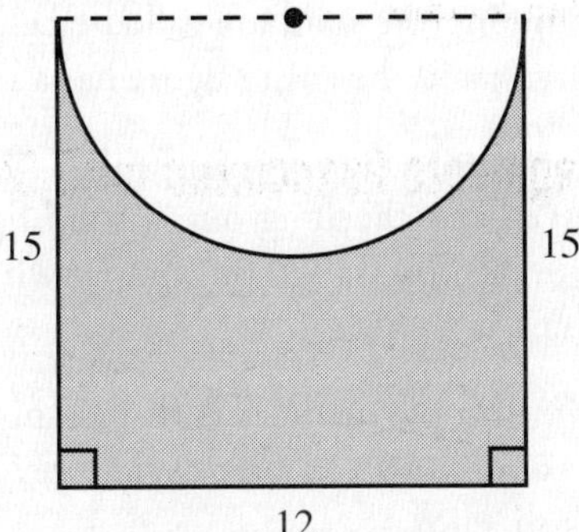

The dotted line completes the rectangle, whose area is 12 × 15 = 180 square units. The radius of the arc must be 6, since its diameter is 12. The area of the whole circle would be $\pi r^2 = \pi(6)^2 = 36\pi$. Hence, the area of the semicircle is half of that, or 18π. Subtracting, the area of the shaded region is $180 - 18\pi$.

Notice that most of the time you are allowed or even encouraged to leave the answer in a form that contains π, rather than being asked to multiply it out. Now let's try another one:

The larger circle shown in the diagram below has an area of 36π. Find the circumference of the smaller circle.

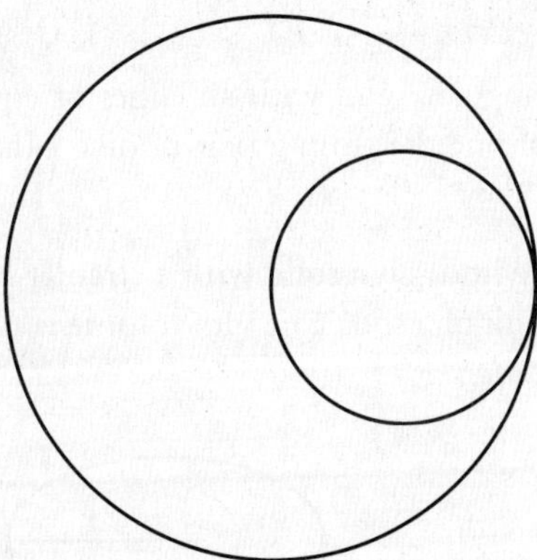

The larger circle has an area of $A_L = \pi r^2 = 36\pi$. This means that $r^2 = 36$ and $r = 6$. The diameter of the smaller circle equals the radius of the larger one, so its radius is $\frac{1}{2}(6) = 3$. Therefore, its circumference must be $2\pi(3) = 6\pi$.

Turning up the Volume

A solid (three-dimensional) figure with straight line edges and flat surfaces is called a *polyhedron.* The surfaces bounding the solid are called faces. The edges of a polyhedron have lengths; its faces have areas; and the entire figure has a *surface area,* which is the sum of the areas of all its faces.

Unlike the plane figures we've been checking out, a solid figure also has a *volume.* Volumes are expressed in cubic units. You should be familiar with the following formulas for volumes of regular polyhedra:

- A *rectangular solid* is a polyhedron with rectangular faces at right angles to one another. It is also known as a *rectangular prism*. (Think of a typical cardboard box, like a shoebox.)

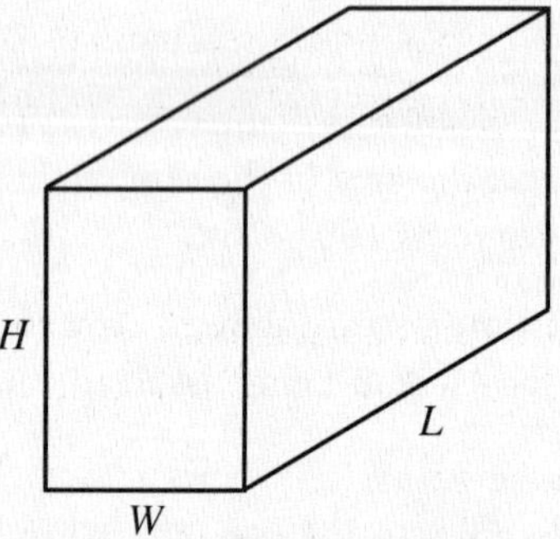

- Its volume is determined by the formula $V = LWH$ = Length × Width × Height
- A *cube* is a rectangular solid with all edges of equal length; that is $L = W = H = s$. (Think of one die from a pair of dice.) Its volume is found using the formula $V = s^3$.
- A right circular cylinder is a solid with a circular base and sides perpendicular to the base. (Think of a soda can.) Its volume is the area of the base times the height, or $V = \pi r^2 h$.

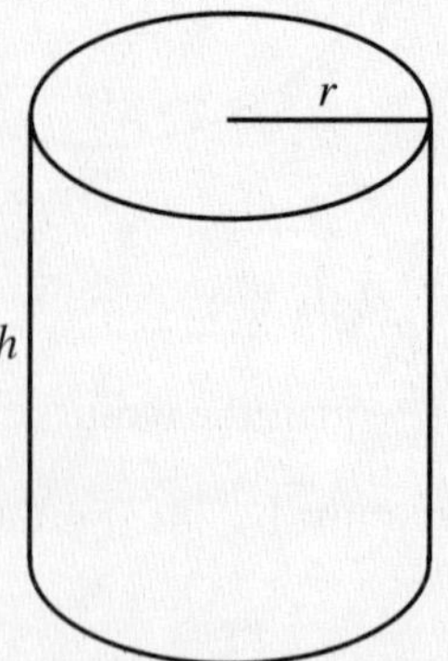

OK. Let's try the first example:

> Find the length of a rectangular solid with a height of 6 that is twice as long as it is wide, if its volume is the same as that of a cube with a total surface area of 864 square inches.

Did you take your time and work this through?

Let x = the width of the rectangular solid. Now, $2x$ = length. The volume of the rectangular solid is $V = 6(x)(2x) = 12x^2$. Since the cube has six square faces, its total surface area is 6 times the area of one face. In symbols, $6s^2 = 864$. Dividing by 6, $s^2 = 144$, and $s = 12$. Therefore, the volume of the cube is $12^3 = 1{,}728$. Since the two solids have the same volume, $12x^2 = 1728$; $x^2 = 144$; $x = 12$. The length of the rectangular solid, which is twice the width, is thus 24.

Let's try one more just to be sure that you understand volume:

> Which has the greater volume, a rectangular solid that is 6 feet long and has a square base with sides 4 feet long, or a cylinder with a length of 7 feet and a diameter of 4 feet?

Here's the solution:

> The volume of the rectangular solid is $V = (4)(4)(6) = 96$ square feet. The radius of the cylinder is 2, so its volume is: $V = \pi\ (2)^2(7) = 28\pi$.

Here's a case where you're going to have to work it out. Since π = about 3.14, $28\ \pi$ = 87.92, or about 88. Therefore, the rectangular solid is larger.

Pop Quiz

You know what time it is, right? Time for another Pop Quiz.

1. 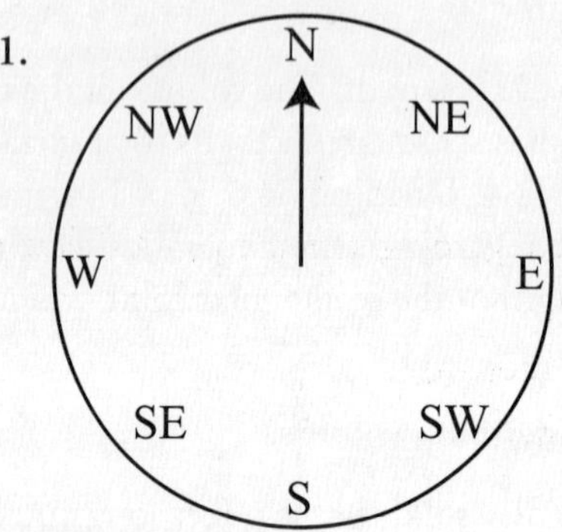

The compass above currently points north. If the needle were to move 2070° in a clockwise direction, in which direction would it point?

(A) North
(B) South
(C) East
(D) West

2. Given isosceles triangle ABC, prove that the altitude drawn from point B cuts the triangle into two congruent smaller triangles.

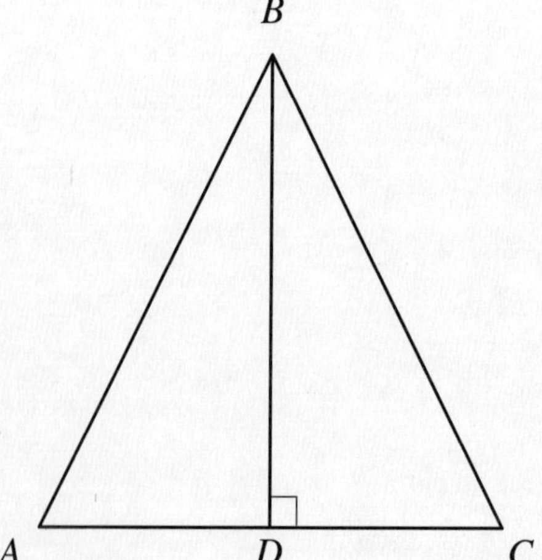

3. What is the length of the diagonal of a rectangle with sides of length 5 and 8?

   (A) $\sqrt{13}$

   (B) $\sqrt{39}$

   (C) $\sqrt{40}$

   (D) $\sqrt{89}$

4. Which of the following statements regarding a rectangle is NOT true?
   (A) The diagonals are congruent.
   (B) The diagonals are also angle bisectors.
   (C) Opposite angles are congruent.
   (D) Adjacent angles are congruent.

5. If O is the center of a circle, AD is a chord, and $AD = 12$, what is the circle's area?

6. What is the volume (rounded to the nearest cubic centimeter) of a rectangular prism with length of 2.3 centimeters, width of 7.8 centimeters, and height of 4.4 centimeters?
   (A) 13 cubic centimeters
   (B) 64 cubic centimeters
   (C) 68 cubic centimeters
   (D) 79 cubic centimeters

Answers and Explanations

1. **The correct answer is (D).** There are 360° in a circle, so you first want to figure out how many complete revolutions the needle makes and if there are any degrees left over. Use your calculator to divide 2070 by 360; the answer is 5.75. That means the needle makes five complete revolutions and 0.75 (or three quarters) of a sixth revolution. Since 0.75 times 360° equals 270°, the needle makes its way 270° clockwise and ends up facing west. (Note: Be sure to differentiate clockwise from counterclockwise; if you go in the wrong direction, you'll get choice (C), East, instead.)

2. You can prove that the two smaller triangles, ΔABD and ΔCBD, are congruent using Angle-Angle-Side.

Statements	**Reasons**
1. ΔABC is an isosceles triangle.	1. Given
2. $\angle A \cong \angle C$	2. Definition of isosceles triangle
3. $\overline{BD}$ is an altitude.	3. Given
4. $\overline{BD}$ is perpendicular to $\overline{AC}$.	4. Definition of altitude
5. $\angle ADB$ and $\angle BDC$ are right angles.	5. Definition of right angles
6. $\angle ADB \cong \angle BDC$	6. All right angles are congruent
7. $\overline{BD} \cong \overline{BD}$	7. Reflexive Property of Congruence
8. $\Delta ABD \cong \Delta CBD$	8. AAS ≅ AAS

3. **The correct answer is (D).**

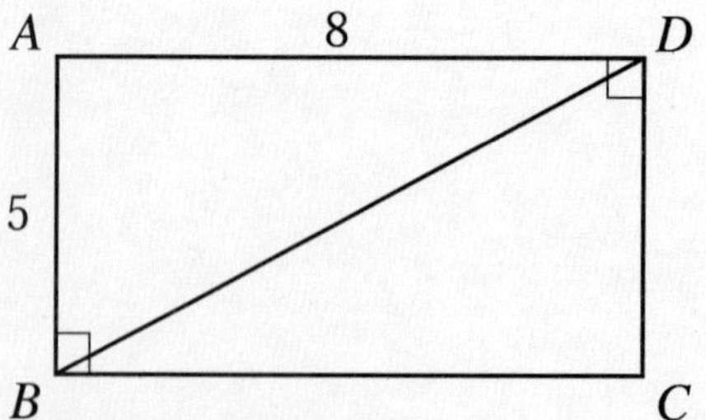

Think of the rectangle's diagonal as the hypotenuse of a right triangle (so you can use the Pythagorean Theorem!):

$$(BD)^2 = (AB)^2 + (AD)^2$$
$$(BD)^2 = 5^2 + 8^2$$
$$(BD)^2 = 25 + 64$$
$$(BD)^2 = 89$$
$$BD = \sqrt{89}$$

4. **The correct answer is (B).** The diagonals of a rectangle are congruent, and rectangles have four right angles, so it must be true that opposite and adjacent angles all equal each other (90° each). However, not all diagonals are angle bisectors; in fact, this only happens when the rectangle is a square.

5. The formula for the area of a circle is $A = \pi r^2$, whereby r is the radius of the circle. Since AD goes through O, the center of the circle, you know that AD is a diameter. Since the radius is the measure from the center of the circle, the radius is 6. Plug 6 into the formula, and you get $\pi(6)^2$, or 36π square units.

6. **The correct answer is (D).** The formula for the volume of a rectangular prism is $A = l \times w \times h$, in which l is the length, w is the width, and h is the height. The area of this prism is therefore $2.3 \times 7.8 \times 4.4$, or 78.936 cubic centimeters. When you round this off (remember Your Best Estimate from Chapter 2) to the nearest cubic centimeter, you get 79.

CHAPTER 6

REVIEWING SEVERAL OTHER TOPICS

There are several smaller topics that will appear on your math exit-level exam, each of which would deserve at least a chapter or two in a regular math text but does not merit that much space in a review. The first few we'll deal with here involve coordinate geometry. That's a fancy way of saying points on a piece of graph paper with coordinate *x*- and *y*-axes drawn.

Coordinate Geometry

Coordinate geometry is the use of line segments to illustrate the position and direction of an object. When is it used, you ask? No, not when you are getting dressed in the morning and are trying to match your clothes. It is used to tell us how to solve a variety of problems ranging from the length of a side of a triangle to how far an object has traveled in a certain amount of time.

> Any object on a plane can be plotted using two points (x,y), while any object in space can be plotted using three points (x,y,z).

MATH

The Midpoint Formula, or Are We There Yet?

Some questions on your exit-level math exam will ask you to find the point that is exactly between two other points. For example, you may need to find a line that divides (bisects) a given line segment into equal halves. This middle point is called the "midpoint."

Given two points $P(x_1,y_1)$ and $Q(x_2,y_2)$, the midpoint M of the line segment PQ has the following coordinates:

$$x_M = \frac{x_1 + x_2}{2},\ y_M = \frac{y_1 + y_2}{2}$$

The midpoint formula is a simple one. Here's a quick explanation: To find the coordinates of the midpoint of a line segment, average the coordinates of the segment's end points. For example, the midpoint between (3, 4) and (2, –2) is

$$x_M = \frac{3+2}{2} = \frac{5}{2},\ y_M = \frac{4+(-2)}{2} = \frac{2}{2} = 1$$

Thus, the midpoint is $\left(\frac{5}{2}, 1\right)$, or (2.5, 1).

Now, take a shot at this sample question:

> If (2, 6) is the midpoint of the line segment connecting (–1, 3) to $P(x,y)$, which is larger, $2x$ or y?

Here's how we solved it:

We know that the average of x and -1 must be 2. That is, $2 = \frac{x+(-1)}{2}$, or $4 = x - 1; x = 5$.

Similarly, we know that the average of y and 3 must be 6, which means that $6 = \frac{y+3}{2}$, or $12 = y + 3; y = 9$. Since $2x = 10, 2x > y$.

Ready for another one?

If $b < 6$, is $(3, b)$ closer to $P(0, 2)$ or $Q(6, 10)$?

We can quickly find that (3, 6) is the midpoint of PQ. Therefore, in the x-direction, $(3, b)$ will be equidistant (an equal distance) from both P and Q. However, if $b < 6$, then b must be closer to 2 than to 10. Therefore, $(3, b)$ is closer to $P(0, 2)$ than to $Q(6, 10)$.

The Formula for Going the Distance

Given two points $P(x_1, y_1)$ and $Q(x_2, y_2)$, the distance from P to Q is given by the formula:

$$d = \sqrt{(x_1 - x_2)^2 + (y_1 - y_2)^2}$$

The formula above is known as the *distance formula.* It merely says that distance is the square root of the sum of the change in x squared plus the change in y squared.

Suppose you wanted to know the distance from (6, 3) to (3, –1). You would find it this way:

$$\begin{aligned} d &= \sqrt{(6-3)^2 + (3-(-1))^2} \\ &= \sqrt{3^2 + 4^2} \\ &= \sqrt{9+16} \\ &= \sqrt{25} \\ &= 5 \end{aligned}$$

Does that look like something you've seen before? Well, we should certainly hope so. Picture any oblique (slanty) line on a piece of graph paper. It's nothing more or less than the hypotenuse of a right triangle whose base runs along the horizontal coordinate of the lowest point and whose height runs down from the highest point until it meets the vertical coordinate of the lowest point. Did you just say, "Good grief, isn't this the Pythagorean Theorem?" If so, you are right. That's exactly what it is— a restatement of the Pythagorean Theorem referring to the length of the hypotenuse as the distance being traveled in slightly unfamiliar terms.

> The distance formula is a variant of the Pythagorean Theorem that you used back in geometry.

Think about it and then try the example below.

The point $(4, t)$ is equidistant from points $(1, 1)$ and $(5, 3)$. What is the value of t?

Since the distances from the two given points are the same, we use the distance formula twice and equate the results, thus:

$$\sqrt{(4-1)^2+(t-1)^2}=\sqrt{(5-4)^2+(3-t)^2}$$
$$\sqrt{9+(t^2-2t+1)}=\sqrt{1+(9-6t+t^2)}$$
$$\sqrt{10-2t+t^2}=\sqrt{10-6t+t^2}$$

Squaring both sides:

$$10-2t+t^2=10-6t+t^2$$

Subtracting $t^2 + 10$ from both sides leaves:

$$-2t=-6t$$

$$4t=0;\ t=0$$

So What Does the Distance Formula Have to Do with Circles?

Funny you should ask! Since all points on a circle are equidistant from its center, you can use the distance formula to prove that the equation for a circle whose radius is r and whose center is at the origin is $x^2 + y^2 = r^2$.

Similarly, the equation for a circle whose radius is r and whose center is at (h, k), two arbitrary coordinates, is $(x-h)^2 + (y-k)^2 = r^2$.

Here's an example:

The point $(t, -1)$ lies on a circle whose radius is 5 and whose center is at $(4, 2)$. What are the possible values of t?

Since every point on the circle must be 5 units from the center, we know that $(t, -1)$ must be 5 units from $(4, 2)$. Using the equation for the circle with $h = 4$ and $k = 2$, and $r = 5$, we have:

$$(x-4)^2+(y-2)^2=25$$

Letting $x = t$ and $y = -1$:

$$(t-4)^2+(-1-2)^2=25$$

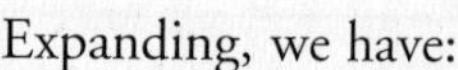

Expanding, we have:

$$t^2 - 8t + 16 + 9 = 25$$

We subtract 25 from both sides to yield:

$$t^2 - 8t = 0$$

This factors as $t(t - 8) = 0$, with two possible solutions, $t = 0$ or $t = 8$.

The most common mistake made when using the formula is to accidentally mismatch the x-values and y-values. Read between the lines and make sure you pair the numbers properly. Don't subtract an x from a y, or vice versa.

Up and Down the Slippery Slope

Slope is the technical term for how slanty or steep a line is. If the slope of a line is 0, it is perfectly flat; that is, it has no slant at all. Given two points, *P* with coordinates (x_1, y_1) and *Q* with coordinates (x_2, y_2), the slope of the line passing through *P* and Q is given by the formula:

$$M = \frac{y_1 - y_2}{x_1 - x_2}$$

In plain words, this says that the slope is the change in *y* divided by the change in *x*, or $M = \frac{\Delta y}{\Delta x}$. The Greek letter Δ (delta) is often used to stand for "difference."

The key point to remember is that slope tells you how much y is changing for every x that is changing.

Here's an example, using numbers. The slope of the line passing through (6, 4) and (3, –1) is

$$\frac{4-(-1)}{6-3} = \frac{5}{3}.$$

Notice that it doesn't matter which point you consider the first point and which the second, as long as you are consistent in the top and bottom of the fraction. Try it!

The slope we just found tells us that for every three it moves to the right, the line rises five. A slope of 2 would tell us that for every graph line it moves to the right, it rises 2. What would a slope of –1 mean? Think about it. Do you have it? For every one that line moves to the right, it goes down one. A negative slope moves from upper left to lower right; a positive slope slants the other way.

Now try this:

> The points (–1, –1), (3, 11), and (1, *t*) lie on the same line. What is the value of *t*?

Think you got it? Here's the solution:

> Since the slope of a line is the same for any two points on the line, and since
>
> $M = \dfrac{y_1 - y_2}{x_1 - x_2}$, using (–1, –1) and (3, 11), we must have:
>
> $$M = \frac{11-(-1)}{3-(-1)} = \frac{12}{4} = 3$$

Now, using the pair (–1, –1) and (1, *t*), $3 = \dfrac{t-(-1)}{1-(-1)} = \dfrac{t+1}{2}$.

Multiplying by 2, $6 = t + 1$; $t = 5$.

> This fact is always true for straight lines: given a point on the line, you can use the slope to get to the next point by counting so many up or down, and then so many over to the right.

That slope wasn't so slippery after all, was it? By the way, we hope that you noticed that *M*, or often *m* is used to represent the slope. Would you like to know why? Well, so would we, but no one seems to know why the letter *m* was chosen.

Equations for Standing in Line—Well, for Drawing Lines, Anyway

If you read the title above and thought you were about to get more algebra pointers, you were right.

The equation that defines a straight line is usually represented as $y = mx + b$, where m is the slope and b is the y-intercept. Note that x and y are the coordinates of the point that is the solution to the equation. When $m = 0$, we have the equation $y = b$, which has as its graph a horizontal straight line crossing the y-axis at $(0, b)$. The exceptional case is the vertical line, which is defined by the equation $x = a$, where a is the common x-value of all the points on the line. (Of course, $x = 0$ is the equation of the y-axis, and, naturally, $y = 0$ is the x-axis.)

Quick—what's the slope of a vertical line? That's a trick question since a vertical line has no slope. If you see "slope is undefined," that means that the line is vertical.

Parallel lines have the same slope. This is due to the fact that slope is the measure of the angle of a line from horizontal, and parallel lines have the same angle. Perpendicular lines (other than the vertical and horizontal ones), on the other hand, have slopes that are negative reciprocals of one another. Yes, we said negative reciprocals, and yes, you will need to know that.

Let's plunge in with an example:

> Find the equation of a straight line parallel to the line with equation $y = 2x - 5$ that passes through the point $(-1, 4)$.

Based on what we just learned ($y = mx + b$), the given line has a slope of 2. Any line parallel to it must also have a slope of 2 and, therefore, must have equation $y = 2x + b$. To determine b, we use the fact that any point that lies on the line must satisfy the equation. Therefore, by substituting the coordinates of the point $(-1, 4)$ for x and y in the equation, we get the following:

$$4 = 2(-1) + b$$

$$4 = -2 + b$$

$$b = 6$$

The equation must be $y = 2x + 6$.

Ready for another one?

Find the equation of a straight line perpendicular to the line with equation $y = \frac{2}{3}x - 4$ that has y-intercept 9.

Remember our trick using stepping stones? The given line has slope $\frac{2}{3}$, so to get to the next "stone," you determine that any line perpendicular to it must have as its slope the negative reciprocal of $\frac{2}{3}$, that is, $-\frac{3}{2}$. Since the line we want has y-intercept 9, the next "stone" shows you that its equation must be $y = -\frac{3}{2}x + 9$. It is possible to multiply this equation by 2 to get $2y = -3x + 18$, which could also be written $3x + 2y = 18$.

Got it? How about one more to make sure?

Find the equation of the line that is the perpendicular bisector of the line segment connecting points $P(-1, 1)$ and $Q(3, 5)$.

Now this one is going to take some fancy footwork. $\overline{PQ}$ has a slope of $M = \frac{5-1}{3-(-1)} = \frac{4}{4} = 1$. That means that the perpendicular bisector must have as its slope the negative reciprocal of 1, which is –1. Thus, its equation must be $y = -x + b$. Since the line bisects the segment, it must pass through the midpoint of $\overline{PQ}$, which we find by averaging the coordinates of the endpoints to get (1, 3). Substituting: $3 = -1 + b$; $b = 4$, and the equation is $y = -x + 4$.

Invasion of the Locus

Actually, locusts invade—not **locus.** Locus is a Greek word meaning location. The locus of points is a way of describing the location of points that make up some geometric entity. Here are three examples:

1. The locus of points in a plane equidistant from a straight line is two parallel lines, one on either side of the original.
2. The locus of points in a plane equidistant from a single point is a circle. Think about that; we just studied it, earlier in this chapter.
3. Finally, the locus of points in a plane equidistant from a given point and a given line in that plane is a **parabola**. What's a parabola? Read on, and find out.

The Graphic Stuff

This section is about graphing *quadratic equations,* or equations of the second degree. Do you know what the most common equation in intermediate algebra is? That's right—it's the quadratic equation.

The graph of the quadratic function $y = ax^2 + bx + c$ is a *parabola.* Visually, the graph of a parabola will "open upward" if $a > 0$ and will "open downward" if $a < 0$. In either case, the point where the parabola changes direction is called the *vertex* and it will be found at $x = \frac{-b}{2a}$. The curve will be symmetrical with respect to the line $x = \frac{-b}{2a}$.

Naturally, there is a strong relationship between the graph and the solution to the equation $ax^2 + bx + c = 0$, which must be solved to find the *x*-intercepts of the graph.

> The points where the parabola crosses the axes are called the "intercepts." The x-intercept is the point at which the line crosses the x-axis, and the y-intercept is where the line crosses the y-axis.

If the equation has two real distinct roots (and not all of them do), then the curve crosses the *x*-axis at two points. If there are two identical roots, then that value will be the *x*-coordinate of the vertex, and the curve will be tangent (touching at only one point) to the axis at that point. If the roots are both complex, then the curve will never cross the *x*-axis.

Here's an example:

Find the coordinates of the vertex of the parabola $y = x^2 - 4x + 3$.

To solve this, first determine the *x*-coordinate of the vertex. The *x*-coordinate of the vertex is $x = \frac{-b}{2a} = \frac{-(-4)}{2(1)} = 2$. Substituting, the *y*-coordinate is $y = (2)^2 - 4(2) + 3 = -1$.

So, the vertex is (2, –1).

Just for the sake of completeness, you should see that the curve opens up (because $a = 1$, which is greater than 0) and that it has *y*-intercept (0, 3) and *x*-intercepts (1, 0) and (3, 0). Take very careful note of the fact that at the *x*-intercepts, $y = 0$, and at the *y*-intercept, $x = 0$. The graph is shown at the top of the next page.

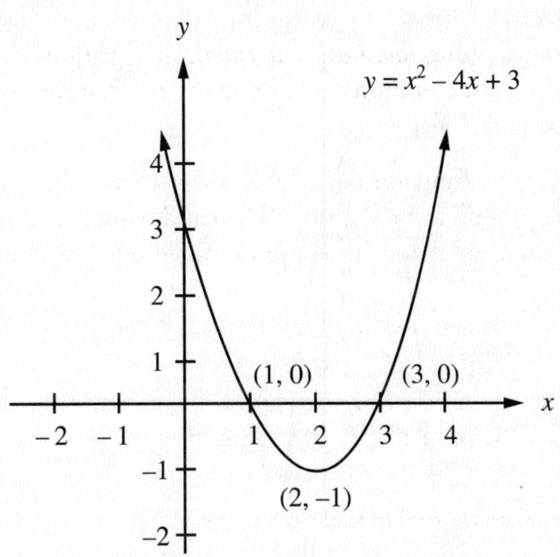

That wasn't so bad, right? Let's try one more to feel comfortable with solving quadratic equations.

Find the x-intercepts and coordinates of the vertex for the parabola $y = -2x^2 - 4x + 6$.

"Find the x-intercepts" means find the values of x for which $y = 0$; that is, the roots of the equation $-2x^2 - 4x + 6 = 0$. Dividing by -2 will make the equation easier to work with. That gives us $x^2 + 2x - 3 = 0$, which factors as $(x - 1)(x + 3) = 0$. Since one of those factors must actually be equal to zero in order to get zero as the value of the entire equation, we'll set each of them equal to zero:

$x - 1 = 0$ and $x + 3 = 0$

Therefore, $x = 1$ and $x = -3$.

The x-intercepts are (1, 0) and (–3, 0). The x-coordinate of the vertex is $\frac{-b}{2a} = \frac{-(-4)}{2(-2)} =$ –1. By substitution, the y-value is 8. Hence, the coordinates are (–1, 8). It is not an accident that the x-coordinate of the vertex falls halfway between the roots. That is a result of the symmetry of the curve. Again, for the sake of completeness, the graph is shown on the next page. Notice that it opens down because $a = -2$ (which is less than 0).

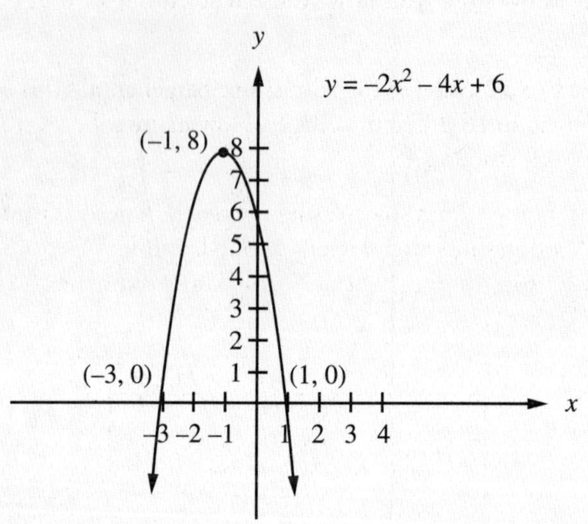

Analyze This

A *set* is a group of related things, objects, letters, or numbers known as *members* or *elements*. It is usually named by an uppercase italic letter, such as Set *F*, but it may be named just by its description. For example, 3 is a member of the set of odd counting numbers; 3 is also an element of real numbers. It follows then that the set of odd counting numbers must be a *subset* of the set of real numbers, since the latter must contain even numbers as well as odd ones.

If set A has m elements, set B has n elements, and the two sets have no elements in common, then the total number of elements in the two sets combined is $m + n$. But if there are k elements common to the two sets, then the total in the combined set is $m + n - k$. In other words, when summing the two sets, you must take into account the double counting of elements common to both groups.

Here's where your analyzing talents come in. This kind of situation is usually handled most easily by displaying the given information in a *Venn Diagram*. A Venn Diagram is made up of two or more overlapping circles. It is often used to show relationships between sets as well as to describe and compare the characteristics of items (from people, events, concepts, etc.—you may even be able to use the Venn Diagram on other exams).

> A simple Venn diagram is one in which no three (or more) curves intersect at a common point.

The examples that follow show you how to use it for different types of exit-level math questions.

> Helena applied to 12 colleges for admission. Sergei applied to 10. Between them they applied to 16 different colleges. How many colleges received applications from both students?

First, create your "stepping stones" by creating the diagram needed to solve this question. Let H be the set of colleges to which Helena applied, and let S be those to which Sergei applied. Letting x be the number that are common to both sets, the diagram shown below displays the data.

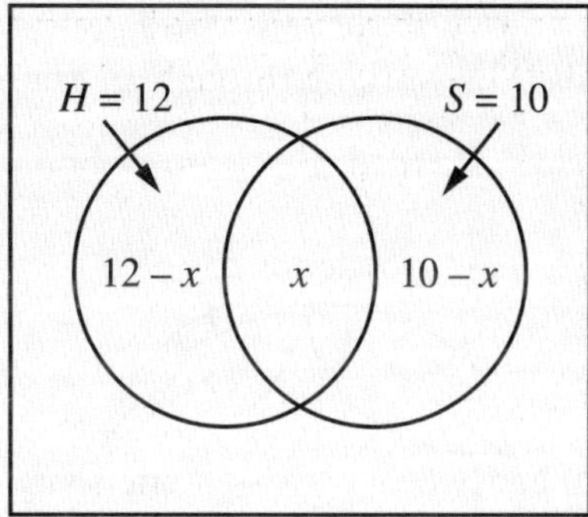

The central region is common to both sets, and we can see that the total is $(12 - x) + x + (10 - x) = 16$. Removing parentheses and combining like terms, we find $22 - x = 16$; therefore, $x = 6$.

Let's try another example:

> A survey of voters shows that 43% listen to radio news reports, 45% listen to TV news reports, and 36% read a daily newspaper. What is the maximum possible percent that do all three?

Again use "stepping stones," but this time use them to determine the sum of the percentages based on the overlap of the sets. If the three sets were totally disjointed (that is, they had no overlap), the sum of the percentages would be 100%. The extent of various kinds of overlap will show up as an excess over 100%. Everyone in two of the three categories will be counted twice, and everyone in all three categories will be counted three times.

If we total 43 + 45 + 36, we find that we have accounted for 124% of the voters, a 24% overcount. Therefore, the number common to all three cannot be greater than one third of that, or 8%. This maximum of 8% is reached only if no one falls into two out of three categories, so that the entire overcount is the result of people in all three categories.

It's the Principle of the Thing

Suppose a process can be broken down into two steps. If the first step can be performed in m ways and if, for each of those ways, the second step can be performed in n ways, then the total number of ways of performing the operation is $T = mn$. This is known as the *multiplication principle for counting.*

Here's an example: Suppose that a jar contains five blocks of different colors. We pick a block, record the color, and then pick a second block without replacing the first. The number of possible color combinations is (5)(4) = 20. There are five possible colors to be drawn from in the first step and four possible colors in the second step. This process extends to more than two steps in the natural way.

The best way to illustrate this is by working through an example:

> The diagram shown below is a road map from Abbottsville to Cartersburg.

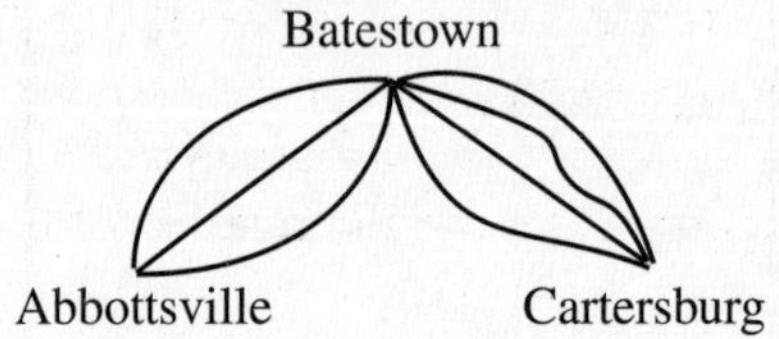

> How many different routes can you follow to drive from Abbottsville to Cartersburg if you go through Batestown only once?

To solve this, note that you have 3 choices for a road from Abbottsville to Batestown and 4 roads from Batestown to Cartersburg. Hence, by the multiplication principle, the total number of routes is $3 \times 4 = 12$.

Let's try another one:

> How many different 3-digit license plate numbers can you form if the first digit cannot be 0?

This one was easy, right? By just extending the multiplication principle to a three-step process, we see that you have 9 choices for the first digit (1, 2, 3, … 9), 10 choices for the second digit (0, 1, 2,. . . 9), and the same 10 choices for the third digit. Thus, the total is $9 \times 10 \times 10 = 900$.

As a natural extension of the multiplication principle, it is not hard to show that the number of distinct arrangements of n distinguishable objects in a row is *n factorial,* which is calculated as follows:

$$n! = n(n-1)(n-2) \ldots (2)(1)$$

For example, there are $4! = 4 \times 3 \times 2 \times 1 = 24$ ways of arranging the four symbols ♣, ♦, ♥, and ♠ in a straight line.

Here's another example:

> If the five starting members of a basketball team are lined up randomly for a photograph, what is the chance that they will be in order of height from shortest to tallest, left to right?

Ready for the solution?

There are 5 distinguishable people, who can be arranged in $5! = 5 \times 4 \times 3 \times 2 \times 1 = 120$ ways. In only one of these ways will they be in the correct order. Therefore, the chance is $\frac{1}{120}$. Does that sound very probable to you? What do we mean by that? Funny you should ask! Take a look at the following section.

Probability

Probability of something occurring is a ratio. To find the probability of an event, divide the number of favorable outcomes of the event by the total number of possible outcomes. For example, if a bag contains 12 blue marbles and 9 red marbles, the probability that a marble selected at random is blue is the number of blue marbles divided by the total number of marbles, which is $\frac{12}{21} = \frac{4}{7}$.

Certainly, you've seen and heard all the stories about a $\frac{1}{2}$ probability of getting heads when flipping a coin, and the same for getting tails. The probability of flipping 2 heads in a row, 2 tails in a row, or a head and a tail are all the same, $\frac{1}{2} \times \frac{1}{2} = \frac{1}{4}$, because the probability remains the same each time you flip. Try something a little different in the example below.

> A box contains five blocks numbered 1, 2, 3, 4, and 5. Johnnie picks a block and replaces it. Lisa then picks a block. What is the probability that the sum of the numbers on the blocks they picked is even?

Since each had 5 choices, there are 25 possible pairs of numbers. The only way the sum could be odd is if one person picked an odd number and the other picked an even number. Think about that for a minute. Suppose that Johnnie chose the odd number and Lisa the even one. Johnnie had 3 possible even numbers to select from, and for each of these, Lisa had 2 possible choices, for a total of (3)(2) = 6 possibilities. However, you could also have had Johnnie pick an even number and Lisa pick an odd one, and there are also 6 ways to do that. Hence, out of 25 possibilities, 12 have an odd total and 13 have an even total. The probability of an even total, then, is $\frac{13}{25}$.

Making Progress—Arithmetically Speaking

An arithmetic progression is a sequence (finite or infinite list) of real numbers for which each term is the previous term plus a constant (called the common difference). For example, starting with 1 and using a common difference of 4, we get the finite arithmetic sequence: 1, 5, 9, 13, 17, 21 and also the infinite sequence:

$$1, 5, 9, 13, 17, 21, 25, 29, \ldots, 4n + 1, \ldots$$

A sequence of numbers $a_1, a_2, a_3, \ldots a_n$ is also known as an arithmetic progression. It is formed if there is a constant (unchanging) difference between successive terms. If we call this difference d, then $a_n = a_1 + (n - 1)d$. Let's find the 9th term of the sequence that starts 1, 5, 9, . . . The common difference, d is 4, so:

$$a_n = a_1 + (n - 1)d \text{ becomes } a_9 = 1 + (9 - 1)4$$

Combine to get $a_9 = 1 + (8)4 = 33$

Now let's check and see whether that's really the 9th term of that sequence:

1, 5, 9, 13, 17, 21, 25, 29, <u>33</u>

That's it!

Let's try an example to make sure you understand progressions:

Find the 20th term of this sequence: 8, 14, 20, 26, . . .

Did you really work it out? Then this is what you should have found:

Solution: $a_1 = 8$, $n = 20$, and $d = 6$, so $a_n = a_1 + (n - 1)d$ becomes $a_{20} = 8 + (20 - 1)6$

Combine to get $a_{20} = 8 + (19)(6) = 8 + 114 = 122$.

Now Let's Get Series!

The sum of all the terms in progression of fixed length is called a *series*. That sum is nothing more than the average of the first and last terms times the number of terms. As a formula, there are two possible approaches:

1. If you know the first and last terms, use $S_n = \frac{n}{2}(a_1 + a_n)$.

2. If all you have is a sequence, use $S_n = \frac{n}{2}[2a_1 + (n - 1)d]$, which incorporates the equation for finding the *nth* term into the sum formula.

Example:

What is the sum of the first ten terms of the sequence –5, –2, 1, 4, . . . ?

(A) 17.5

(B) 22

(C) 40.5

(D) 85

Solution:

The correct answer is (D). The first term is –5. The common difference is $d = 3$ and $n = 10$. So, $S_n = \frac{n}{2}[2a_1 + (n - 1)d]$ becomes $S_{10} = \frac{10}{2}[2(-5) + (10 - 1)3]$. Simplifying, we get $S_{10} = 5[-10 + 9(3)] = 5(-10 + 27) = 5(17) = 85$.

Making Progress—Geometrically Speaking

A geometric sequence is a sequence (finite or infinite) of real numbers for which each term is the previous term multiplied by a constant (called the common ratio). For example, starting with 3 and using a common ratio of 2, we get the finite geometric sequence: 3, 6, 12, 24, 48 and also the infinite sequence:

$3, 6, 12, 24, 48, \ldots, 3 \bullet 2^n \ldots$

A sequence of numbers $a_1, a_2, a_3, \ldots a_n$ is said to form a geometric progression if each term is obtained by multiplying the preceding one by a constant. That is, the ratio of successive terms is a constant. Using r to represent the common ratio, we have the formula:

$$a_n = a_1 r^{n-1}$$

You can find the value of r by taking any term in the sequence and dividing it by the previous term.

> In general, the terms of a geometric sequence have the form $a_n = ar^n$ ($n = 0, 1, 2, \ldots$) for fixed numbers a and r.

Here's an example:

Find the common ratio and determine the 9th term in the sequence 1, 3, 9, 27, . . .

Here's how we solved it:

Since $r = a_2 \div a_1$, $r = 3 \div 1 = 3$

Now substitute into the formula: $a_n = a_1 r^{n-1}$ becomes $a_9 = 1(3^{9-1}) = 3^8 = 6561$

Now Seriesly, Folks . . .

Just in case you haven't guessed, a geometric series is the sum of a geometric sequence or progression. If the sequence has a definite number of terms and the common ratio is known, then the following formula may be used:

$$S_n = a_1\left(\frac{1-r^n}{1-r}\right)$$

Let's try an example:

If the fourth term of a geometric progression is 5 and the seventh term is –40, what is the sum of the first five terms?

(A) $\frac{-55}{8}$

(B) $\frac{19}{8}$

(C) 3

(D) $\frac{33}{8}$

Did you get it? Here's a breakdown of the solution:

If the fourth term is 5 and the seventh term is –40, then we have two equations (from the earlier formula, $a_n = a_1 r^{n-1}$): $a_1 r^3 = 5$ and $a_1 r^6 = -40$. From them, we can find the value of r.

Dividing the second by the first, we have:

$$\frac{a_1 r^6}{a_1 r^3} = \frac{-40}{5};\ r^3 = -8$$

This means $r = -2$. Since $a_1 r^3 = 5$ and $r^3 = -8$, $a_1 = \frac{-5}{8}$

Now, we can find the sum of the first five terms:

Remember $S_5 = -\frac{5}{8}\left(\frac{1-(-2)^5}{1-(-2)}\right)$

Therefore, $S_5 = -\frac{5}{8}\left(\frac{33}{3}\right) = -\frac{55}{8}$

The correct answer is (A).

We need an aspirin after that one. You probably need a drink of cold water.

The Matrix—Not to Be Confused with the Film of the Same Name

A *matrix* (plural *matrices)* is an ordered set of numbers listed in rectangular form. The rows of the matrix are numbered from top to bottom, and the columns are numbered from left to right. Matrices with the same "shape," that is, having the same numbers of rows and columns, can be added and subtracted by adding or subtracting entries in corresponding positions.

Ready to try an example?

Find the sum of these two matrices:

$$A = \begin{bmatrix} 2 & 6 \\ 3 & -1 \end{bmatrix} \qquad B = \begin{bmatrix} 4 & 0 \\ 2 & 1 \end{bmatrix}$$

Here's the solution.

The two matrices are both the same shape (2 × 2), so we can simply add the entries to get:

$$A + B = \begin{bmatrix} 6 & 6 \\ 5 & 0 \end{bmatrix}$$

To multiply a matrix by a real number, we multiply each element with this number.

To multiply a matrix A by a *scalar* (number) k, multiply every entry in A by k. For example:

$$3\begin{bmatrix} 2 & 6 \\ 3 & -1 \end{bmatrix} = \begin{bmatrix} 6 & 18 \\ 9 & -3 \end{bmatrix}$$

You can also determine the product of a row matrix (a matrix with one row) and a column matrix (a matrix with one column). The product, RC, of a row matrix R with a column matrix C can be defined only if the number of entries in each is the same. When this occurs, the product is a number that is the sum of the products of the respective entries.

Here's the first example:

If $R = (1\ 2\ 3)$ and $C = \begin{bmatrix} 4 \\ 5 \\ 6 \end{bmatrix}$, then

$$RC = (1\ 2\ 3)\begin{bmatrix} 4 \\ 5 \\ 6 \end{bmatrix} = (1)(4) + (2)(5) + (3)(6) = 32$$

If you found this one confusing until you saw it worked out, don't worry. Take a look at the second example and its solution; then go back to the first example again. Given two matrices A, which is $m \times n$, and B, which is $n \times p$, their product, AB, can be formed because the number of columns in the first matrix is equal to the number of rows in the second. The resulting matrix will be $m \times p$, and the entry in row number i, column number j is the product of row i of A and column j of B. Confused? All right, try the following:

If $A = \begin{bmatrix} 2 & 6 \\ 3 & -1 \end{bmatrix}$ and $B = \begin{bmatrix} 4 & 3 & -2 \\ 2 & 1 & 5 \end{bmatrix}$, then the entry in the second row, third column of AB will be

(A) −11

(B) −1

(C) 1

(D) 11

To solve this, you need to find the product of the second row of A and the third column of B, that is:

$$(3\ -1)\begin{bmatrix} -2 \\ 5 \end{bmatrix} = (3)(-2) + (-1)(5) = -11$$

The correct answer is (A). Get it now?

Matrices Have Their Uses

Matrices can be used to organize the solution to a system of equations. Consider this system: $\begin{cases} 2x+5y=19 \\ 4x-y=5 \end{cases}$

The solution can be organized by making a matrix of the coefficients and constants, like this:

$$\begin{cases} 2x+5y=19 \\ 4x-y=5 \end{cases} \quad \rightarrow \quad \left[\begin{array}{cc|c} 2 & 5 & 19 \\ 4 & -1 & 5 \end{array}\right]$$

The aim here, is to use row multiplication and addition to create an equivalent matrix that looks like this:

$$\left[\begin{array}{cc|c} a & b & c \\ 0 & d & e \end{array}\right] \quad \text{or like this:} \quad \left[\begin{array}{cc|c} a & b & c \\ d & 0 & e \end{array}\right]$$

Remember, the matrix just gives us a more organized format for solving the system of equations by the addition method. The easiest way to accomplish this would be to multiply the second row by 5, so as to give us the right-hand matrix (above). In other words, it will make the middle term drop out.

$$\left.\begin{array}{r} 2x+5y=19 \\ 4x-y=5 \end{array}\right\} \quad \rightarrow \quad \left[\begin{array}{cc|c} 2 & 5 & 19 \\ 4 & -1 & 5 \end{array}\right] \text{ Multiply 2nd row by 5.}$$

$$\begin{array}{r} \text{Rewrite Row 1} \rightarrow \\ \text{Write the sum of Row 1 and } 5\times \text{ Row 2} \rightarrow \end{array} \quad \left[\begin{array}{cc|c} 2 & 5 & 19 \\ 22 & 0 & 44 \end{array}\right]$$

This new matrix now represents the system: $2x + 5y = 19$

$22x = 44$

Therefore, it follows that $x = 2$

Now substitute 2 for x in the first equation, and get: $2x + 5y = 19$

$2(2) + 5y = 19$

$5y = 15$

$y = 3$

There you have the solution set: $x = 2$, $y = 3$.

Minding Our P's and Q's

The saying, "To mind one's P's and Q's" comes from the days when liquids did not come in pre-measured containers but were sold in bulk and poured into the customers' vessels. One would not stay in business for long if he or she gave out Q's (quarts) while charging for P's (pints), which as you may know are half the size of the former.

Let's start out with traditional units of distance, which are based on the foot. An inch is $\frac{1}{12}$ of a foot, a yard is 3 feet, and, if you can fathom this, there are 2 yards (6 feet, or 72 inches) in a fathom. When playing baseball, don't let anybody tell you that you were out by a mile, since a mile is 5280 feet, or 1728 yards.

Moving along to liquid measure, we have the basic quart, half of which is a pint. But a pint consists of 2 cups, each of which contains 8 fluid ounces. By applying what we just said, we can see that a pint contains 16 fluid ounces and a quart contains 32 of the same. What about a gallon, you ask? Well, a gallon contains 4 quarts, or $4 \times 32 = 128$ fl. oz., the abbreviation for fluid ounces.

Be sure to read between the lines when answering measurement and distance questions. You need to know what unit the answer should be in so you can focus on that particular unit when solving questions on your exit-level math exam.

Just Weight and See

Traditional units deal with weight, which scientists will tell you depends upon the mass of an object and the amount of acceleration exerted upon it. Since you are unlikely to be concerned about the weight of anything except here in the Earth's atmosphere during the course of this exam, we can let the nuances slide. The basic traditional unit of weight (not to be confused with units of *wait,* which are usually expressed in hours, days, weeks, and years) is the pound. Each pound may be subdivided into 16 ounces.

Think of it this way: If this book contained a ton of information, it would weigh 2000 lbs. (pounds).

Quick weight summary:
traditional unit of weight = pound
1 pound = 16 ounces
1 ton = 2000 pounds

Watch the Meter—Literally

After the chaos of traditional measurement, the metric system is pure poetry. There are three basic units:

1. *Meter* (distance)
2. *Liter* (capacity)
3. *Gram* (mass, but as long as we're on this planet, equivalent to weight)

All the relationships are controlled by powers of 10, and all fractional or larger units are denoted by prefixes. The most common ones are:

Prefix	Multiplier
milli	0.001
centi	0.01
deci	0.1
none	1
deka	10
hecto	100
kilo	1000

For example, a millimeter is a thousandth of a meter, a centiliter is a hundredth of a liter, and a kilogram is 1000 grams (a bit more than 2 pounds). To convert a kilo- quantity to a milli- quantity, move the decimal point 6 places to the right. That's because milli is 6 places away from kilo (count on the chart), and since milli is smaller than kilo, there'll be more of them.

To go from a centi- unit to a hecto- unit, move the decimal point 4 places to the right. If you can't see why, ask yourself:

- How many prefixes apart are the old and the new ones?
- Are my new units smaller (requiring more) or larger (requiring fewer)?

THE SOHCAHTOA RESERVATION

There is no Sohcatoa tribe of Native Americans, yet it is a name you had best remember for your exit-level math exam. It is the mnemonic device for the trigonometric functions of either acute angle of a right triangle. For either acute angle, the side opposite that angle is known as the **opposite side**. The angle is formed by the **hypotenuse** of the triangle and its (the angle's) **adjacent side**. The three standard trigonometric functions are **sine** (abbreviated sin), **cosine** (abbreviated cos), and **tangent** (abbreviated tan). The are constructed as follows:

$$\sin = \frac{\text{opposite}}{\text{hypotenuse}}$$

$$\cos = \frac{\text{adjacent}}{\text{hypotenuse}}$$

$$\tan = \frac{\text{opposite}}{\text{adjacent}}$$

Using these relationships, it is possible to determine the degree-measure of an angle of a right triangle knowing only two sides. For instance, the sine of a 30° angle is 0.5, so for any right triangle in which the opposite side of an angle is half the size of the hypotenuse, that must be a 30°, 60°, 90° triangle.

Also, knowing the degree measure of any angle and the length of one side, it is possible to determine the other two sides. Consider the same 30° angle with an opposite side of length 5 inches. The following must be true:

We have the opposite side, so use $\sin 30^\circ = \frac{5}{\text{hypotenuse}}$

But we know the sine of 30° is 0.5, so: $\frac{0.5}{1} = \frac{5}{\text{hypotenuse}}$

By cross-multiplying, we get: $(0.5)(\text{hypotenuse}) = 5$

Divide both sides by 0.5 $\quad$ hypotenuse = 10 inches.

By using the Pythagorean theorem, we could then find the third side of the triangle.

The functions sine and cosine may have values from –1 to +1. The *y*-values of the graph of sine begin with 0° at 0 (on the *x*-axis) and goes up as high as a *y*-value of 1 at 90°. Then it drops back to zero at 180°, down to –1 at 270° and back up to 0 at 360°. It looks kind of like an elongated letter "S" lying on its side.

The graph of the function cosine begins at a *y*-value of +1, crosses the *x*-axis at 90°, continues down to –1 at 180°, then comes back up to cross the *x*-axis at 270°, and finishes at y = 1 at 360°. It's a big curvy "U" shape.

The range of the tangent function reaches from $-\infty$ to $+\infty$.

There are three more trigonometric functions. They are the inverses of the three we have already seen (shown with abbreviations):

$$\text{cosecant (csc)} = \frac{1}{\text{sine}}$$

$$\text{secant (sec)} = \frac{1}{\text{cosine}}$$

$$\text{cotangent (cot)} = \frac{1}{\text{tangent}}$$

You may also think of them this way:

$$\text{cosecant (csc)} = \frac{\text{hypotenuse}}{\text{opposite}}$$

$$\text{secant (sec)} = \frac{\text{hypotenuse}}{\text{adjacent}}$$

$$\text{cotangent (cot)} = \frac{\text{adjacent}}{\text{opposite}}$$

All right! Do you remember yet what SOHCAHTOA means? It means:

Sin:Opposite/Hypotenuse Cos:Adjacent/Hypotenuse, Tan:Opposite/Adjacent. It is very powerful, so use it carefully.

That wraps up the last chapter in the review section. One more Pop Quiz and you will be ready to go on to the Mixed Practice chapters.

Pop Quiz

1. Which of the following equations represents a circle with radius 4 that is centered around the point (3, –1)?
   (A) $(x-3)^2+(y+1)^2=16$
   (B) $(x-3)^2+(y+1)^2=4$
   (C) $(x+3)^2+(y-1)^2=16$
   (D) $(x+3)^2+(y-1)^2=4$

2. What equation represents the axis of symmetry of the graph of the equation $y=x^2-2x-24$?
   (A) $x=-1$
   (B) $x=1$
   (C) $y=-1$
   (D) $y=1$

3. When John rolled a six-sided die ten times, he got a five each time. If he were to roll the die an eleventh time, what would be the odds that he would roll a five again?
   (A) 0
   (B) $\frac{1}{6}$
   (C) $\frac{1}{2}$
   (D) $\frac{5}{6}$

4. Find the 20th term of the progression: 2, 8, 14, 20, . . .

5. Which of the following is not a unit of volume?
   (A) milliliter
   (B) cubic inch
   (C) gallon
   (D) square foot

Answers and Explanations

1. **The correct answer is (A).** The formula for a circle with center (h, k) and radius r is

$$(x-h)^2+(y-k)^2=r^2$$

Since the radius of the circle is 4, you know that the $r^2 = 4^2$, or 16. The key to the rest of this question is remembering the minus signs in the formula above. If you substitute (3, –1) for (h, k) in the formula, you get:

$$(x-3)^2+[y-(-1)]^2=16$$
$$(x-3)^2+(y+1)^2=16$$

2. **The correct answer is (B).** The parabola is in standard form $(y=ax^2+bx+c)$, so you can find the axis of symmetry using the equation: $x=-\frac{b}{2a}$. The equation is $y=x^2-2x-24$, so a = 1, b = –2, and c = –24. The equation for the axis of symmetry is

$$x=-\frac{-2}{2(1)}$$
$$=\frac{2}{2}=1.$$

The axis of symmetry is the line x = 1.

3. **The correct answer is (B).** When determining probability, find the number of desired outcomes (what you *want* to happen) and divide it by the number of possible outcomes (all the things that *could* happen). No matter how many times you roll a die, the probability that you will get a specific number will always be one out of six. It doesn't matter what has happened before because past results have no influence on future results.

4. **The correct answer is (116).** The progression is an arithmetic sequence, for which you must first find the common difference between terms. That number is 6, since 8 – 2 = 6, 14 – 8 = 6, etc.

In order to find the 20th term of this progression, use the formula: $a_n = a_1 + (n-1)d$.

Substituting, we find: $a_{20} = 2 + (20 - 1)6 = 2 + (19)6 = 2 + 114 = 116$

5. Each of the answer choices is a measure of volume except "square foot," which is a measure of area.

PART III

EXERCISES

MIXED PRACTICE 1

Each of the final two chapters contains a mixture of different types of problems that are similar to those you will encounter on your exit-level math exam. Rather than overwhelm you with a flood of problems, we're arranging them in groups of about ten to twelve at a time. Next, you'll find the solutions to them so you won't be in suspense for too long. The solutions explain the way the problems should be approached in order to maximize your success in solving them.

Now, get yourself some blank sheets of scrap paper, have a glass of water, and find a comfortable place to work. Not too comfortable, though. We don't want you falling asleep.

Okay! It's time to take the plunge.

Questions 1 and 2 refer to the table below, which lists the percentage of New Englanders who live in each of the six New England states:

State	Percentage
Connecticut	20%
Maine	8%
Massachusetts	32%
New Hampshire	13%
Rhode Island	12%
Vermont	15%

1. What kind of graph should be used to show the data in this table?
   (A) Circle
   (B) Bar
   (C) Line
   (D) Pictograph

   Ⓐ Ⓑ Ⓒ Ⓓ

2. Which of the following statements regarding the data in the table is false?
   (A) New Hampshire and Rhode Island account for one quarter of New England's population.
   (B) One fifth of all New Englanders live in Connecticut.
   (C) More people live in New Hampshire than live in Vermont.
   (D) Four times as many people live in Massachusetts as live in Maine.

   Ⓐ Ⓑ Ⓒ Ⓓ

Questions 3–5 refer to the chart below, which lists the results of a poll in which people were asked to name their favorite ice cream:

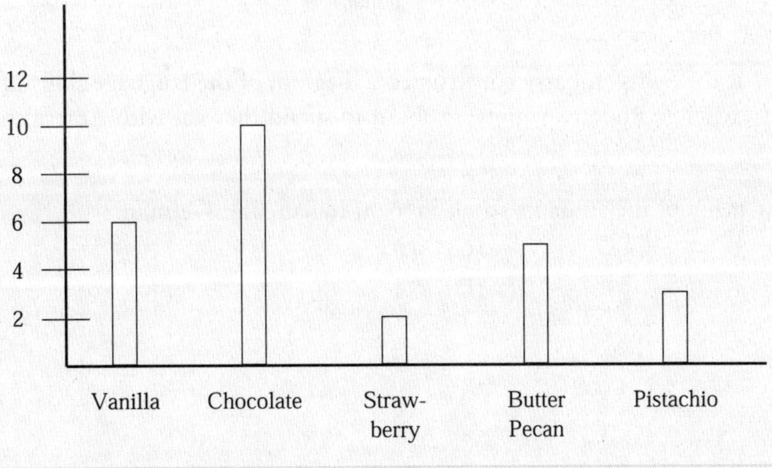

MATH

3. The number of people who prefer chocolate is how much greater than the number of people who prefer vanilla?

(A) 1 (C) 4
(B) 2 (D) 6

Ⓐ Ⓑ Ⓒ Ⓓ

4. What is the ratio of those who prefer strawberry to those who prefer vanilla?

(A) 1:3 (C) 3:1
(B) 1:2 (D) 4:1

Ⓐ Ⓑ Ⓒ Ⓓ

5. Approximately what percent of the group prefers vanilla ice cream?

(A) 15% (C) 35%
(B) 23% (D) 40%

Ⓐ Ⓑ Ⓒ Ⓓ

Questions 6–7 refer to the diagram below.

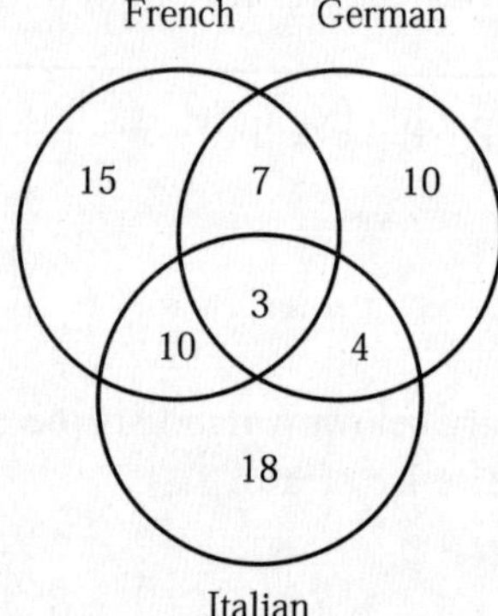

A worker at the Swiss embassy constructed a diagram of the language skills of this year's group of exchange students who were about to spend the year with American families.

6. How many of the students speak French, Italian, and German?

(A) 3 (C) 10
(B) 4 (D) 24

Ⓐ Ⓑ Ⓒ Ⓓ

7. How many students speak only French?

(A) 10
(B) 12
(C) 15
(D) 18

Questions 8–9 refer to the following:

The students in Mr. Phelps's geometry class earned the following scores on the midterm exam: 71, 78, 69, 61, 91, 78, 85, 63, 93, 78, 81, 90, 71.

8. What is the range of the exam scores in the class?

(A) 32
(B) 30
(C) 28
(D) 26

9. What is the mode of the exam scores in the class?

(A) 71
(B) 78
(C) 82
(D) 85

10. Arlene bought three purses for a total cost of \$91.50, and Janice bought four purses for a total cost of \$130.40. Which of the following statements is true?

(A) The average price of Arlene's purses is greater than the average price of Janice's purses.
(B) The average price of Janice's purses is greater than the average price of Arlene's purses.
(C) The average price for the purses of both women are the same.
(D) The average price of the women's purses cannot be determined.

Answers and Explanations

Let's check out the solutions to this first group. Don't ever think that there is only one way to solve a problem because there are usually many alternative approaches. You may have come up with one different from ours. The test will be whether your answer matches ours.

1. **The correct answer is (A).** When a data table shows a number of percentages, and those percentages add up to 100% (that is, all representatives are accounted for), then the best graph to use to display this information is a pie chart like the one here.

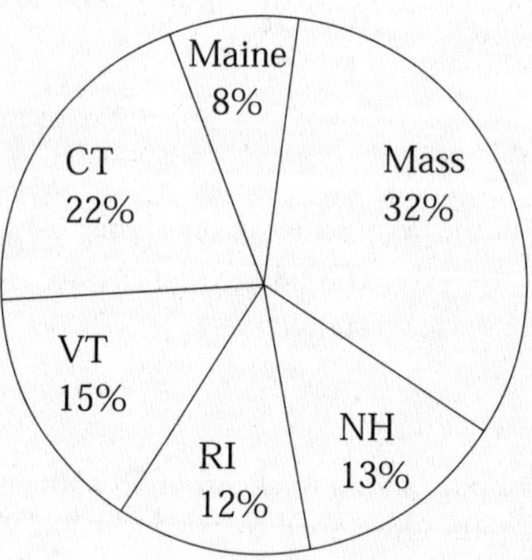

2. **The correct answer is (C).** Be careful here, because the question asked you which of the answer choices is *false* (you see this when you read between the lines to determine what you are being asked). That means the other distracter answer choices are all true. Now you can use the Elimination Game to eliminate the answer choices that are true. Choice (A) is correct because the percentages of New Hampshire (13%) and Rhode Island (12%) total 25%, which is the same as one quarter. Choice (B) is true because Connecticut's percentage (20%) is the same as $\frac{1}{5}$. Choice (D) is true because Massachusetts' percentage equals 4 times the percentage of Maine ($4 \times 8 = 32$). Choice (C) is incorrect, however, because Vermont's percentage is 15%, but New Hampshire's percentage is only 12%; therefore, more people live in Vermont than live in New Hampshire.

3. **The correct answer is (C).** According to the chart, 10 people said they like chocolate best, while only 6 said that vanilla is their favorite. $10 - 6$ equals 4.

4. **The correct answer is (A).** According to the chart, 2 people said they like strawberry best, while 6 said that vanilla was their favorite. This means the ratio of strawberry to vanilla is 2:6. Since both of these numbers are divisible by 2, you can reduce this ratio to 1:3. Don't fall for choice (C), which has the ratio in reverse order. In ratios, order matters.

5. **The correct answer is (B).** Percents require knowledge of two amounts: the part and the whole. To find the total number of respondents to the poll, add up all of the individual columns: $6 + 10 + 2 + 5 + 3 = 26$ people who were polled. There were 6 who said they liked vanilla, so that's the part. Therefore, the fractional amount is $\frac{6}{26}$, which you can reduce to $\frac{3}{13}$ (since both 6 and 26 are divisible by 2). Among the answer choices, the closest percent to this fraction is 23%.

6. **The correct answer is (A).** The diagram is a larger version of a Venn diagram; instead of two intersecting circles, there are three. Each circle represents one language, and the little part in the center—which looks like a triangle with rounded sides—represents those who speak all three languages (since anyone standing in that little triangle is part of all three circles). There are three people in that little triangle.

7. **The correct answer is (C).** The number of students that speak only French is found in the part of the French circle (on the upper left) that doesn't overlap with any other circle. For example, there are 7 students who speak French and German and 10 students who speak French and Italian. The number off by itself in the French circle is 15; therefore, there are 15 people who speak only French.

8. **The correct answer is (A).** The range of any list of numbers is the difference between the greatest and the smallest number in the list. The highest score on the test was 93, and the lowest score was 61. The range is therefore $93 - 61$, or 32.

9. **The correct answer is (B).** The mode of any list of numbers is the number that appears most often. Since three students scored 78 on the test, 78 appears the most often.

10. **The correct answer is (B).** There are three important values when determining the average of a series of numbers: the number of elements you are averaging, the average value of those elements, and the total value of those elements. To find the average price of the purses, divide the total values ($91.50 and $130.40) by the number of purses (three and four): $91.50 ÷ 3 = $30.50, and $130.40 ÷ 4 = $32.60. Therefore, the average price of Janice's purses is greater.

We can tell that you're ready for another batch of problems, and we certainly don't want to disappoint you, so here they are:

11. Solve for p: $-3p + 4 < 43$

(A) $p > -13$ (C) $p > 13$
(B) $p < -13$ (D) $p < 13$

Ⓐ Ⓑ Ⓒ Ⓓ

12. One mile equals 5,280 feet. If Allenburg and Lipperton are 3.6 miles apart, how many feet apart are they?

(A) 1,467 (C) 8,880
(B) 4,342 (D) 19, 008

Ⓐ Ⓑ Ⓒ Ⓓ

Questions 13–15 refer to the following table, which lists the Smog Index—defined as the average annual level of smog particulates (in parts per million)—for each of seven major American cities.

City	Smog Index
Chicago	0.35
Houston	0.61
Los Angeles	0.49
Miami	0.26
New York	0.32
Providence	0.17
San Diego	0.04

13. Based on the above chart, which of the four cities below has the greatest amount of smog in its atmosphere?

(A) Chicago (C) Los Angeles
(B) Houston (D) New York

Ⓐ Ⓑ Ⓒ Ⓓ

14. Based on the above chart, which of the following statements is correct?
    (A) Providence averages more than four times as much smog as San Diego does.
    (B) There is the same average amount of smog in Miami as there is in New York.
    (C) Houston averages more than twice as much smog as Chicago does.
    (D) The average levels of smog in Miami and Chicago combined equal the same average amount of smog in Los Angeles.

15. If a person who is highly sensitive to smog had to move to one of the seven cities in the chart, which one would she most likely choose?

Questions 16 and 17 refer to the following pictogram, which shows the numbers of different brands of cars sold in Phoenix, Arizona, in 1998.

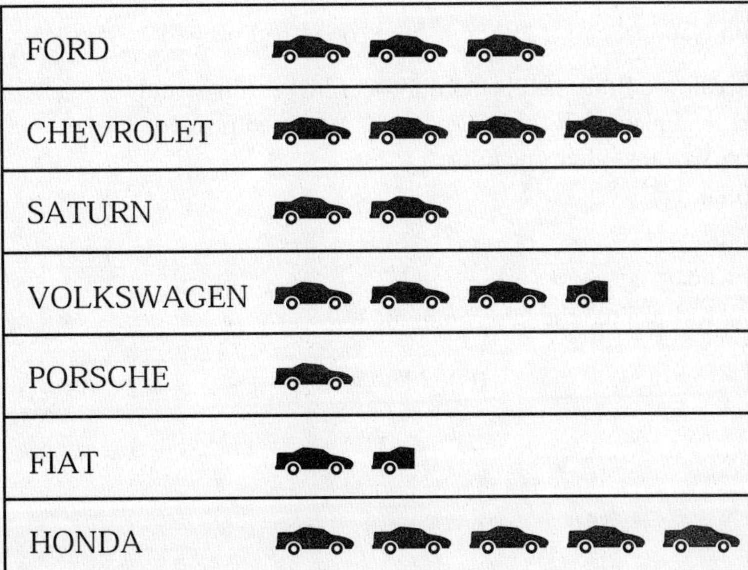

16. Which were the two most popular brands of cars sold in Phoenix in 1998?

(A) Porsche and Saturn
(B) Honda and Chevrolet
(C) Fiat and Honda
(D) Porsche and Fiat

Ⓐ Ⓑ Ⓒ Ⓓ

17. How many cars among the three top-selling brands were sold in 1998?

(A) 2,500
(B) 7,000
(C) 12,500
(D) 20,000

Ⓐ Ⓑ Ⓒ Ⓓ

18. While preparing an order, a pharmacist realizes that two green pills weigh the same as four red pills and that two red pills weigh the same as three purple pills. One green pill therefore weighs the same as how many purple pills?

(A) 1
(B) 2
(C) 3
(D) 4

Ⓐ Ⓑ Ⓒ Ⓓ

19. Three Boy Scouts set out to plant 200 seedlings each at Florham National Park. After one hour, Brian had planted $\frac{3}{8}$ of his seedlings, Bruce had planted 39% of his seedlings, and Brendan had planted 72 of his seedlings. Who had planted the most seedlings after one hour?

(A) Brian
(B) Bruce
(C) Brendan
(D) All had planted the same amount.

Ⓐ Ⓑ Ⓒ Ⓓ

Answers and Explanations

11. **The correct answer is (A).** First, subtract 4 from both sides (you can do this for both equalities and inequalities):

$$-3p + 4 - 4 < 43 - 4$$

$$-3p < 39$$

Whenever you solve an inequality by dividing or multiplying by a negative number, be sure to flip the arrow in the other direction when you're done:

$$-3p < 39$$

$$\frac{-3p}{-3} > \frac{39}{-3}$$

$$p > -13$$

12. **The correct answer is (D).** The first sentence gives you the first relationship (between miles and feet). In order to determine the number of feet between Allenburg and Lipperton, set up a proportion that relates miles and feet and be sure to keep your units straight $\left(\frac{miles}{feet}\right)$: $\frac{1}{5{,}280} = \frac{3.6}{x}$.

Whenever two fractions are equal to each other, you can cross multiply:

$$1 \times x = 5{,}280 \times 3.6$$

$$x = 19{,}008$$

13. **The correct answer is (B).** The greatest decimal among the four cities listed in the answer choices is 0.61, which is the level of smog in Houston.

14. **The correct answer is (A).** The level of smog in Providence is 0.17, and the level of smog in San Diego is 0.04. Since $0.04 \times 4 = 0.16$, it is true that Providence averages more than four times as much smog as San Diego.

15. If someone who was sensitive to smog had to move to one of these seven cities, it is logical to assume that he or she would choose the one with the lowest level of smog, which is San Diego (0.04).

16. **The correct answer is (B).** Based on the pictogram, the car brands with the most icons next to them are Honda (five) and Chevrolet (four).

17. **The correct answer is (C).** Based on the pictogram, the three car brands with the most little icons next to them are Honda (five), Chevrolet (four), and Volkswagen (three and a half). Add up these three numbers: $5.0 + 4.0 + 3.5 = 12.5$. Since each little icon represents 100 cars sold, there must have been 12.5×100, or 12,500 of these three cars sold in 1998.

HIGH STAKES

18. The correct answer is (C). Look at the first part of the problem first. Since two green pills weigh the same as four red pills, you can set up a ratio: $2g = 4r$. Since both numbers are divisible by 2, you can divide both sides of the equation to determine that $g = 2r$. Moving on to the second half, we know that two red pills weigh the same as three purple pills, or $2r = 3p$. Since $2r$ is a term that appears in both of these equations, you can put the two together like this: $g = 2r = 3p$. By this rationale, all three of these terms are equal to each other. This means that g must equal $3p$. In other words, one green pill weighs the same as three purple pills.

19. The correct answer is (B). Brian planted $\frac{3}{8}$ of his 200 seedlings. Since "of" always means "multiply" in word problems, you can determine the actual number by multiplying:

$$\frac{3}{8}\times 200 = \frac{3}{8}\times\frac{200}{1} = \frac{600}{8}.$$

Since $600 \div 8 = 75$, you know that Brian planted 75 seedlings.

Second, Bruce planted 39% of his seedlings. Since "percent" means "out of 100," you can rewrite 39% as $\frac{39}{100}$ and multiply once again:

$$\frac{39}{100}\times 200 = \frac{39}{100}\times\frac{200}{1} = \frac{7800}{100} = 78$$

Bruce planted 78 seedlings, which is more than Brian's 75 or Brendan's 72.

And just one more batch of questions before you take a nap:

20. In how many points do the graphs of the equations $x^2 + y^2 = 25$ and $y = 3x - 1$ intersect?

(A) 0

(B) 1

(C) 2

(D) The figures do not intersect.

Ⓐ Ⓑ Ⓒ Ⓓ

Questions 21 and 22 refer to the following pictogram, which indicates the average monthly rainfall in the Boola Boola Islands over the course of a year.

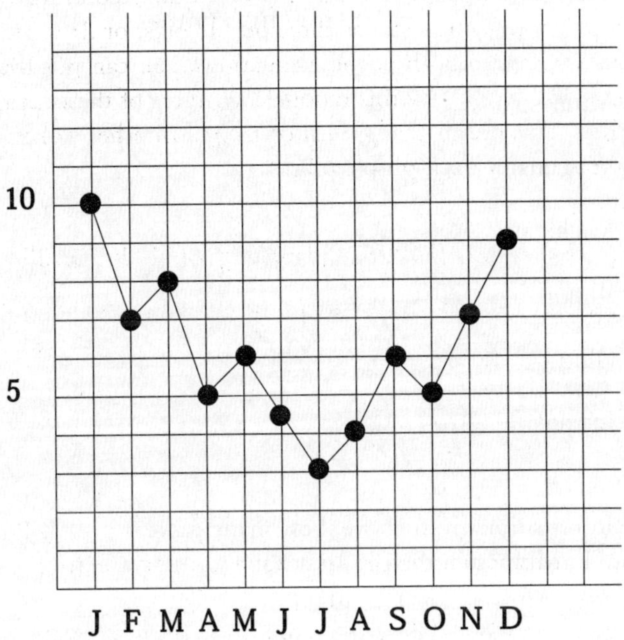

21. Based on the information in the graph, less than 7 inches of rain fell in how many months last year?
    (A) 2
    (B) 5
    (C) 7
    (D) 9

Ⓐ Ⓑ Ⓒ Ⓓ

22. The most rain fell during which month of the year?
    (A) January
    (B) April
    (C) August
    (D) December

Ⓐ Ⓑ Ⓒ Ⓓ

23. The pictogram below refers to the following pictogram, which shows the approximate mosquito populations in five U.S. states.

= 100,000 mosquitoes

Minnesota

Wisconsin

Michigan

Illinois

Ohio

Indiana

Based on the Information given above, how many more mosquitoes are in Minnesota than in Indiana?

(A) 4.5
(B) 9
(C) 450,000
(D) 900,000

24. Which of the following units of measure would be the most appropriate to use in order to measure the amount of water in a swimming pool?

(A) Square feet
(B) Centimeters
(C) Yards
(D) Liters

25. At a softball tournament, 4 points are awarded for a home run, 3 points are awarded for a triple, 2 points are awarded for a double, 1 point is awarded for a single, and 3 points are deducted for every out. If a team hits a home run, two doubles, and a single and also registers three outs, how many points does the team receive?

(A) 0
(B) 1
(C) 4
(D) 6

26. Nikolai made $8.80 per hour this summer selling hot dogs at the baseball stadium. If union rules require that each stadium employee receive a raise of between 10% and 20% each year, what is the acceptable range for Nikolai's hourly wage next summer?

(A) $7.04–$7.92
(B) $9.68–$10.56
(C) $8.88–$9.32
(D) $10.56–$11.44

Ⓐ Ⓑ Ⓒ Ⓓ

27. Carla bought two rectangular carpets for her living room. The purple carpet measured 4 feet by 6 feet, and the pink carpet measured 5 feet by 7 feet. How do the areas of the two carpets compare?

(A) The pink carpet and the purple carpet are the same size.
(B) The pink carpet is 2 square feet larger than the purple carpet.
(C) The pink carpet is 9 square feet larger than the purple carpet.
(D) The pink carpet is 11 square feet larger than the purple carpet.

Ⓐ Ⓑ Ⓒ Ⓓ

28. If $x > 4$ and $y > -3$, which of the following inequalities expresses the value of $x + y$?

(A) $x + y > 1$
(B) $x + y > 7$
(C) $x + y < -1$
(D) $x + y < -7$

Ⓐ Ⓑ Ⓒ Ⓓ

Answers and Explanations

20. **The correct answer is (C).** The first equation, $x^2 + y^2 = 25$, is a circle with a radius of 5 units and has its center at the point (0, 0). The second graph, $y = 3x - 1$, is a line that's in the $y = mx + b$ format, so you can tell it intersects the y-axis at (0, –1) and has a slope of 3. Your graph should look like this:

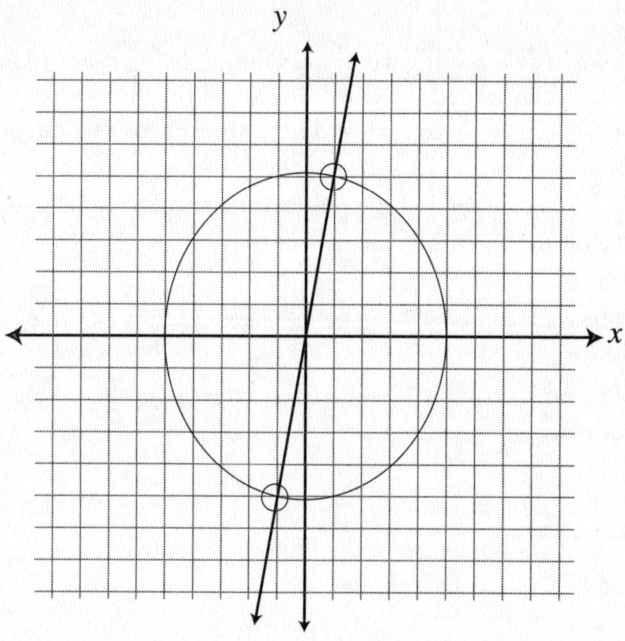

There are two points of intersection.

21. **The correct answer is (C).** According to the graph, less than 7 inches of rain fell during the months of April (5 inches), May (6 inches), June (5 inches), July (3 inches), August (4 inches), September (6 inches), and October (5 inches). Remember that you want *less* than 7 inches, so February and November (7 inches each) don't count.

22. **The correct answer is (A).** According to the graph, the most rain (10 inches) fell in January.

23. **The correct answer is (C).** Minnesota has 6 little bug icons next to it in the pictogram, and each bug stands for 100,000 actual mosquitoes. Therefore, there are $6 \times 100{,}000$, or 600,000 mosquitoes in Minnesota. Indiana has one and a half icons next to it, and $1.5 \times 100{,}000 = 150{,}000$. The difference between the two values is 600,000 – 150,000, or 450,000 mosquitoes.

24. **The correct answer is (D).** Read between the lines here. Water is measured in terms of three-dimensional units, since things that hold water (bathtubs, tea kettles, swimming pools) are three-dimensional. The only unit of volume among the answer choices is liters, which are part of the metric system and are slightly larger than a quart.

25. **The correct answer is (A).** If the team hits a home run (4 points), two doubles (2 × 2, or four points), and a single (1 point), it earns a total of 4 + 4 + 1, or 9 points. However, it also registers three outs, so 3 × 3, or 9 points, are taken away. Since 9 – 9 = 0, the hits are completely negated by the outs.

26. **The correct answer is (D).** Start with Nikolai's salary this year: $8.80. Next year, he will have to earn at least 10% more but less than 20% more. So you need to find 10% of $8.80 and 20% of $8.80. Since "per cent" means "out of 100" and "of" means "multiply," you can rewrite "10% of $8.80" like this:

$$\frac{10}{100} \times 8.80 = \frac{10}{100} \times \frac{8.80}{1} = \frac{88}{100} = 0.88$$

A 10% raise equals another $0.88 per hour. If you add $0.88 to $8.80, you get $9.68. You can rewrite the second term, "20% of $8.80," in a similar way:

$$\frac{20}{100} \times 8.80 = \frac{20}{100} \times \frac{8.80}{1} = \frac{176}{100} = 1.76$$

A 20% raise equals another $1.76 per hour. If you add $1.76 to $8.80, you get $10.56. The range is therefore $9.68–$10.56.

27. **The correct answer is (D).** The formula for the area of a rectangle is $l \times w$, in which l is the length of the rectangle and w is the width. Use this formula to find the area of Carla's two new carpets: The purple carpet's area is 4 × 6, or 24 square feet, and the area of the pink carpet is 5 × 7, or 35 square feet. The pink carpet is 35 – 24, or 11 square feet larger than the purple carpet.

28. **The correct answer is (A).** When adding inequalities like these, you can add both sides individually (as long as the inequality signs are pointing in the same direction) like this:

$$x > 4, y > -3 \rightarrow x + y > 4 + -3$$

Since $4 + -3 = 1$, it is therefore true that $x + y > 1$.

Now that wasn't too bad, was it? If you want to continue, we have plenty more for you, but this is as good a place to take a breather as any.

MIXED PRACTICE 1

OK, break's over. Are you ready for some more practice? We haven't changed the rules. We'll still give you problems, then follow up with the answers and explanations.

Questions 29–32 pertain to quadrilateral *ABCD* with the coordinates *A*(–6, 3), *B*(2, 7), *C*(5, 1), and *D*(–3, –3):

29. Graph *ABCD* on a sheet of graph paper.

30. Find the length of side *AB*.

31. Find the slope of side *AB*.

32. Prove that $\angle ABC$ is a right angle.

33. If an acre of corn requires 100 gallons of water per day, how many gallons of water are required to irrigate 12 acres of corn for a week?

(A) 700
(B) 1,200
(C) 4,200
(D) 8,400

Ⓐ Ⓑ Ⓒ Ⓓ

34. Which of the following is closest to 1.3?

(A) $\frac{1}{3}$
(B) $\frac{2}{3}$
(C) $\frac{4}{3}$
(D) $\frac{6}{3}$

Ⓐ Ⓑ Ⓒ Ⓓ

35. At its Grand Opening sale, an electronics store offers 8% off the listed price and a $100 rebate on the new, lower price for all new merchandise. Under this policy, if the listed price of a DVD changer is $260, what is the best estimate of the amount that a customer will actually pay?

(A) $80
(B) $100
(C) $120
(D) $140

Ⓐ Ⓑ Ⓒ Ⓓ

36. A certain couch costs $400, but the same couch with a fold-out bed inside costs 40% more. How much does the couch with the fold-out bed cost?

(A) $240
(B) $416
(C) $460
(D) $560

Ⓐ Ⓑ Ⓒ Ⓓ

37. If Earl's Auto Zone sold eight used cars at a mean price of $6,250 on Saturday, what was the total value of the cars that were sold on Saturday?

(A) $50,000
(B) $48,200
(C) $25,000
(D) $780

Ⓐ Ⓑ Ⓒ Ⓓ

Answers and Explanations

29.

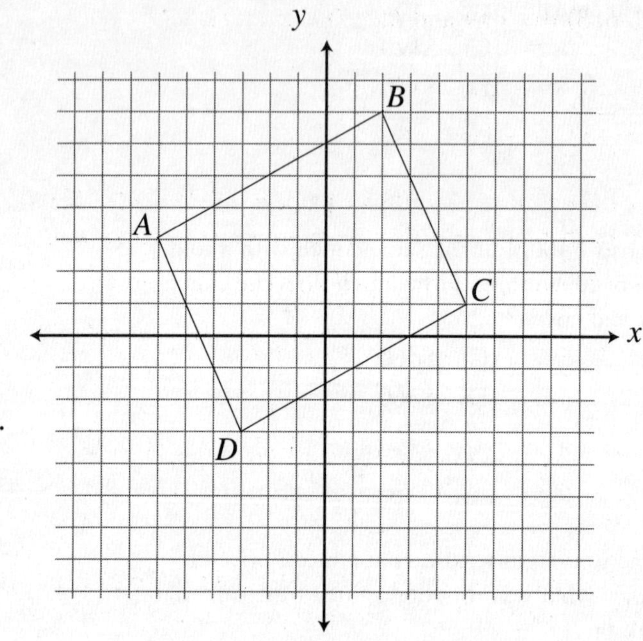

30. To find the length of a line segment on the coordinate axes, use the distance formula: $d = \sqrt{(x_2 - x_1)^2 + (y_2 - y_1)^2}$. It doesn't matter which coordinate is (x_1, y_1) and which is (x_2, y_2), as long as you keep it consistent. To find the length of side *AB*, let $A(-6, 3) = (x_1, y_1)$ and $B(2, 7) = (x_2, y_2)$. Plug the coordinates into the formula (be careful not to use them in the wrong order), and solve for *d*:

$$
\begin{aligned}
d &= \sqrt{(x_2 - x_1)^2 + (y_2 - y_1)^2} \\
&= \sqrt{[2 - (-6)]^2 + (7 - 3)^2} \\
&= \sqrt{8^2 + 4^2} \\
&= \sqrt{64 + 16} \\
&= \sqrt{80} = 4\sqrt{5}.
\end{aligned}
$$

31. To find the slope of a line (or line segment), use the slope formula, $m = \frac{y_2 - y_1}{x_2 - x_1}$, and assign the coordinates consistently. To find the slope of AB, let $A(-6, 3) = (x_1, y_1)$ and $B(2, 7) = (x_2, y_2)$:

$$\text{Slope } = \frac{y_2 - y_1}{x_2 - x_1} = \frac{7-3}{2-(-6)} = \frac{4}{8} = \frac{1}{2}.$$

32. If an angle drawn on the coordinate plane is a right angle, then the slopes of the two lines that make up that angle are negative reciprocals (this will be more apparent later on in this answer). The slope of $\overline{AB}$ is ½, so use the same slope formula to find the slope of $\overline{BC}$: $= \frac{y_2 - y_1}{x_2 - x_1} = \frac{1-7}{5-2} = \frac{-6}{3} = -2.$

The slope of $\overline{BC}$ is –2, and the slope of $\overline{AB}$ is ½. These slopes are negative reciprocals, so these lines are perpendicular to each other. Thus, the angle measures 90° and is a right angle.

33. **The correct answer is (D).** If it takes 100 gallons to irrigate one acre, then it takes 100 × 12, or 1,200 gallons, to irrigate 12 acres. Don't be tempted to choose choice (B), however, because you're not done yet. To irrigate these 12 acres for a *week*, you have to multiply 1,200 gallons per day times seven days: 1,200 × 7 = 8,400.

34. **The correct answer is (C).** Since you're looking for a fraction that is greater than one, you can eliminate answer choices (A) and (B) because each of those is less than one. Furthermore, $\frac{6}{3}$ is the same as 6 ÷ 3, or 2, which is not very close to 1.3. To verify that the remaining response, $\frac{4}{3}$, is correct, either use long division (4 ÷ 3, which equals 1.3333) or use your calculator.

35. **The correct answer is (D).** If a DVD player costs $260, an 8% discount from this price is 260 × 0.08, or $20.80. Since we're dealing with estimation here, you can use your best estimate and round this off to $20; this means the reduced price is $260 – $20, or $240. When you apply the $100 rebate to the new, lower price, you get a final price of $240 – $100, or $140.

36. **The correct answer is (D).** You can use the elimination game and eliminate choice (A) right away since the problem states the fold-out couch costs more than the other one, which is $400. 40% of 400 is 0.40 × 400 = 160. Adding this to 400 gives $560.

37. **The correct answer is (A).** The mean (or average) value of a number of items is determined by dividing the total value of the items by the number of items involved. In this case, the total value divided by 8 equals the mean value, \$6,250. Therefore, you can find the total value by multiplying the mean value by 8: \$6,250 × 8 = \$50,000.

Those weren't that bad, now, were they? You really will find that the more you practice the easier they become, and that's not because you're getting easier questions. It's because you're getting more comfortable with them. Moving right along ...

Questions 38–40 pertain to the following table, which lists the number of people who attended baseball games at McCoy Stadium during the past week:

Day	Number
Sunday	29,243
Monday	17,681
Tuesday	15,102
Wednesday	18,395
Thursday	5,802
Friday	24,653
Saturday	28,313

38. Which of the following is the median value of the data above?

(A) 5, 802
(B) 18,395
(C) 19,511
(D) 29, 243

Ⓐ Ⓑ Ⓒ Ⓓ

39. One day last week, it rained for almost the entire day and night. According to the data in the table, which day was most likely the day when all the rain came?

(A) Sunday
(B) Tuesday
(C) Thursday
(D) Friday

Ⓐ Ⓑ Ⓒ Ⓓ

40. According to the data in the table, the days on which the most people went to McCoy Stadium were Saturday and Sunday. Why do you suppose this was the case?

41. The number 349 *most likely* represents a(n)

(A) area code.
(B) zip code.
(C) phone number.
(D) age.

Ⓐ Ⓑ Ⓒ Ⓓ

42. Which of the following is the best way to simplify the algebraic expression $\frac{3x + 2xy - 5xz}{x}$ if x, y, and z are not equal to zero?

(A) $3x + 2y - 5$
(B) $3 + 2y - 5z$
(C) $10yz$
(D) It cannot be simplified.

Ⓐ Ⓑ Ⓒ Ⓓ

43.

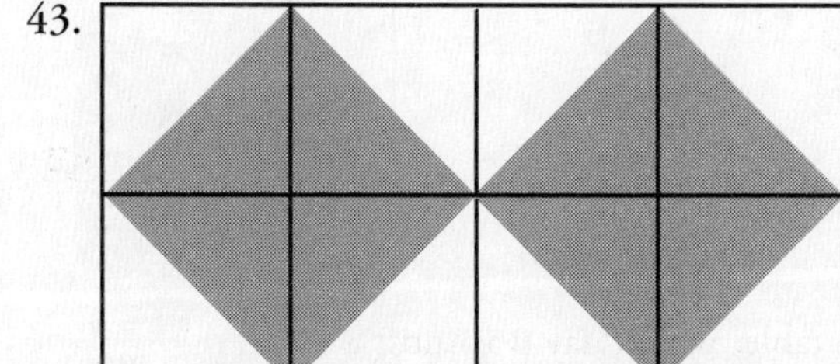

If the figure above is made up of 8 identical squares measuring 3 cm. on a side, what is the area of the shaded region?

(A) 18
(B) 27
(C) 36
(D) 72

Ⓐ Ⓑ Ⓒ Ⓓ

44. A square is cut into four rectangles with the following areas:

	30
6	10

What is the area of the last rectangle?

(A) 12
(B) 16
(C) 18
(D) 20

Ⓐ Ⓑ Ⓒ Ⓓ

Questions 45–46 refer to the following:

Maximum Fun Toy Company sells an action figure that is packaged in a cubic box that measures 3 inches on a side. There are eight figures in all, and the company wants to offer them in a complete packaged set. The two options for the packaging of the full set appear below:

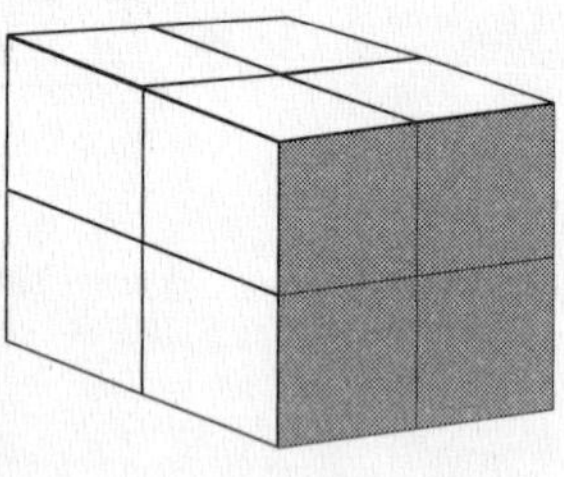

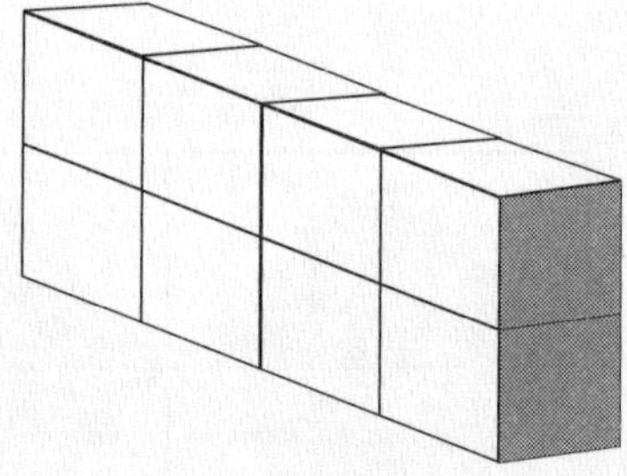

45. Which box will cost more to make?

46. If the packaging material costs $0.20 per square inch, how much more expensive will one box be than the other?

47. Before flying from Chicago to Kansas City, Mrs. O'Boyle wanted to figure out how many miles she was about to fly. She opened a map of the United States and found that Chicago and Kansas City were $4\frac{3}{4}$ inches apart. If each inch on the map represents 50 miles, how many miles did Mrs. O'Boyle fly?

(A) 23.75 miles
(B) 118.75 miles
(C) 237.5 miles
(D) 475 miles

Ⓐ Ⓑ Ⓒ Ⓓ

48. Which answer represents 25% written as a fraction?

(A) $\frac{1}{4}$
(B) $\frac{2}{5}$
(C) $\frac{3}{8}$
(D) $\frac{1}{2}$

Ⓐ Ⓑ Ⓒ Ⓓ

Answers and Explanations

38. **The correct answer is (B).** To find the median of a group of numbers, put them all in order, from least to greatest, and find the middle value of those numbers. If you put the numbers in the data table in order, they look like this: 5,802; 15,102; 17,681; 18,395; 24,653; 28,313; and 29,243. The middle value of these numbers is 18,395.

39. **The correct answer is (C).** It stands to reason that fewer people would go out to watch a baseball game if it were very rainy outside—especially since it had been raining all day, so the rain didn't come as much of a surprise. Since Thursday's number is so much less than all of the other ones, Thursday was most logically the rainiest night.

40. A number of answers could work here. The most common one might be that, since Saturday and Sunday games are usually played during the daytime, many more people, including a lot more younger people, were able to go to the game. Also, most adults work on weekdays but are free to go to ballgames on the weekend (perhaps with their children). Another answer might be that a popular visiting team played the home team, or perhaps the other team was from a neighboring town, making it easy for the other team's fans to come and watch.

41. **The correct answer is (A).** Since (telephone) area codes in the United States have three digits, the number 349 is most likely an area code. Using the Elimination Game, you can see that the other choices are not possible: Zip codes have five digits, phone numbers have seven digits, and no one can live to be 349 years old (not in this galaxy, anyway).

42. **The correct answer is (B).** In order to simplify the given algebraic expression, you need to be able to divide each of the terms in the top by the x in the bottom. Since every term in the top has an x in it, you can simplify it—therefore, cross out choice (D). Simplify the expression like this:

$$\frac{3x+2xy-5xz}{x}=\frac{3x}{x}+\frac{2xy}{x}-\frac{5xz}{x}=3+2y-5z.$$

43. **The correct answer is (C).** The most basic way to solve this is to find the area of all eight triangles and add them up. And that's easy enough since all you have to do is use the formula for the area of a triangle, $A=\frac{1}{2}bh$, and plug in 3 for both the base and the height. Each triangle measures 4.5 square cm., and $8 \times 4.5 = 36$.

44. The correct answer is (C).

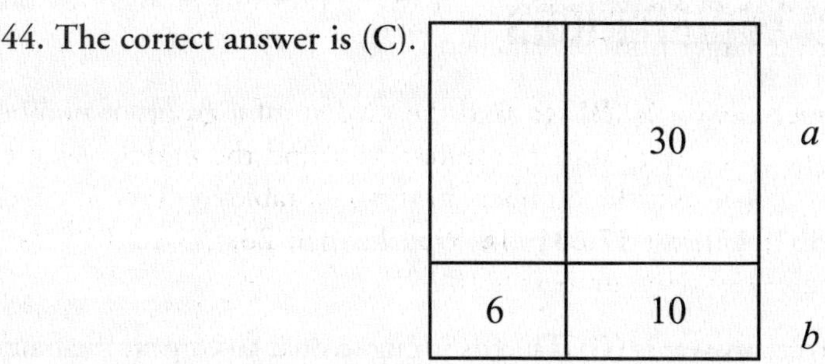

Here's the diagram again, only we've labeled a few of the sides to make it a little easier to work with. According to the diagram (and using the formula for the area of a rectangle, which is $l \times w$), we're looking for the area of the rectangle in the upper left corner, which has the area of $a \times d$, or ad. Let's start on the right side: $ac = 30$ and $bc = 10$. From this, we know that $\frac{ac}{bc} = \frac{30}{10} = 3$.

If you cancel the c's from the numerator and the denominator, you get $\frac{a}{b} = 3$, or $a = 3b$. (OK so far? Take another look if you're still a little confused.) Now, take a look at the rectangle in the lower left corner: $bd = 6$, so $b = \frac{6}{d}$. Substitute this equation in the $a = 3b$ equation, and you get $a = 3 \times \frac{6}{d}$, or $a = \frac{18}{d}$. After you cross multiply, you get $ad = 18$.

45. **The correct answer is Box B.** This question involves figuring out the surface area of a rectangular prism, and the formula for finding the surface area is: $SA = 2lw + 2lh + 2wh$, whereby l, w, and h are the length, width, and height of the prism. Box A is a cube, so you can use the other formula, which applies only to cubes: $SA = 6s^2$, whereby s is the length of a side. Since each little box measures 3 inches, the side of the big box is 6 inches long. That makes the surface area equal to $6 \times (6)^2$, or 216. Box B is a rectangular prism with height 3, width 6, and length 12. That means its surface area is $[2 \times (12 \times 6)] + [2 \times (12 \times 3)] + [2 \times (6 \times 3)]$, or 252. Box B has a greater surface area, so it will cost more to make (assuming they're made of the same stuff).

46. Multiply each of the results you got in the previous problem by \$0.20 and subtract the larger from the smaller:

Box B: 252 × \$0.20 = \$50.40 Box A: 216 × \$0.20 = \$43.20

\$50.40 – \$43.20 = \$7.20

Box B will cost **\$7.20** more to make than Box A.

47. The correct answer is (C). The first thing to do is to convert the fraction $4\frac{3}{4}$ into a decimal. Since $\frac{3}{4}$ can be converted to 0.75 (because 3 divided by 4, by long division, equals 0.75), $4\frac{3}{4} = 4.75$. Each of those 4.75 inches represents 50 miles, so set up a proportion like this:

$\frac{1}{50} = \frac{4.75}{x}$, in which x is the actual distance between the two cities. Whenever two fractions are across an equal sign from each other, cross multiply them like this: $x \times 1 = 4.75 \times 50$. When you simplify this, you get $x = 237.5$.

48. The correct answer is (A). Whenever you have to convert a percent into a fraction, the percent sign means "per 100." Therefore, 25% is the same thing as "25 per 100," or $\frac{25}{100}$. When you reduce this fraction by dividing both the top and the bottom numbers by 25, the answer becomes $\frac{1}{4}$.

How did you do on those questions? There were some good tips in there. All right, we know; you can't wait to do some more. Go ahead, we won't try to stop you.

Questions 49–51 are based on the graph below:

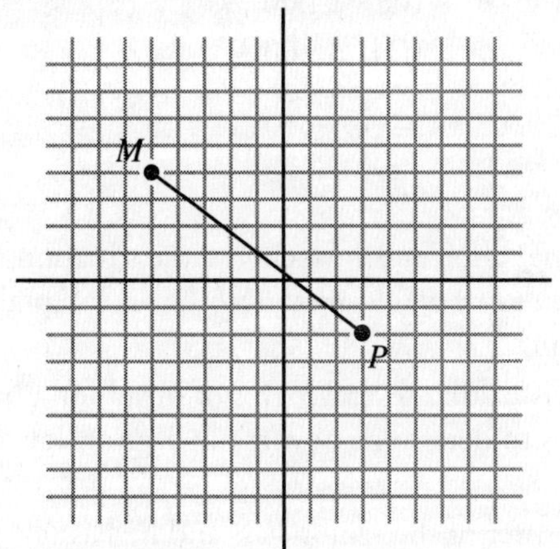

49. What are the coordinates of point *M*?
    (A) (5, 4)
    (B) (–5, 4)
    (C) (5, –4)
    (D) (–5, –4)

Ⓐ Ⓑ Ⓒ Ⓓ

50. What are the coordinates of point *P*?
    (A) (3, 2)
    (B) (–3, 2)
    (C) (3, –2)
    (D) (–3, –2)

Ⓐ Ⓑ Ⓒ Ⓓ

51. What is the length of line segment *MP*?
    (A) $2\sqrt{2}$
    (B) $\sqrt{38}$
    (C) $\sqrt{66}$
    (D) 10

Ⓐ Ⓑ Ⓒ Ⓓ

52. Carlos borrowed $8,000 from his local bank at a fixed simple interest rate of 5.5%. If he repaid the loan in full after two years, how much did he end up paying back to the bank?
    (A) $880
    (B) $8,080
    (C) $8,440
    (D) $8,880

Ⓐ Ⓑ Ⓒ Ⓓ

53. What is the best estimate for a 16 percent tip on a meal that cost $24.00?

(A) $1.00
(B) $2.00
(C) $4.00
(D) $6.00

Ⓐ Ⓑ Ⓒ Ⓓ

54. From the list of answer choices below, choose the situation in which *approximate numbers* would *most likely* be an acceptable method of calculation.

(A) Mrs. Marquez is baking several loaves of bread for a bake sale and she has to determine how many bags of flour she will need.
(B) William is treasurer of the senior class and he has to make sure there is enough money in the account to pay for the new yearbooks.
(C) As a project for his economics class, Dwayne created a bar graph comparing the gross domestic product of every European nation.
(D) Diana has a part-time job at the library and she submitted the number of hours she worked to her manager so she could get paid.

Ⓐ Ⓑ Ⓒ Ⓓ

55. From the list of answer choices below, choose the situation in which *exact numbers* would *most likely* be an acceptable method of calculation.

(A) When selecting a new computer, Dave wondered how many gigabytes of memory he would need for all of his gaming software.
(B) After the guest speaker gave a lecture in the main auditorium, he wondered how many students had been in attendance during his speech.
(C) The ranger at a local wildlife sanctuary kept a list of the number of rare Egyptian tortoises over each of the last ten years in order to determine their breeding habits.
(D) Backstage at the rock concert, Gina asked the lead singer how many autographs he had signed in his life.

Ⓐ Ⓑ Ⓒ Ⓓ

56. Mirabella has ten T-shirts in her dresser drawer; seven of them are red, and the rest are not. If she were to reach in and randomly select a shirt from drawer, what would be the probability that she would select a red shirt?

(A) $\frac{1}{10}$ (C) $\frac{7}{10}$

(B) $\frac{3}{10}$ (D) 1

Ⓐ Ⓑ Ⓒ Ⓓ

57. Each person who receives a score of greater than or equal to 60 will pass the final exam. Which of the graphs below correctly describes this statement?

(A) 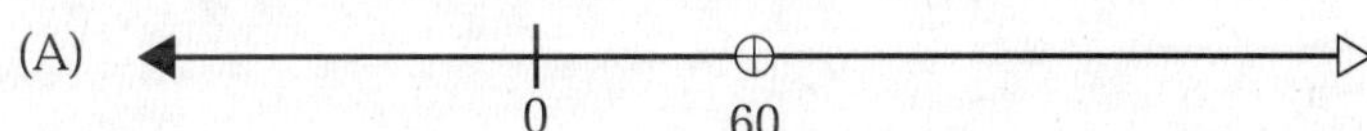

(B) 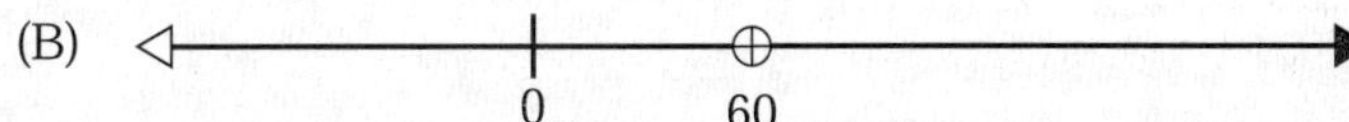

(C) 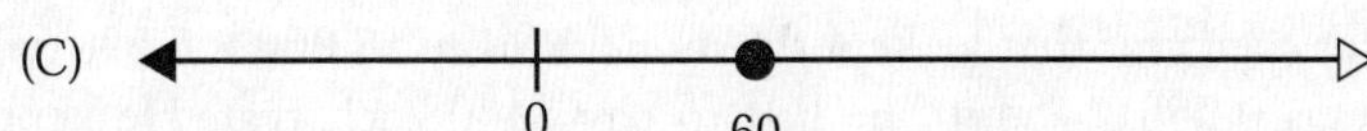

(D) 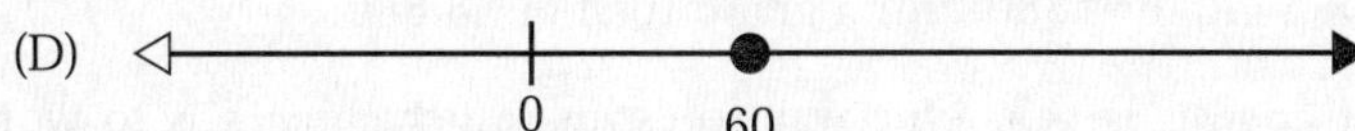

Ⓐ Ⓑ Ⓒ Ⓓ

Answers and Explanations

49. **The correct answer is (B).** The numbers themselves are the same throughout all four choices—the only difference is whether they are negative or positive. When a point is in Quadrant II, the *x*-coordinate is negative and the *y*-coordinate is positive. Therefore, the coordinates of point *M* are (–5, 4).

50. **The correct answer is (C).** The numbers themselves are the same throughout all four choices—the only difference is whether they are negative or positive. When a point is in Quadrant IV, the *x*-coordinate is positive and the *y*-coordinate is negative. Therefore, the coordinates of point *P* are (3, –2).

51. **The correct answer is (D).** To find the length of a line segment, use the distance formula:

$$d = \sqrt{(x_2 - x_1)^2 + (y_2 - y_1)^2}$$
$$= \sqrt{(-5-3)^2 + [4-(-2)]^2}$$
$$= \sqrt{(-8)^2 + 6^2}$$
$$= \sqrt{64+36}$$
$$= \sqrt{100} = 10.$$

52. **The correct answer is (D).** Carlos had to pay 5.5% interest on the \$8,000 he borrowed for each year that he kept the money. Since \$8,000 × 5.5% (which is the same as 0.055) = \$440, he had to pay \$440 each year. He kept the money for two years, so he paid back all of the principal (\$8,000) plus the interest (2 × \$440, or \$880), for a grand total of \$8,880.

53. **The correct answer is (C).** One way to estimate percentages is to work in increments of 10%. For example, 10% of \$24.00 is \$2.40 (you calculate this by moving the decimal point one place to the left), and 20% is the same as 2 × 10%, which is the same as 2 × \$2.40 (or \$4.80). Since 16% falls between 10% and 20%, the tip must be somewhere between \$2.40 and \$4.80. Choice (C) is the only one in that range. Another way to look at this problem is that 16% is the same as $\frac{16}{100}$, which is close to $\frac{1}{6}$. Since $\frac{1}{6} \times 24 = \frac{24}{6} = 4$, then \$4 is a good estimate.

54. **The correct answer is (A).** To solve this, you need to read between the lines. For choices (B), (C), and (D), each person has to use exact numbers. Although baking is an exact science, Mrs. Marquez will have to make a rounded-off guess of how many bags of flour she will need, and she will make as many loaves of bread as those bags will allow. Therefore, an approximation will be adequate.

55. **The correct answer is (C).** Of the four scenarios given, the most likely case for using exact numbers is with the tortoises, since the problem states that they are rare (meaning that there are probably very few of them and are thus easy to count). The rest of the choices do not require as much of an exacting touch.

56. **The correct answer is (C).** If Mirabella reaches in and grabs a T-shirt at random, there are ten possible outcomes. Furthermore, there are seven desired outcomes (seven red shirts). Therefore, the probability that she will select a red shirt from her drawer (since she is such a fan of red shirts) is $\frac{7}{10}$.

57. **The correct answer is (D).** Each of the line graphs singles out 60 as a key number in this equation, since those who fail will be on one side and those who pass will be on another. Since all students who receive grades greater than 60 will pass, the arrow should include all numbers greater than 60 and should thus point to the right. Eliminate choices (A) and (C). The other point is whether the dot at 60 should be colored in. Since the question says that all students who earn grades greater than or equal to 60 will pass, 60 is a passing grade. The circle should therefore be colored in.

Feel like taking a break now, or are you ready to move on to the next set of questions? If you need to take a breather, that's all right. Go ahead.

Ready now? Let's try just a few more before your eyelids get too magnetic to keep apart:

58. Benjamin arrived at school at 8:15 a.m. and left at 3:00 p.m. If he left school for half an hour to get a sandwich for lunch, what was the total length of time that he was at school?

(A) 5.75 hours
(B) 6.25 hours
(C) 6.5 hours
(D) 6.75 hours

Ⓐ Ⓑ Ⓒ Ⓓ

59. If Petra makes a 210-mile trip in 3.5 hours, what is her average speed for the trip?

(A) 50
(B) 52
(C) 58
(D) 60

Ⓐ Ⓑ Ⓒ Ⓓ

60. In physics, the formula for the force exerted by a moving object is $f = m \times a$, in which m is the mass of the object and a is the object's acceleration. If a stone weighs 8.2 grams and is accelerating at a rate of 5.5 feet/sec^2, what is the force that stone would exert?

(A) 13.7
(B) 41.0
(C) 45.1
(D) 248.05

Ⓐ Ⓑ Ⓒ Ⓓ

61. If an object weighs 5.6 pounds, how many kilograms does it weigh? (one pound = 2.2 kilograms)

(A) 2.54 kilograms
(B) 6.16 kilograms
(C) 7.80 kilograms
(D) 12.32 kilograms

Ⓐ Ⓑ Ⓒ Ⓓ

62. Fig. A Fig. B

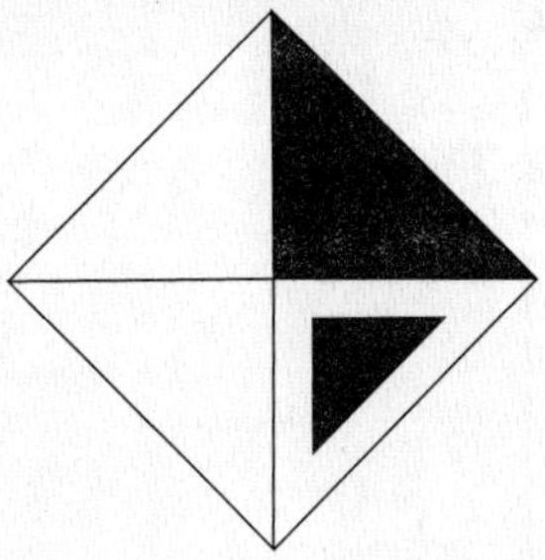

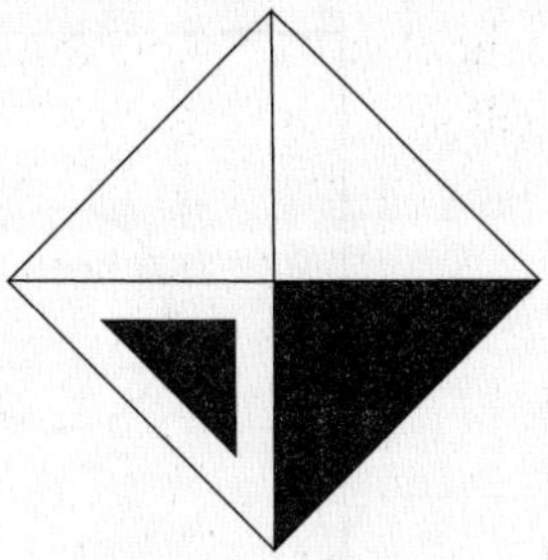

Study figures A and B. Which transformation, if any, of Figure A is shown in Figure B?

(A) Rotation
(B) Reflection
(C) Translation
(D) No transformation

Ⓐ Ⓑ Ⓒ Ⓓ

63. Fig. M Fig. N

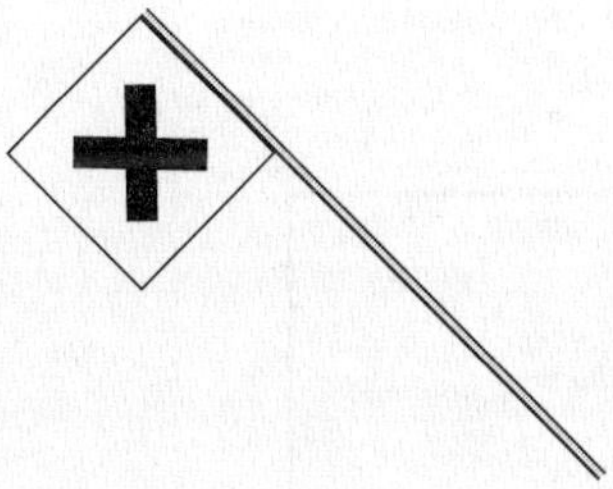

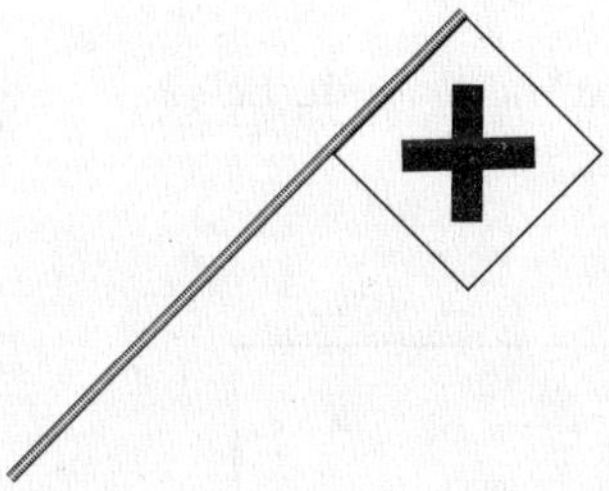

Study figures M and N. Which transformation, if any, of Figure M is shown in Figure N?

(A) Rotation
(B) Reflection
(C) Translation
(D) No transformation

Ⓐ Ⓑ Ⓒ Ⓓ

64. Fig. Y Fig. Z

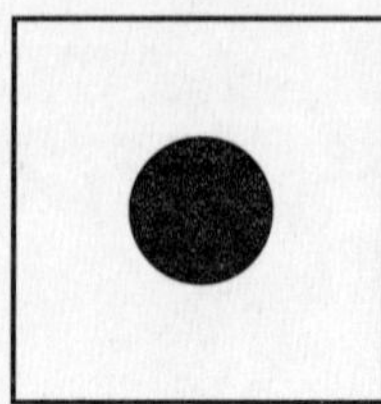

Study figures Y and Z. Which transformation, if any, of Figure Y is shown in Figure Z?

(A) Rotation
(B) Reflection
(C) Translation
(D) No transformation

Ⓐ Ⓑ Ⓒ Ⓓ

Questions 65–66 refer to the diagram below:

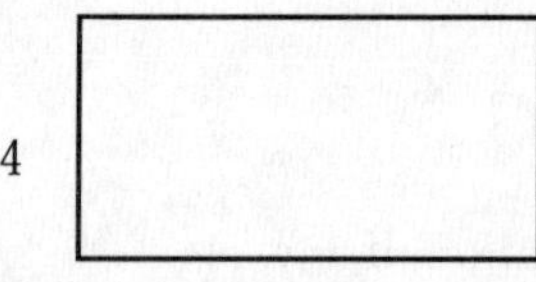

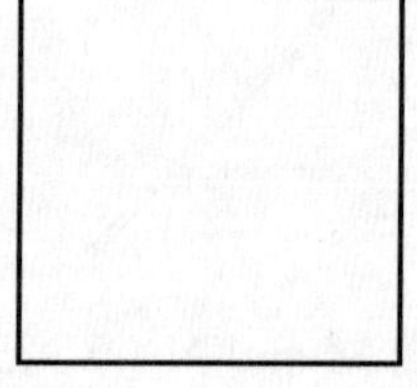

65. If the perimeters of the rectangle *R* and square *S* above are equal, what is the length of a side of square *S*?

(A) 6 cm. (C) 8 cm.
(B) 7 cm. (D) 14 cm.

Ⓐ Ⓑ Ⓒ Ⓓ

66. What is the difference in the areas of the two quadrilaterals?

(A) 6 cm.^{2} (C) 18 cm.^{2}
(B) 9 cm.^{2} (D) 0 cm.^{2}

Ⓐ Ⓑ Ⓒ Ⓓ

67. The formula for the volume of a cylinder is $V = \pi r^2 h$. What is the volume of a cylinder with a radius of 5 ft. and a height of 3 ft.?
   (A) 15π ft.^{3}
   (B) 45π ft.^{3}
   (C) 60π ft.^{3}
   (D) 75π ft.^{3}

Ⓐ Ⓑ Ⓒ Ⓓ

68. What is the surface area of a cube with a side of length 5 in.?
   (A) 25 in.^{2}
   (B) 125 in.^{2}
   (C) 150 in.^{2}
   (D) 225 in.^{2}

Ⓐ Ⓑ Ⓒ Ⓓ

69. What is the volume of a cube with a side of length 5 in.?
   (A) 25 in.^{3}
   (B) 125 in.^{3}
   (C) 150 in.^{3}
   (D) 225 in.^{3}

Ⓐ Ⓑ Ⓒ Ⓓ

Answers and Explanations

58. The correct answer is (B). The length of time between 8:15 a.m. and 3:00 p.m. is a total of 6 hours and 45 minutes. However, he spent half an hour, or 30 minutes, away from school during lunch. Therefore, we should subtract 30 minutes from the total; the result is 6 hours and 15 minutes. To determine the decimal value of 15 minutes out of a total of 60, set up the following proportion:

$$\frac{15}{60} = \frac{x}{100}$$

Whenever two fractions are equal to each other, you can cross multiply terms like this:

$$60 \times x = 15 \times 100$$

$$60x = 1{,}500$$

$$x = 25$$

The fraction now reads $\frac{25}{100}$, which is the same as 0.25. Therefore, the final answer is 6 hours plus 0.25 hours, or 6.25 hours.

59. The correct answer is (D). To solve any problem regarding distance, rate, and time, use the formula that relates all of them: rate times time equals distance, or $r \times t = d$. You have been given two of these values (the distance, d, is 210, and the time, t, is 3.5) and you need to find the third, the rate. Plug the values you know into the equation and solve:

$$r \times 3.5 = 210 \qquad r = \frac{210}{3.5} \qquad r = 60$$

60. The correct answer is (C). There is a lot of physics-related jargon in this problem, but you don't have to worry about units or strange terminology. The only thing to do is plug the numbers into their proper places in the given formula and solve (the mass, m, is 8.2, and the acceleration, a, is 5.5):

$$f = m \times a$$

$$f = 8.2 \times 5.5$$

$$f = 45.10$$

61. **The correct answer is (D).** The conversion factor has been provided for you: one pound equals 2.2 kilograms. To find the value of 5.6 pounds in kilograms, set up a proportion that relates pounds to kilograms and let x = the number of kilograms:

$$\frac{lbs}{kgs} = \frac{1}{2.2} = \frac{5.6}{x}$$

Whenever two fractions are equal to each other, you can cross multiply terms like this:

$$x \times 1 = 2.2 \times 5.6$$

$$x = 12.32$$

From this calculation, 5.6 pounds equals 12.32 kilograms.

62. **The correct answer is (A).** The two diamond-shaped figures appear to be similar, because they each feature one quadrant that has been colored in and another quadrant that has a little triangle in it. The colored-in triangle goes from the upper right in Figure A to the lower right in Figure B. The little triangle makes a similar move one quadrant over, from the lower right to the lower left. Therefore, Figure B has been rotated 90° clockwise.

63. **The correct answer is (B).** These flags look identical because the plus sign is in the middle of both. The only difference is that the flag hangs to the left in Figure M, and it hangs to the *right* in Figure N. It's almost as if Figure M is a mirror image of Figure N, and this suggests that the two are reflections of each other.

64. **The correct answer is (D).** Figures Y and Z are both squares, and they both have circles in them. However, Figure Y is larger than Figure Z. Since rotations, reflections, and translations all preserve the size of an image, Figure Z represents none of those transformations.

65. **The correct answer is (B).** The formula for the perimeter of a rectangle is $2l + 2w$, in which l is the length of the rectangle and w is the width of the rectangle. Therefore, the perimeter of rectangle R is 2(10) + 2(4), or 28 cm. Secondly, the formula for the perimeter of a square is $4s$, in which s is the length of each side of the square. Since the two perimeters are equal, you can set the formula for the perimeter of square S equal to 28:

$$4s = 28$$

$$s = 7$$

Each side of the square is 7 cm. long.

66. **The correct answer is (B).** The formula for the area of a rectangle is $l \times w$, in which l is the length of the rectangle and w is the width of the rectangle. Therefore, the area of rectangle R is 10×4, or 40 cm^2. Secondly, the formula for the area of a square is s^2, in which s is the length of each side of the square. Since the length of the side of the square is 7, the area of the square is 7^2, or 49 cm^2. The difference between the two areas is 49 – 40, or 9 cm^2.

67. **The correct answer is (D).** You've been given the formula for a cylinder, so the only thing to do is to be sure you plug the values in all the right places. You've been asked for the volume, V, and you've been given the radius ($r = 5$) and the height ($h = 3$). Plug in those values and solve for V:

$$V = \pi r^2 h$$

$$V = \pi(5)^2(3)$$

$$V = \pi(25)(3) = 75\pi$$

68. **The correct answer is (C).** The formula for the surface area of a cube is $6s^2$ (or the sum of the areas of the 6 square-shaped sides), in which s is the length of a side of the cube. Therefore, the surface area of a cube with a side of length 5 in. equals 6×5^2, which equals 6×25, or 150 in^2.

69. **The correct answer is (B).** The formula for the volume of a cube is s^3, in which s is the length of a side of the cube. Therefore, the volume of a cube with a side of length 5 in. equals 5^3, which equals $5 \times 5 \times 5$, or 125 in^3.

You did it! You completed the first set of drill questions. This is probably another excellent place to take a break. By the way, you can go back and do the same set of questions a second or even a third time if you're still unsure of yourself. Practice may or may not make perfect, but it certainly makes you much more likely to succeed and more comfortable with answering exit-level math questions.

MIXED PRACTICE 2

Here is another chapter of drill questions designed to help you get a better handle on your exit-level math tests. As before, we'll give you a group of questions at a time before pausing to examine the strategies and tactics that are used solve them.

Just keep repeating to yourself, "The more practice I get, the more confident I will be on test day."

1. Arthur has a backyard garden that is 4 yards longer than it is wide. He wants to put in a walkway that is two yards wide around the entire perimeter of the garden. If the area of the entire garden, including the walkway, is 320 square yards, what will be the total surface area of the walkway?

   (A) 72 (C) 192

   (B) 128 (D) 320

   Ⓐ Ⓑ Ⓒ Ⓓ

2. What are the roots of the equation $2x^2 + 7x + 6 = 0$?

MATH

3. What are the roots of the equation $2x^2 + 7x + 4 = 0$?

4. Albemarle University has 400 sophomores, x of whom are English majors. If there are three times as many computer science majors as English majors and half as many history majors as computer science majors, which expression represents (in terms of x) the number of students who have declared a different major than the three mentioned?

(A) $400 - 5\frac{1}{2}x$

(B) $400 - 6x$

(C) $5\frac{1}{2}x$

(D) $6x$

Ⓐ Ⓑ Ⓒ Ⓓ

5. Bert's Bait Shop sells night crawlers and fly-fishing lures. The Starter set contains 10 lures and 20 night crawlers and costs \$9.50, and the Executive set contains 20 lures and 50 night crawlers and costs \$20.00. If there is no discounting involved, what is the price of one lure?

6.

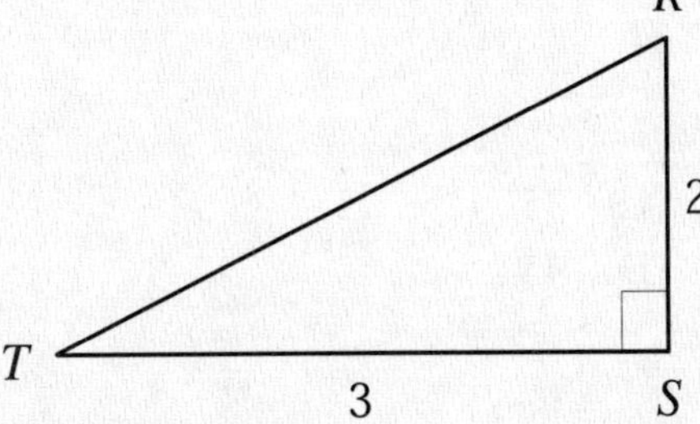

In the accompanying diagram of right triangle RST, what is $\tan \angle T$?

(A) $\frac{2}{3}$

(B) $\frac{\sqrt{13}}{3}$

(C) $\frac{3}{2}$

(D) It cannot be determined.

Ⓐ Ⓑ Ⓒ Ⓓ

Questions 7–9 apply to the circle with center M.

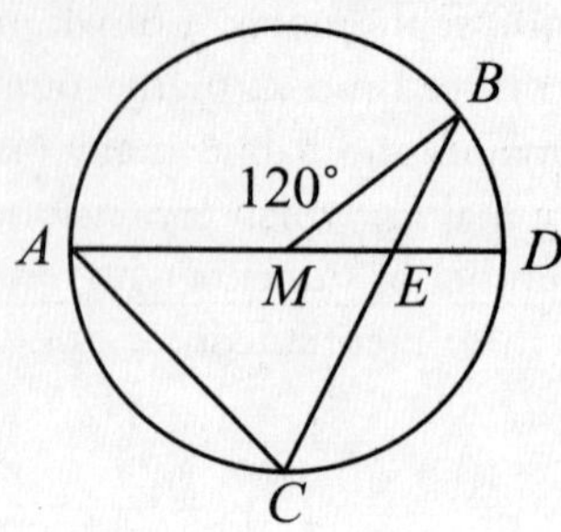

7. What is m$\angle ACB$?

(A) 30
(B) 60
(C) 90
(D) 120

Ⓐ Ⓑ Ⓒ Ⓓ

8. If arcs AC and CD are the same length, what is m$\angle CAD$?

(A) 30
(B) 45
(C) 60
(D) 90

Ⓐ Ⓑ Ⓒ Ⓓ

9. What is m$\angle MBE$?

(A) 15
(B) 25
(C) 35
(D) 45

Ⓐ Ⓑ Ⓒ Ⓓ

10. Solve for the integer x:

$$\frac{4x+5}{-18}=\frac{x}{x-3}$$

Answers and Explanations

1. **The correct answer is (B).**

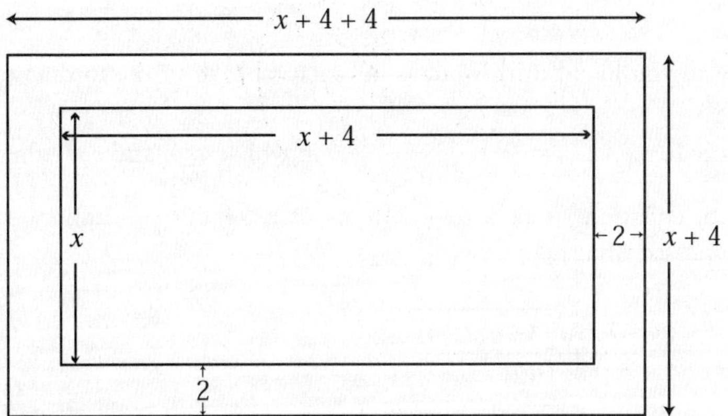

You have to use some Stepping Stones to solve this question. Let the width of the garden be x. Since the garden is 4 yards longer than it is wide, let the length equal $x + 4$. Next, add the width of the walkway, which adds two meters *to both sides* of the garden. Therefore, the new width is $x + 4$, and the new length is $x + 8$. Since the total area is 320, you can multiply the measurements like this:

$$(x+4)(x+8)=320$$
$$x^2+12x+32=320$$
$$x^2+12x-288=0$$

Now factor this, either using the Quadratic Formula or using trial and error:

$$x^2+12x-288=0$$
$$(x-12)(x+24)=0$$
$$x=\{12,-24\}$$

Since you're dealing with an actual measurement, you can throw out the –24. Thus, the backyard must be 12 yards long and 12 + 4, or 16, yards wide. If the dimensions of the yard itself are 12 × 16, then its total area is 192 square yards. Since the total area is 320, you can subtract the area of the yard to find the area of the walk: 320 – 192 = 128 square yards.

2. This one is factorable: $2x^2 + 7x + 6 = (2x + 3)(x + 2)$.

Set each factor equal to zero:

$2x + 3 = 0$ $\qquad$ $x + 2 = 0$

$2x = -3$ $\qquad$ $x = -2$

$$x = -\frac{3}{2}$$

So, we find the values of x are $-\frac{3}{2}$ and -2.

3. Try all you like, but this one is not factorable. It's time to drag out the quadratic formula: $x = \frac{-b \pm \sqrt{b^2 - 4ac}}{2a}$, in which a, b, and c are the coefficients of the equation $y = ax^2 + bx + c$. In this case, $a = 2$, $b = 7$, and $c = 4$. Plug them in and see what happens:

$$x = \frac{-7 \pm \sqrt{7^2 - 4(2)(4)}}{2(2)}$$
$$= \frac{-7 \pm \sqrt{49 - 32}}{4}$$
$$= \frac{7 \pm \sqrt{17}}{4}.$$

The two roots are $\frac{-7 + \sqrt{17}}{4}$ and $\frac{-7 - \sqrt{17}}{4}$.

4. **The correct answer is (A)**. Algebra is an option here, but the easiest way to solve this is to plug in a number for x. Let's say $x = 20$ English majors. If there are three times as many computer science majors, then there are 3×20, or 60 computer science majors. There are half as many history majors as computer science majors, so half of 60 is 30. That makes a total of $20 + 60 + 30$, or 110 sophomores who are accounted for. The number of other majors equals $400 - 110$, or 290. This is the number you're aiming for when you plug 20 into the answer choices. Since $400 - 5\frac{1}{2}(20) = 400 - 110$, or 290.

5. **The lures cost 75 cents ($0.75) a piece.** You've been given two unknown quantities (the price of lures and the price of night crawlers), and two equations involving those quantities. In other words, you've got "two equations and two unknowns," or simultaneous equations. The key to this is making sure you set up your equations properly. Let l = the number of lures and n = the number of night crawlers:

10 lures + 20 night crawlers = $9.50 becomes $10l + 20n = 9.5$
20 lures + 50 night crawlers = $20.00 becomes $20l + 50n = 20$

In order to find l, you have to make the n's cancel out. Therefore, multiply the top equation by –5 and the bottom one by 2:

$$-5\ (10l + 20n = 9.5) = -50l - 100n = -47.5$$
$$2\ (20l + 50n = 20) = 40l + 100n = 40$$

Add the two equations, and the n's are gone:

$$-10l = -7.5;\ l = 0.75.$$

6. **The correct answer is (A).** The tangent function involves the "TOA" portion of the memory trick "SOHCAHTOA"; the tangent equals $\frac{opposite}{adjacent}$. The length of the side opposite $\angle T$ is 2, and the length of the adjacent side is 3. The tangent must therefore be $\frac{2}{3}$.

7. **The correct answer is (B).** Since point C, the vertex of $\angle ACB$, is on the circumference of circle O, $\angle ACB$ is an inscribed angle. By rule, the measure of an inscribed angle that intercepts the same arc as a central angle is exactly half the measure of the central angle. Therefore, $m\angle ACB = \frac{1}{2}(120)$, or 60°.

8. **The correct answer is (B).** First, remember that the measure of arc ABD is 180°. That means the measure of the other half of the circle, arc ACD, also measures 180° (remember that the whole circle measures 360°). If arcs AC and CD are the same length, they must both measure 90°. $\angle CAD$ is also an inscribed angle, so it's measure must be half the measure of the arc that it intercepts. Thus, $m\angle CAD = 45°$.

9. **The correct answer is (D).** Here's a real test of your knowledge of triangles and angle measure. Center your attention on ΔACE since you know a lot about it. The total measure of the three angles in a triangle is 180° and you know the measure of two of them. Figure out the measure of $\angle AEC$ like this:

$$m\angle CAE + m\angle ACE + m\angle AEC = 180$$
$$45 + 60 + m\angle AEC = 180$$
$$m\angle AEC = 75.$$

Now look at ΔMEB. Since the measure of arc BD is 60, you know $m\angle BME = 60$ (because it's a central angle). Furthermore, $\angle MEC$ (the same angle as $\angle AEC$, which measures 75°) and $\angle MEB$ are supplementary angles, so their sum is 180°. That makes the measure of $\angle MEB$ equal to 180 – 75, or 105°.

Find the measure of $\angle DBE$ by using the following formula:

$$m\angle BME + m\angle MEB + m\angle MBE = 180$$
$$60 + 105 + m\angle MBE = 180$$
$$m\angle MBE = 15.$$

10. **The correct answer is $x = 1$.** You can cross multiply here, and you'll have to factor the result:

$$\frac{4x+5}{-18}=\frac{x}{x-3}$$
$$(4x+5)(x-3)=-18x$$
$$4x^2-12x+5x-15=-18x$$
$$4x^2-7x-15=-18x$$
$$4x^2+11x-15=0.$$

It might take some doing, but you can factor the quadratic:

$$4x^2+11x-15=0$$
$$(4x+15)(x-1)=0$$
$$x=\left\{-\frac{15}{4},1\right\}$$

Note that you're only supposed to solve for the *integer x*.

Whew! Some of those were tough. Then again, we're really trying to find out what you know. And, remember, the better the workout we give you here, the easier the test will be later. Ready for some more challenges? Try these:

11. A 12-inch by 18-inch mirror is placed in a frame of uniform width. If the area of the picture and the frame is 280 square inches, how many inches wide is the frame?

(A) 1
(B) 2
(C) 3
(D) 4

Ⓐ Ⓑ Ⓒ Ⓓ

12. Which of the following is the greatest quantity?

(A) $\sqrt{185}$
(B) 0.13×10^2
(C) 15% of 90
(D) $\frac{182}{13}$

Ⓐ Ⓑ Ⓒ Ⓓ

13. Rank the following numbers from least to greatest: 12.3, 4π, $\sqrt{161}$, and $\frac{50}{4}$

(A) 12.3, 4π, $\sqrt{161}$, $\frac{50}{4}$

(B) 12.3, $\frac{50}{4}$, 4π, $\sqrt{161}$

(C) 4π, 12.3, $\sqrt{161}$, $\frac{50}{4}$

(D) 4π, 12.3, $\frac{50}{4}$, $\sqrt{161}$

Ⓐ Ⓑ Ⓒ Ⓓ

14. In a produce shipment, each crate of melons contains between 20 and 25 fruit. If each melon costs $1.40, what is the range of the possible cost of a crate of melons?

(A) $25–$28
(B) $28–$35
(C) $35–$42
(D) $42–$50

Ⓐ Ⓑ Ⓒ Ⓓ

15. A store offers a promotion whereby anyone who buys two cans of artichoke hearts can get a third can for one-third off. If each can of artichoke hearts costs $3.90, how much will three cans cost?

16. The Maverick Bus Company estimates that three out of every four passengers, on average, use tokens to ride the bus, and the remainder use cash. If 4,216 people rode the bus on Thursday, how many people would the company assume paid with a token?

(A) 1,054
(B) 2,108
(C) 3,162
(D) 4,216

Ⓐ Ⓑ Ⓒ Ⓓ

17.

The wheel shown above is spun twice, and the two results are added together. Which of the following sums is the most likely result?

(A) 6
(B) 7
(C) 9
(D) 12

Ⓐ Ⓑ Ⓒ Ⓓ

18. Microfine Metallurgists manufactures a ball bearing of a specific diameter to be used in skateboard wheels. The ball bearing is to be 15 mm in diameter, and that diameter cannot vary by more than 0.3% (larger or smaller). Which of the following diameters is therefore unsatisfactory?

(A) 14.94
(B) 14.96
(C) 15.03
(D) 15.04

Ⓐ Ⓑ Ⓒ Ⓓ

19. In the 2002 budget, the city of Declanburg increased its percentage allotted to sanitation to 11% from 8% in 2001. Due to cutbacks, however, the size of the overall budget declined to $32.1 million from 39.0 million in 2001. Which of the following is true regarding the actual amount of money that Declanburg spent on sanitation in 2002 compared to 2001?

(A) Increased
(B) Stayed the same
(C) Decreased
(D) Cannot be determined

Ⓐ Ⓑ Ⓒ Ⓓ

Questions 20–21 relate to the following problem:

Marcus signs up for an MP3 downloading service that offers the following four membership options:

Package 1—Monthly fee: \$3.95; Price per MP3: \$0.39
Package 2—Monthly fee: \$4.95; Price per MP3: \$0.26
Package 3—Monthly fee: \$6.95; Price per MP3: \$0.17
Package 4—Monthly fee: \$8.95; Price per MP3: \$0.10

20. If Marcus plans to download 20 MP3s per month, which package is the least expensive?

(A) Package 1
(B) Package 2
(C) Package 3
(D) Package 4

Ⓐ Ⓑ Ⓒ Ⓓ

21. What is the least number of MP3s that Marcus would have to download per month in order for Package 4 to be the least expensive?

(A) 27
(B) 28
(C) 29
(D) 30

Ⓐ Ⓑ Ⓒ Ⓓ

Answers and Explanations

11. The correct answer is (A).

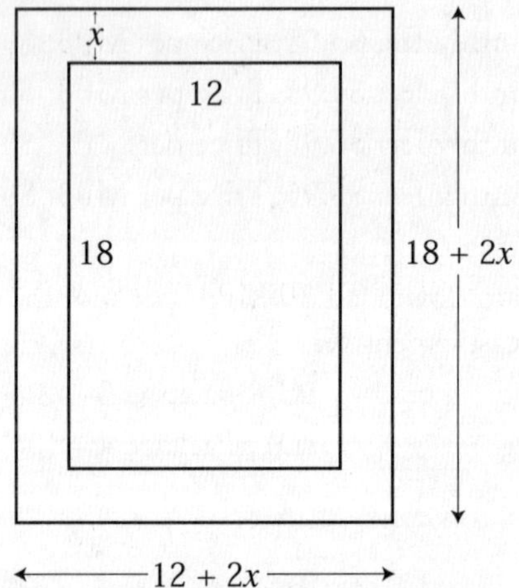

The dimensions of the mirror are 12 × 18, and there is a frame around it of uniform width, x. The outer dimension of the width is $12 + 2x$, and the exterior length is $18 + 2x$. Use the formula for the area of a rectangle ($l \times w$) and plug in the dimensions you just figured out: $(12 + 2x)(18 + 2x) = 280$. Using FOIL, you get: $216 + 36x + 24x + 4x^2 = 280$. Combine the terms, and you get:

$$4x^2 + 60x + 216 = 280$$
$$4x^2 + 60x - 64 = 0$$

When you divide each term by 4, you can simplify the quadratic to $x^2 + 15x - 16 = 0$. Now factor it:

$(x + 16)(x - 1) = 0$; so $x = -16$ or 1.

The width of the frame has to have a positive value, so the width of the frame must be 1 inch.

12. **The correct answer is (D).** Use your calculator to find the value of each of the answer choices: $\sqrt{185} \approx 13.6$; $0.13 \times 10^2 = 13$; 15% of 90 = 13.5; and $\frac{182}{13} = 14$.

13. **The correct answer is (B).** Use your calculator to find the value of the three terms (other than 12.3): $4\pi \approx 12.56$; $\sqrt{161} \approx 12.68$; and $\frac{50}{4} = 12.5$. The order is, therefore: 12.3, $\frac{50}{4}$, 4π, $\sqrt{161}$.

14. **The correct answer is (B).** At the very least, there are 20 melons in a crate. Since the price of each fruit is \$1.40, the very least the crate will cost is 20 × \$1.40, or \$28. Similarly, 25 × \$1.40 = \$35. The range is \$28–\$35.

15. **The correct answer is \$10.40.** The first two cans will cost \$3.90 a piece. To find the price of the third can, multiply the price by $\frac{1}{3}$: $\left(\frac{1}{3}\times 3.90 = 1.30\right)$. Subtract that from \$3.90, and you'll find that the discounted can costs \$2.60. Add up the three prices: \$3.90 + \$3.90 + \$2.60 = \$10.40.

16. **The correct answer is (C).** Multiply the total by $\frac{3}{4}$ to find the answer: $4{,}216\times\frac{3}{4} = \frac{4{,}216}{1}\times\frac{3}{4}$. Now, multiply and divide: $\frac{4{,}216}{1}\times\frac{3}{4} = \frac{12{,}648}{4}$, and 12,648 divided by 4 equals 3,162.

17. **The correct answer is (B).** This is a great question for the Elimination Game. There are six numbers on the wheel; therefore, if you spin the wheel twice, there are 6^2, or 36 possible results. The smallest result is 1 + 1, or 2, and the largest result is 6 + 6, or 12. Each of those can occur only once, so you can cross off choice (D). To figure out all the possibilities, the fastest way is to simply count them. There are six ways to get the sum of 7: 1 + 6, 2 + 5, 3 + 4, 4 + 3, 5 + 2, and 6 + 1.

18. **The correct answer is (A).** Figure out the percentage of the variance. Since $0.3\% = \frac{0.3}{100}$, or 0.003, you can multiply that by 15 mm. to get 0.045 mm., which is the maximum by which the diameter can vary. In other words, the diameter must be between 15 – 0.045, or 14.955, and 15 + 0.045, or 15.045. The only one of the answer choices that is not between those two numbers is 14.94.

19. **The correct answer is (A).** Figure out the actual amount by applying the relevant percentages to each year (and be sure not to confuse them). In 2001, 8% of the \$39 million, or \$3.12 million, was spent on sanitation. In 2002, the amount changed to 11% of \$32.1 million, or \$3.531 million. Therefore, the amount of money spent *increased*.

20. **The correct answer is (B).** Multiply the fee per MP3 by 20, and then add the monthly fee in order to find the total amount:

    Package 1—\$3.95 + (20 × \$0.39) = \$3.95 + \$7.80 = \$11.75
    Package 2—\$4.95 + (20 × \$0.26) = \$4.95 + \$5.20 = \$10.15

Package 3—$6.95 + (20 × $0.17) = $6.95 + $3.40 = $10.35
Package 4—$8.95 + (20 × $0.10) = $8.95 + $2.00 = $10.95

If Marcus wants to download 20 MP3s, Package 2 is the least expensive.

21. **The correct answer is (C).** You could plug in all four choices starting with choice (A) until Package 4 was the least expensive, but that could take a lot of time. The key point to realize is that Package 4 has the highest fee but the lowest cost per MP3; therefore, at some point, the cost savings on the MP3s will offset the higher fee. In order words, let x = the number of MP3s that Marcus has to order. The money spent on Package 3, in cents, equals $17x + 695$, and the money spent on Package 4 equals $10x + 895$. To find out when Package 4 costs less than Package 3, set up the inequality:

$17x + 695 > 10x + 895$

$7x > 200$

$x > 28.57$

Therefore, the first answer greater than 28.57, or 29, is the point at which Package 4 is cheapest.

Our head's spinning thinking about all those MP3s, and how obsolete they're soon going to be. MP4s anyone? And throw in a couple of DVDs as well. But not right now.

First, let's work through the next set of practice problems.

22. The following chart shows the number of students who play four sports at four different high schools:

School	Football	Tennis	Soccer	Track
Knightsbridge	41	17	31	27
Lincoln	46	31	22	18
Mayfair	52	14	26	31
Newcastle	49	22	14	35

Which of the following statements regarding the data above is *not* true?

(A) More students run track at Knightsbridge High than play soccer at Mayfair High.

(B) At Newcastle High, the number of students on the football team equals the number of players on the track and soccer teams combined.

(C) At Mayfair High, there are twice as many players on the football team as there are on the soccer team.

(D) Among the four schools, Mayfair High has the most students that play sports.

Ⓐ Ⓑ Ⓒ Ⓓ

23. Yesterday, Jerome drove 300 miles from Larchville to Morganburg. He drove an average of 60 miles per hour until he got halfway to Morganburg; due to excessive traffic, he only averaged 50 miles per hour for the rest of the trip. How long did the trip take?

24. An ice cream store offers the following prices for gallons of ice cream (and offers a 10% discount to anyone who buys three or more gallons):

Vanilla	$4.00
Chocolate	$4.50
Strawberry	$4.50
Mocha Chip	$5.50
Pistachio	$6.00

If Mrs. Rodriguez buys a gallon of vanilla, two gallons of strawberry, and a gallon of mocha chip, how much will she end up paying?

(A) $12.60
(B) $13.00
(C) $16.65
(D) $18.50

25. Tania's shirt drawer contains three red shirts, four blue shirts, six green shirts, and one yellow shirt. If the red and yellow shirts are long-sleeved, what is the probability that a shirt chosen at random from the drawer will be long-sleeved?

26. The table below shows the approximate number of students who entered medical school in the indicated years:

Year	No. of Students
1965	1,100
1970	1,500
1978	2,700
1985	4,000
1992	6,000
2000	

Complete the following three parts:

Part I: On a sheet of graph paper, plot the five existing data points on a graph (with the y-axis labeled up to 15,000) and connect the points to form a trend line.

HIGH STAKES

Part II: Use the graph from Part I to predict the number of students who enrolled in medical school in 2000, assuming that the current trend remained the same.

Part III: If you were to be told that 8,200 students enrolled in medical school in 1990, how could you explain the huge digression from the trend line?

27. If two sides of a triangle have lengths of 3 and 9, which of the following is not a possible length of the third side?

(A) 5
(B) 7
(C) 9
(D) 11

Ⓐ Ⓑ Ⓒ Ⓓ

28. The table below indicates the average monthly snowfall, in inches, at four American cities:

City	Boulder	Burlington	Billings	Boise
October	1.0	2.7	1.9	3.1
November	4.3	5.6	3.2	7.2
December	5.1	4.9	6.7	10.1
January	6.2	8.9	6.2	4.5
February	4.9	7.1	6.3	4.3

Which of the following statements is *not* true?

(A) Boise and Burlington have the same average aggregate snowfall over the five-month period.
(B) Burlington's average snowfall in January is greater than Boise's average snowfall in December.
(C) Boulder's aggregate snowfall over the five months is the least of the four cities.
(D) Billings's average snowfall in December is more than twice its average snowfall in November.

Ⓐ Ⓑ Ⓒ Ⓓ

29. Alberto has three sons and two daughters. Which of the following expresses the fractional amount of his children that are daughters?

(A) $\frac{2}{5}$
(B) $\frac{2}{3}$
(C) $\frac{3}{5}$
(D) $\frac{5}{3}$

Ⓐ Ⓑ Ⓒ Ⓓ

30. There are m pens and n pencils in a jar on Tran's desk. Which of the following algebraic expressions expresses the fractional amount of pencils to the total?

(A) $\frac{m}{n}$

(B) $\frac{n}{m+n}$

(C) $\frac{m}{m+n}$

(D) $\frac{1}{m+n}$

Ⓐ Ⓑ Ⓒ Ⓓ

Answers and Explanations

22. The correct answer is (D). Here's another question where the Elimination Game can be used. You can work your way through the choices to find the one that is *not* true. Add up the number of students in each school: Knightsbridge High has 116 players, Lincoln 117, Mayfair 123, and Newcastle 120.

23. The correct answer is 5.5 hours. The key to this problem is the formula "rate times time equals distance," or $r \times t = d$. Jerome averaged 60 miles per hour for the first half (or 150 miles) of the trip. Therefore, the rate is 60 and the distance is 150:

$r \times t = d$

$60t = 150$; $t = 2.5$ hours.

For the remaining 150 miles, he averaged only 50 miles per hour:

$r \times t = d$

$50t = 150$; $t = 3$ hours.

The entire trip took 2.5 + 3, or 5.5 hours.

24. The correct answer is (C). Given the price list, Mrs. Rodriguez will spend $4.00 + (2 × $4.50) + $5.50, or $18.50—before the discount (which applies to three or more gallons). Calculating 10% of something is easy; just move the decimal point one place to the left. Therefore, 10% of $18.50 is $1.85, and $18.50 – $1.85 = $16.65.

25. The correct answer is $\frac{2}{7}$. There is a total of 14 shirts in the drawer (3 + 4 + 6 + 1 = 14), and four of them (the reds and the yellow) are long-sleeved. Therefore, the probability that a long-sleeved shirt will be selected is $\frac{4}{14}$, or $\frac{2}{7}$.

26. To solve this question, use your Stepping Stones to create the needed graphs.

Part I.

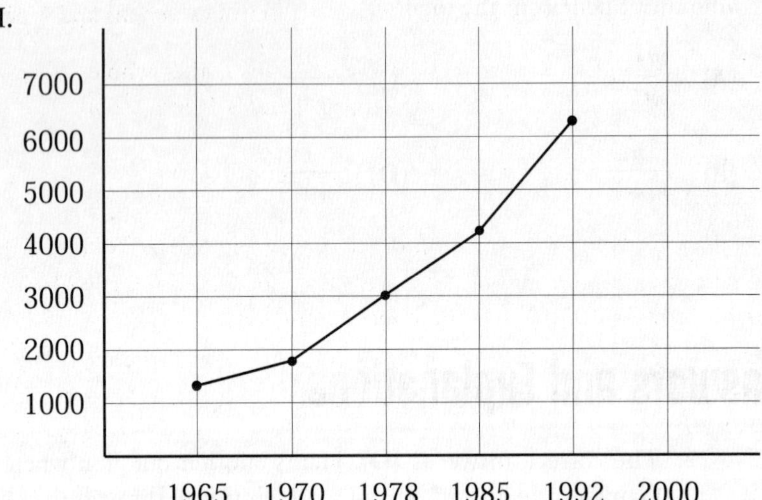

Part II. The test writers don't expect you to get this perfect, but they'll usually have a specific range in mind. In this case, your answer should be anywhere between 9,000 and 11,000; they'd have a hard time rejecting an answer in that range.

Part III. There could be any number of reasons why the number spiked so high in 1990. The test writers will be looking for anything plausible, as long as you recognize that trend lines are merely rough sketches, and that actual results can vary from year to year.

27. **The correct answer is (A).** The length of any side of a triangle is less than the sum of the other two sides and greater than the difference. If the two sides have lengths 3 and 9, then the third side must be greater than 6 and less than 12. Among the choices, only 5 is outside this range.

28. **The correct answer is (B).** Read between the lines on this one. You need to find the answer choice that is *not* true. Burlington gets 8.9 inches in January, and Boise gets 10.1 inches in December, so choice (B) is incorrect.

29. **The correct answer is (A).** Fractions are a way of indicating part of a whole, and they look like this: $\frac{part}{whole}$. If Alberto has three sons and two daughters, then he has a total of five children—this is the "whole." The "part" is that portion of the whole consisting of daughters (there are two). The part is 2, and the whole is 5. Therefore, the fraction is $\frac{2}{5}$.

30. **The correct answer is (B).** Fractions are a way of indicating part of a whole, and they look like this: $\frac{part}{whole}$. If Tran has m pens and n pencils, then he has a total of $m + n$ items in the jar—this is the "whole." The "part" is that portion of the whole consisting of pencils (there are n). The part is n, and the whole is $m + n$. Therefore, the fraction is $\frac{n}{m+n}$.

Hey! That was kind of exhilarating, and the nicest part was we didn't have to shovel any of that snow from Question 28. It may be a good time for a cup of hot cocoa. Unless, of course, you want to practice some more right now.

31. Which value is greatest?
   (A) 3^4
   (B) 4^3
   (C) 2^6
   (D) 6^2

Ⓐ Ⓑ Ⓒ Ⓓ

32. A wheel is divided into 12 wedges of equal size, numbered from 1 through 12. If the pointer is spun counterclockwise, what is the probability that it will land on an even number?
   (A) 0
   (B) $\frac{1}{4}$
   (C) $\frac{1}{2}$
   (D) 1

Ⓐ Ⓑ Ⓒ Ⓓ

33. For which of the following situations would the use of approximate numbers be the most appropriate?
   (A) The cost of a new bus purchased by Fleetwheels Bus Co.
   (B) The number of buses owned by Fleetwheels Bus Co.
   (C) The number of times each Fleetwheels bus is inspected each year
   (D) The number of people who ride a Fleetwheels bus to work each day

Ⓐ Ⓑ Ⓒ Ⓓ

34. The length of a blade of grass is best measured in
   (A) inches.
   (B) yards.
   (C) miles.
   (D) acres.

Ⓐ Ⓑ Ⓒ Ⓓ

Questions 35–37 pertain to the circle with center O.

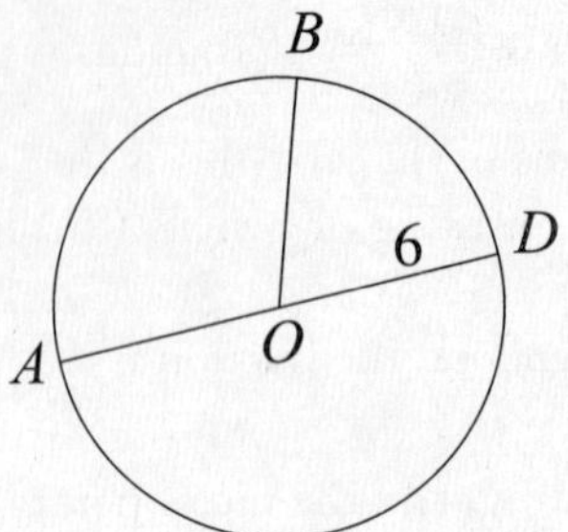

35. What is the circle's circumference?

36. If m$\angle AOB$ = 120º, what is the area of sector AOB?

37. What is the length of minor arc AB?

38. Which one of the following quadratic equations has irrational roots?

(A) $x^2 - 3x - 10 = 0$
(B) $x^2 - 4x - 1 = 0$
(C) $x^2 - 16 = 0$
(D) $x^2 - 5x - 14 = 0$

Ⓐ Ⓑ Ⓒ Ⓓ

39. Simplify the following:

$$\frac{(x+7x+12)}{3x+12} \cdot \frac{x+2x-15}{x^2-9}$$

40. Solve for x:

$$\frac{3x+2}{12} = \frac{x}{3}$$

Answers and Explanations

We're breaking a little early for solutions this time because if we didn't break here, we'd have to wait until question 52.

31. **The correct answer is (A).** Each of these is an exponential representation of a two-digit number. The rule with exponents is: "When in doubt, expand it out." Therefore, 3^4 is the same as 3 multiplied times itself four times, or $3 \times 3 \times 3 \times 3$, which equals 81.

    Find the value of the other three terms the same way:
    (B) $4 \times 4 \times 4 = 64$
    (C) $2 \times 2 \times 2 \times 2 \times 2 \times 2 = 64$
    (D) $6 \times 6 = 36$
    None of these is bigger than the first answer you tried.

32. **The correct answer is (C).** When determining probability, find the number of desired outcomes (what you *want* to happen) and divide it by the number of *all* possible outcomes (all the things that *could* happen). There are six even numbers (2, 4, 6, 8, 10, and 12), and there are 12 numbers overall. Therefore, the probability that the pointer will land on an even number is 6/12, or 1/2. Note that you can use the Elimination Game and eliminate choices (A) and (D) because a probability of 0 means it can never happen; a probability of 1 means it will always happen. Also, don't worry about the counterclockwise reference. We added that to see if you were paying attention. The probability is the same no matter the direction in which you spin the pointer.

33. **The correct answer is (D).** Approximate numbers are best used when situations vary day by day and when the numbers in question are very large. It's important for Fleetwheels to keep exact numbers regarding the cost of each bus it buys, the number of buses it owns, and the number of times each bus is inspected. The exact number of people who ride the bus to work each day is harder to keep track of; usually, an approximation will suffice.

34. **The correct answer is (A).** Grass can cover large areas of land, but individual *blades* of grass are usually quite small. Therefore, the best unit of measure to use is inches.

35. **The correct answer is 12π linear units.** The formula for the circumference of a circle is $C = 2\pi r$. Plug 6 into this equation, and you get $(2)(6)\pi$, or 12π linear units.

36. **The correct answer is 12π square units.** O is the center of the circle, so $\angle AOB$ is a central angle. It measures 120°, and there are 360° in a circle. Therefore, you know that the central angle is one third of the entire circle

because $\frac{120}{360}=\frac{1}{3}$. Since $\angle AOB$ is one third of the circle, the area of the sector bounded by $\angle AOB$ must be one third of the entire area (which is 36π). Divide 36π by 3, and you get 12π square units.

37. **The correct answer is 4π linear units.** O is the center of the circle, so $\angle AOB$ is a central angle. It measures 120°, and there are 360° in a circle. Therefore, you know that the central angle is one third of the entire circle, because $\frac{120}{360}=\frac{1}{3}$. Since $\angle AOB$ is one third of the circle, the length of minor arc AB must be one third of the entire circumference (which is 12π). One third of 12π is 4π linear units.

38. **The correct answer is (B).** The roots of a quadratic are rational if you can factor the equation. Try to factor each of the choices you're given. The one you can't factor is the correct choice.

(A) $x^2-3x-10=0$

$(x+2)(x-5)=0$

$x=\{-2,5\}$

(B) Not factorable

(C) $x^2-16=0$

$(x-4)(x+4)=0$

$x=\{-4,4\}$

(D) $x^2-5x-14=0$

$(x-7)(x+2)=0$

$x=\{7,-2\}$

You have to use the Quadratic Formula to get the roots of answer choice (B).

39. **The correct answer is $\frac{(x+5)}{3}$.** Factor all the complex terms like this:

$x^2+7x+12 = (x+3)(x+4)$

$3x+12 = 3(x+4)$

$x^2-9 = (x+3)(x-3)$

$x^2+2x-15 = (x-3)(x+5)$

Once you've factored everything, you should start seeing a lot of similar terms on both the top and bottom of the fractions:

$$\frac{(x+3)(x+4)}{3(x+4)} \cdot \frac{(x-3)(x+5)}{(x-3)(x+3)}.$$

Cancel out all the factors that appear both on the top and on the bottom and you're left with: $\frac{(x+5)}{3}$.

40. The correct answer is 2 = *x*. Any time two fractions are equal to each other, you can cross multiply:

$$\frac{3x+2}{12} = \frac{x}{3}$$
$$3(3x+2) = 12x$$
$$9x+6 = 12x$$
$$6 = 3x$$
$$2 = x$$

"How about some more problems?" you ask. Sure, help yourself to another dozen!

Questions 41–46 apply to ΔMNP, which has coordinates $M(-1, 4)$, $N(5, 5)$, and $P(3, 1)$.

41. Graph ΔMNP.

42. What is the length of MP?

43. Graph $\Delta M'N'P'$ after ΔMNP is reflected in the y-axis and give the new triangle's coordinates.

44. Use the distance formula to find the length of $\overline{M'P'}$. How does it compare to the length of $\overline{MP}$?

45. Graph $\Delta M'N'P'$ after ΔMNP undergoes a translation of $(-3, -2)$ and give the new triangle's coordinates.

46. Graph $\Delta M'N'P'$ after ΔMNP is rotated around the origin and give the new triangle's coordinates.

Questions 47–48 refer to the following:

If one adds three years to Bill's age and then multiplies that number by two, the result is Jane's age.

47. If Bill is b years old, which of the following represents Jane's age in terms of b?

(A) $2b + 3$
(B) $2(b + 3)$
(C) $b + 6$
(D) $2b - 6$

Ⓐ Ⓑ Ⓒ Ⓓ

48. If Bill is 9 years old, how old is Jane?

(A) 12 years old
(B) 15 years old
(C) 21 years old
(D) 24 years old

Ⓐ Ⓑ Ⓒ Ⓓ

Questions 49–50 refer to the following:

A right triangle has legs of length 8 and 15.

49. What is the area of the triangle?

(A) 30
(B) 60
(C) 90
(D) 120

Ⓐ Ⓑ Ⓒ Ⓓ

50. What is the length of the hypotenuse of the right triangle?

(A) 12
(B) 17
(C) 19
(D) 23

Ⓐ Ⓑ Ⓒ Ⓓ

51. Gwendolyn wants to put a circular concrete patio in her backyard. When she goes to the hardware store, she finds that each bag of concrete mix is enough to cover 50 square feet (assuming that the patio will be 1-inch high). If the patio is to have a radius of 12 feet (and will be 1-inch high), how many bags of concrete must she buy?

(A) 3
(B) 5
(C) 8
(D) 10

52.

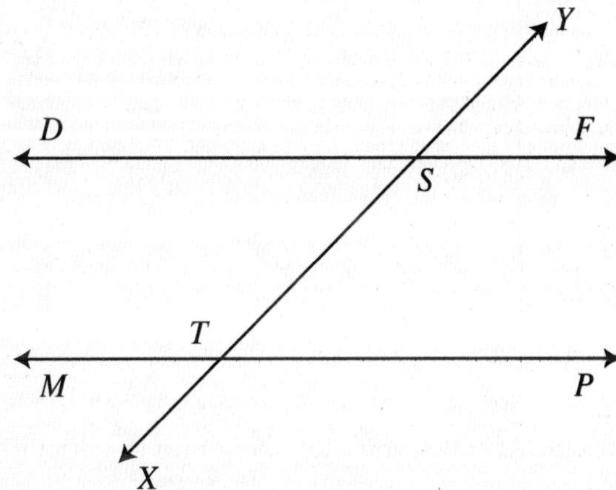

In the accompanying diagram, $\overleftrightarrow{DF}$ is parallel to $\overleftrightarrow{MP}$, and $\overleftrightarrow{XY}$ intersects the two lines at points S and T, respectively. If $m\angle DST = 3x + 20$ and $m\angle PTF = 5x - 10$, what is the value of x?

(A) 5
(B) 10
(C) 15
(D) 20

Answers and Explanations

41.

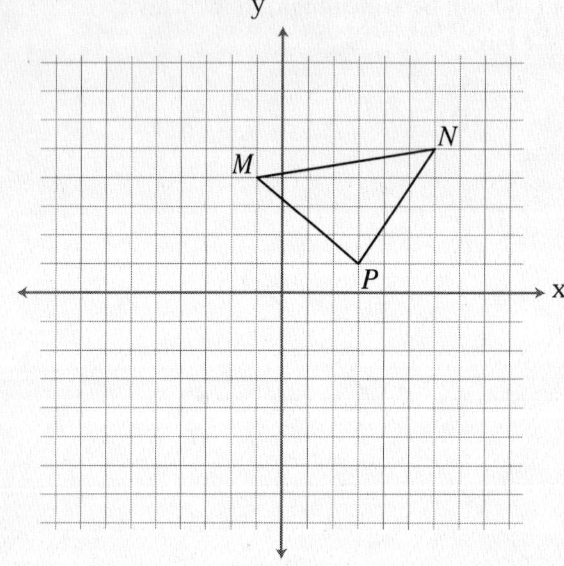

42. Use the coordinates for M and P and plug them into the distance formula:

$$d = \sqrt{(x_2 - x_1)^2 + (y_2 - y_1)^2}$$
$$= \sqrt{[(3-(-1)]^2 + (1-4)^2}$$
$$= \sqrt{4^2 + (-3)^2}$$
$$= \sqrt{16+9}$$
$$= \sqrt{25} = 5.$$

43.

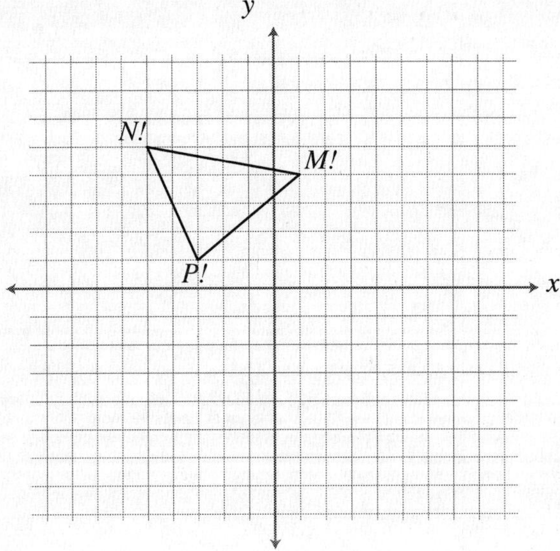

When a polygon undergoes a reflection in the *y*-axis, the *x*-coordinates are multiplied by –1 and the *y*-coordinates remain the same. Therefore, the coordinates of the new triangle in this case are: $M(1, 4)$, $N(-5, 5)$, and $P(-3, 1)$.

44. Plug in the coordinates and use the distance formula:

$$
\begin{aligned}
d &= \sqrt{(x_2 - x_1)^2 + (y_2 - y_1)^2} \\
&= \sqrt{(-3-1)^2 + (1-4)^2} \\
&= \sqrt{(-4)^2 + (-3)^2} \\
&= \sqrt{16+9} \\
&= \sqrt{25} = 5.
\end{aligned}
$$

Since the size of a polygon is not affected by a reflection, translation, or rotation, the image segment $M'P'$ is exactly the same length as its pre-image $\overline{MP}$.

45.

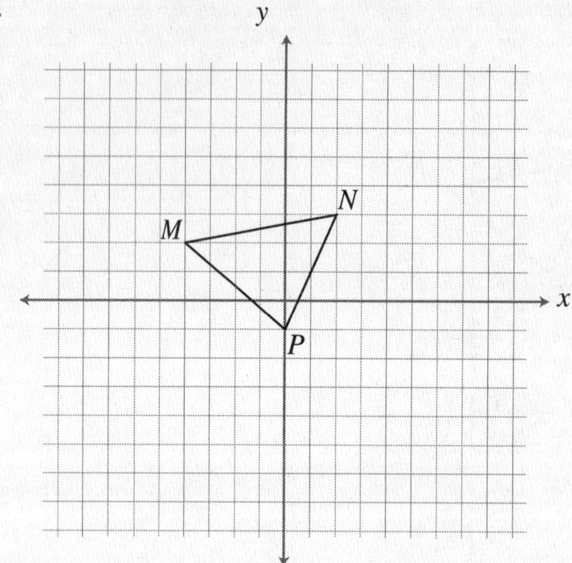

When a polygon undergoes a translation of (x, y), you add x to all of the x-coordinates and y to all the y-coordinates. Therefore, the coordinates of the new triangle in this case are $M(-4, 2)$, $N(2, 3)$, and $P(0, -1)$.

46.

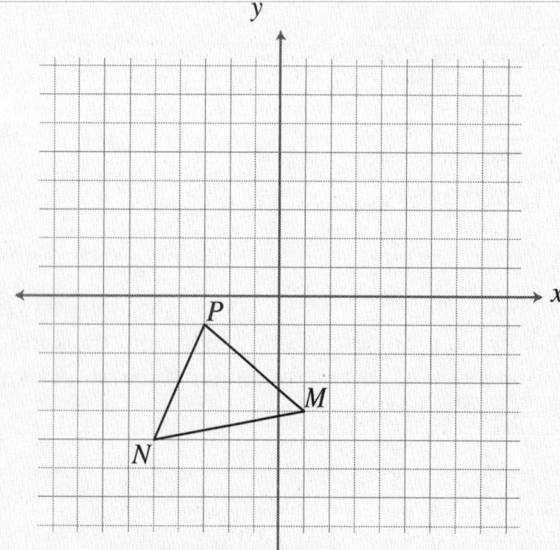

When a polygon undergoes a rotation about the origin, both the x-coordinates and y-coordinates are multiplied by -1. Therefore, the coordinates of the new triangle in this case are $M(1, -4)$, $N(-5, -5)$, and $P(-3, -1)$.

47. The correct answer is (B). Follow the steps carefully. First, "one adds three years to Bill's age"; if 3 is added to b, the resulting term is $b + 3$. Then, one "multiplies that number by 2." When you do this, be sure to multiply everything by 2 using parentheses: $2(b + 3)$.

48. The correct answer is (D). You can either use the algebraic expression you just created in the previous question, or you use the question itself. If you add 3 years to Bill's age (which is 9), you get 9 + 3, or 12. After you double this new number, the result is 2×12, or 24.

49. The correct answer is (B).

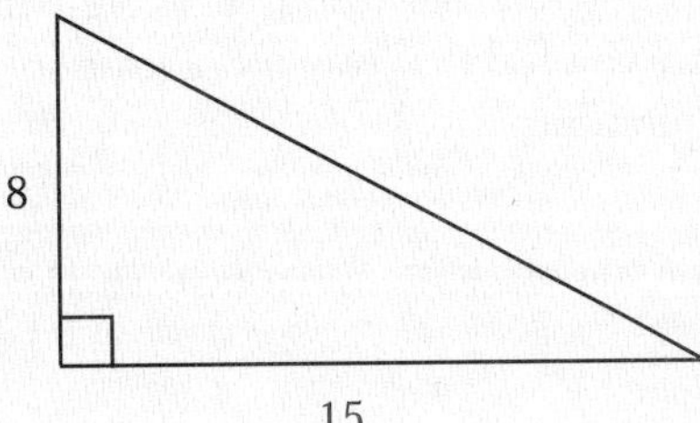

The formula for the area of a triangle is $A = \frac{1}{2}bh$, in which A is the area, b is the length of the base, and h is the height. The base and height of a right triangle are the same as the lengths of the two legs, because these legs are perpendicular (see the figure above). Therefore, the area of this triangle is $\frac{1}{2} \times 8 \times 15$, or 60.

50. The correct answer is (B). Find the hypotenuse of a right triangle using the Pythagorean theorem: $a^2 + b^2 = c^2$, in which a and b are the lengths of the legs and c is the length of the hypotenuse. Since the legs measure 8 and 15, plug these into the formula and solve:

$$8^2 + 15^2 = c^2$$

$$64 + 225 = c^2$$

$$289 = c^2$$

$$17 = c$$

51. The correct answer is (D). To find the total area of the patio that Gwendolyn wants, use the formula for the area of a circle: $A = \pi r^2$. If the radius of the patio is to be 12 feet, then the total area will be $\pi(12)^2$, or 144π. When you substitute 3.14 for π, you get 144×3.14, or 452.16 square feet. Each bag will cover 50 square feet, so divide 452.16 by 50 in order to determine how many bags will be needed: $452.16 \div 50 = 9.0432$. This means that Gwendolyn will need nine full bags, plus a little bit more. Therefore, she will need to buy 10 bags, and she will have a lot left over.

52. **The correct answer is (C).** Since the two lines are parallel, the transversal creates $\angle DST$ and $m\angle PTF$ as alternate interior angles, which, by definition, have the same measure. Set them equal to each other and solve for x:

$$5x - 10 = 3x + 20$$
$$2x = 30$$
$$x = 15$$

We're getting pretty close to the end of this book. This is the penultimate (next to the last) set of practice problems. We feel as if we've become very close through all this practice, and we're sure you feel that way too. Please try not to get too sentimental as you do these last sets of questions.

53. A sphere has a volume of 288π. What is its surface area?

[Volume of a sphere: $V = \frac{4}{3}\pi r^3$;

surface area of a sphere:

$S.A. = 4\pi r^2$]

(A) 36π
(B) 72π
(C) 144π
(D) 288π

Ⓐ Ⓑ Ⓒ Ⓓ

54. The population of Brattleboro was 743,294 in 1990. If the population increased by 254,432 people between 1990 and 2000, which of the following is true?

(A) The population increased by more than 50%.
(B) The population was less than 1 million in 2000.
(C) The population was greater than 1 million in 2000.
(D) The population was greater than 10 million in 2000.

Ⓐ Ⓑ Ⓒ Ⓓ

55.

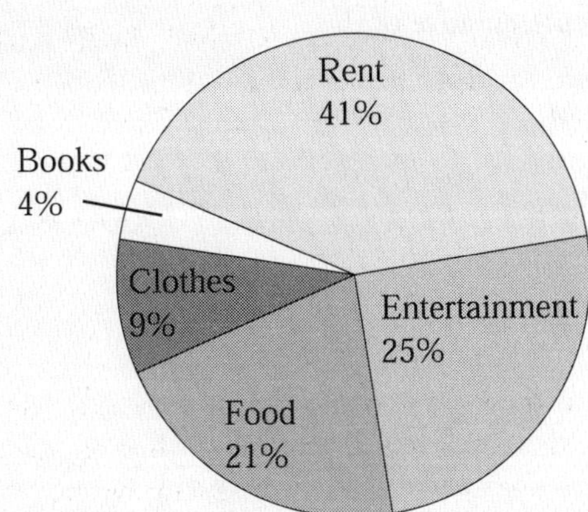

The above pie chart indicates the percentage of Nedra's expenses during her first year at college. Based on the information in the pie chart, which of the following statements is *false*?

(A) Nedra spent exactly half of her money on rent and clothes.

(B) Nedra spent exactly one quarter of her money on entertainment.

(C) Nedra spent more than three times as much on entertainment as she did on clothes.

(D) The amount Nedra spent on food and books combined equaled the amount she spent on entertainment.

56. If the legs of a right triangle measure 4 and $\sqrt{11}$, what is the measure of the triangle's hypotenuse?

(A) $3\sqrt{3}$

(B) 5

(C) 15

(D) 27

57. In order to save up $500, Arnold took a job at a local drug store. If he makes $8.50 per hour, works 15 hours per week, and saves every penny that he earns, how many weeks will he have to work before he reaches his savings goal?

(A) 2

(B) 4

(C) 6

(D) 8

58. Which of the following equations is representative of the multiplicative identity?

(A) $a \times 1 = a$
(B) $a \times b = b \times a$
(C) $a \times a = a^2$
(D) $a \times 0 = 0$

Ⓐ Ⓑ Ⓒ Ⓓ

59.

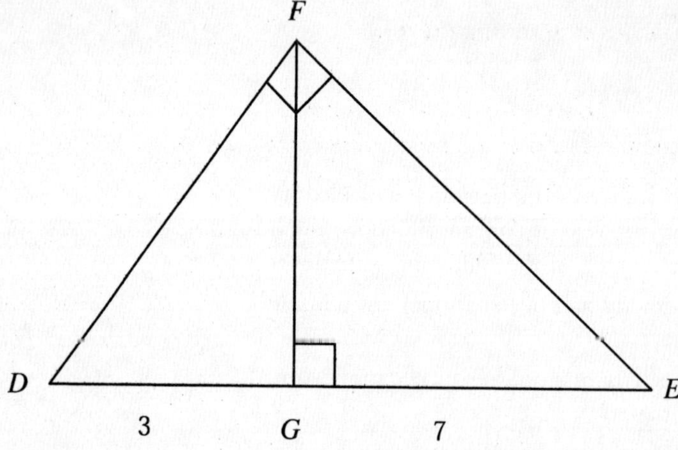

In the above diagram of right triangle DEF and altitude $\overline{FG}$, $DG = 3$ and $GE = 7$. What is the length of $\overline{FG}$?

(A) 2
(B) $\sqrt{21}$
(C) $\sqrt{58}$
(D) 10

Ⓐ Ⓑ Ⓒ Ⓓ

60. An isosceles right triangle ABC has a hypotenuse of length $6\sqrt{2}$. If isosceles right triangle DEF has four times the area of triangle ABC, how long is each leg of triangle DEF?

(A) 6
(B) 9
(C) 12
(D) 24

Ⓐ Ⓑ Ⓒ Ⓓ

61. If the function $a ♣ b$ is defined as $a ♣ b = \frac{a+b-1}{a-2b+1}$, what is the value of $5 ♣ 1$?

62. Malcolm earned $7.30 per hour bagging groceries at the Maximart. His schedule during a particular week was the following:

Monday:	4:00 p.m. – 8:30 p.m.
Tuesday:	4:30 p.m. – 8:30 p.m.
Wednesday:	3:30 p.m. – 7:00 p.m.
Thursday:	Off
Friday:	4:00 p.m. – 9:00 p.m.

How much did Malcolm earn during the week?

63. A carpenter wants to resurface a floor that measures 12 feet by 18 feet. If each section of flooring is a square that measures 18 inches on a side, how many sections will she need?

(A) 36
(B) 96
(C) 108
(D) 216

Ⓐ Ⓑ Ⓒ Ⓓ

64.

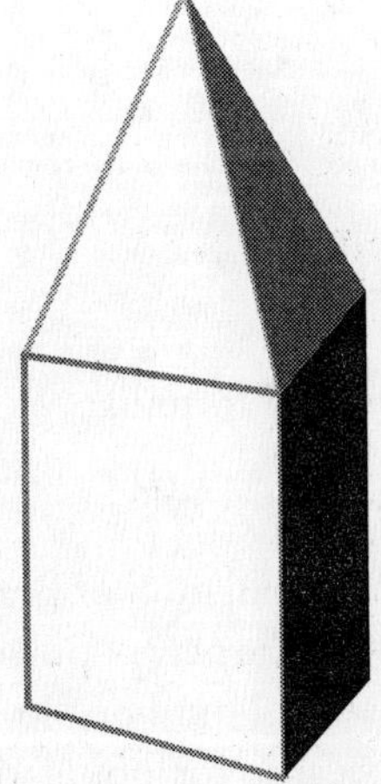

In order to find the volume of the figure above, what two volume formulas must you know?

(A) Pyramid and rectangle
(B) Pyramid and rectangular prism
(C) Cone and cylinder
(D) Triangle and rectangle

Ⓐ Ⓑ Ⓒ Ⓓ

65. The base of ΔMNP is 6 units long, and its altitude is 8 units long. If ΔMNP and ΔRST are similar triangles, and the length of the base of ΔRST is 15 units long, how long is the altitude of ΔRST?

(A) 12
(B) 18.5
(C) 20
(D) 48

Ⓐ Ⓑ Ⓒ Ⓓ

Answers and Explanations

53. **The correct answer is (C).** Start with the first formula, and set it equal to 288π:

$$288\pi = \frac{4}{3}\pi r^3$$
$$\frac{3}{4}\cdot 288\pi = \frac{3}{4}\cdot\frac{4}{3}\pi r^3$$
$$216\pi = \pi r^3$$
$$216 = r^3$$
$$6 = r.$$

Now plug the radius into the second formula:

$$S.A. = 4\pi r^2 = 4\pi(6)^2 = 4\pi(36) = 144\pi.$$

54. **The correct answer is (B).** If the population of Brattleboro was 743,294 and subsequently increased by 254,432, the new population is 743,294 + 254,432, or 997,726. This value is less than 1 million, so the answer is choice (B). Note: Choice (A) is incorrect because the population increased by less than half. Half of 743,294 is 371,647, which is greater than 254,432.

55. **The correct answer is (C).** According to the chart, Nedra spent 25% of her money on entertainment and 9% on clothes. Since $3 \times 9\% = 27\%$, the 25% she spent on entertainment is *less than* three times the 9% she spent on clothes.

56. **The correct answer is (A).** Since the question tells you that the two *legs* measure 4 and $\sqrt{11}$, you can use the Pythagorean Theorem:

$$a^2 + b^2 = c^2$$
$$(4)^2 + (\sqrt{11})^2 = c^2$$
$$16 + 11 = c^2$$
$$27 = c^2$$
$$\sqrt{27} = c.$$

You can simplify your answer by factoring out a 9: $\sqrt{27} = \sqrt{9 \cdot 3} = \sqrt{9} \cdot \sqrt{3} = 3\sqrt{3}$.

57. **The correct answer is (B).** If Arnold makes \$8.50 per hour and works 15 hours per week, then he makes \$8.50 × 15, or \$127.50, per week. Work through the answer choices individually, in order, and see which one takes Arnold over the \$500 mark. Choice (A) is not sufficient because he will only earn 2 × \$127.50, or \$255, in two weeks. In four weeks, however, he will make 4 × \$127.50, or \$510. By using the Elimination Game, you can see that choice (B) brings the amount he will earn over \$500 in four weeks. You don't need to calculate the other answer choices since they are more than four weeks.

58. **The correct answer is (A).** The multiplicative identity states that if you multiply any number by 1, the result is the original number ($4 \times 1 = 4$, $7 \times 1 = 7$, and so forth). In algebraic terms, this is represented by the equation $a \times 1 = a$.

59. **The correct answer is (B).** When an altitude is drawn to the hypotenuse of a right triangle, the length of that altitude is the mean proportional between the two parts of the hypotenuse. (It all relates to similar triangles.) Set $FG = x$ and set up the proportion:

$$\frac{DG}{FG} = \frac{FG}{GE}$$
$$\frac{3}{x} = \frac{x}{7}.$$

When you cross multiply, you'll get $x^2 = 21$, so $x = \sqrt{21}$.

60. **The correct answer is (C).**

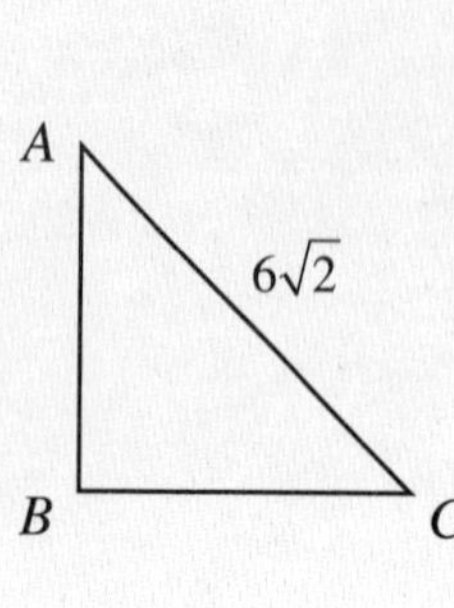

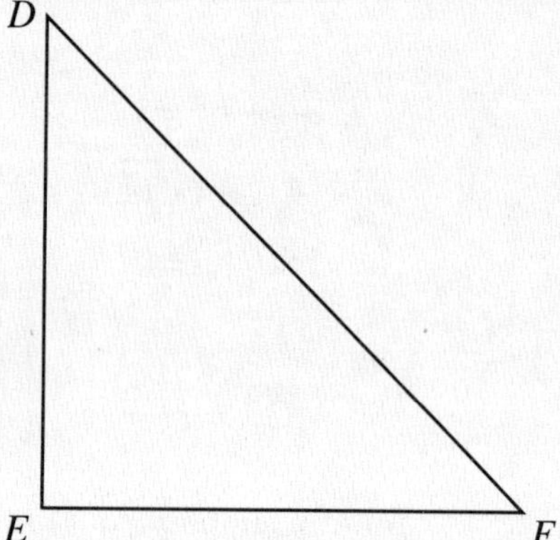

An isosceles right triangle is the same as a 45:45:90 triangle, and the ratio of its sides (leg, leg, hypotenuse) is $1:1:\sqrt{2}$. Therefore, if the hypotenuse measures $6\sqrt{2}$, then each leg measures 6 and the area of ΔABC is $\frac{1}{2}bh$; $\frac{1}{2}(6)(6)=18$. Triangle *DEF* has four times the area of ΔABC, and 4 × 18 = 72. Use the area of a triangle formula in reverse to find the length of a leg of ΔDEF (since it is an isosceles right triangle, the base and the height are the same):

$$\frac{1}{2}(x)(x)=72$$
$$x^2=144$$
$$x=12.$$

61. **The correct answer is 5/4.** They've defined what the ♣ means, so plug in a = 5 and b = 1:

$$\frac{a+b-1}{a-2b+1}=\frac{5+1-1}{5-2(1)+1}=\frac{5}{4}.$$

62. **The correct answer is $124.10.** Calculate the number of hours Malcolm worked for the entire week: Monday, 4.5 hours; Tuesday, 4 hours; Wednesday, 3.5 hours; Thursday, 0 hours; and Friday, 5 hours. The total workweek was 17 hours. Multiply that by $7.30, and you'll get $124.10.

63. The correct answer is (B).

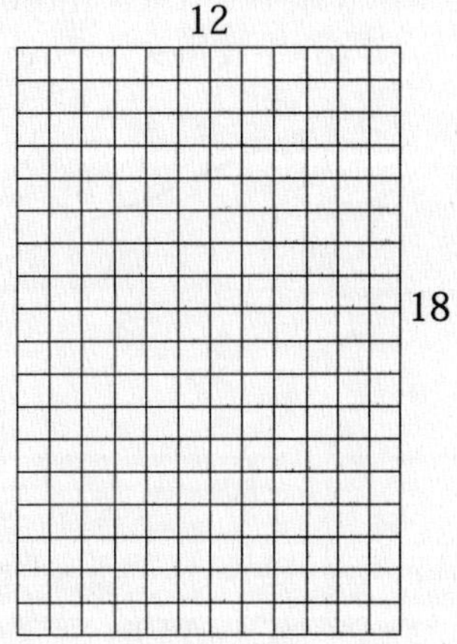

Since there are 12 inches in a foot, 18 inches equals 1.5 feet (because 12 × 1.5 = 18). Now, find out how many 1.5-foot sides fit into 12 feet and 16 feet by dividing. If you divide 12 by 1.5, you get 8; dividing 18 by 1.5 gives you 12. Therefore, you need 8 × 12, or 96 sections.

64. The correct answer is (B). Here's that good old Elimination Game again. You can eliminate choices (A) and (D) right away because a rectangle is not a three-dimensional figure (you find the area of a rectangle, not its volume). Furthermore, there are no rounded edges on the diagram, so you can cross off choice (C). The figure is made up of a pyramid sitting on top of a rectangular prism.

65. The correct answer is (C). The lengths of any corresponding measures of similar triangles are proportional. Set up the proportion to find the altitude of ΔRST:

$$\frac{6}{8} = \frac{15}{x}$$

$$6x = 120$$

$$x = 20$$

Here comes the absolute final set of practice problems. Beg all you want, but this is the end of it. We'll make this one a baker's dozen (that's 13). Of course, as we've already noted, there is no reason why you can't cycle through all of these problems again, or as many times as you want until you feel like you can ace your exit-level math test.

66.

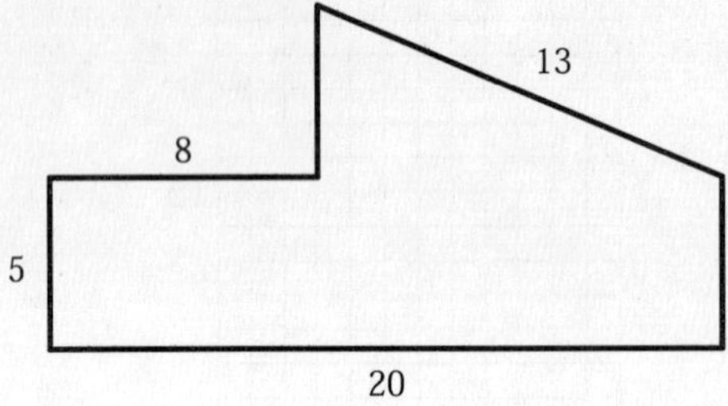

What is the area of the irregularly shaped polygon above?

(A) 56
(B) 85
(C) 130
(D) 160

Ⓐ Ⓑ Ⓒ Ⓓ

67. What is the sum of the degree measures of the interior angles of a regular pentagon?

(A) 180
(B) 360
(C) 540
(D) 720

Ⓐ Ⓑ Ⓒ Ⓓ

68. Which of the following statements regarding a parallelogram is false?

(A) Adjacent angles are supplementary.
(B) Opposite angles are congruent.
(C) Opposite sides are congruent.
(D) Diagonals are congruent.

Ⓐ Ⓑ Ⓒ Ⓓ

69. Which of the following is a simplification of the algebraic equation $2(3a + 4b) - 3(a - 5b)$?

(A) $3a - 7b$
(B) $3a + 23b$
(C) $9a - 7b$
(D) $9a + 23b$

Ⓐ Ⓑ Ⓒ Ⓓ

70. Which of the following statements regarding the algebraic expression $\frac{2a+5b}{5b}$ is correct?

(A) The expression can be reduced to $2a$.
(B) The expression can be reduced to $2a + 1$.
(C) The expression can be restated as $\frac{10ab}{5b}$.
(D) The expression is in its simplest form.

Ⓐ Ⓑ Ⓒ Ⓓ

71. Simplify $x + 4(3x)$.

(A) $5x$
(B) $8x$
(C) $13x$
(D) $3x^2 + 12x$

Ⓐ Ⓑ Ⓒ Ⓓ

72. Each day, Rose's Café sells doughnuts at $0.65 each and muffins at $0.75 each. If the café sells 12 muffins and 15 doughnuts in 1 hour, which of the following expressions represents how much the café made in that hour?

(A) $15(0.65) + 12(0.75)$
(B) $15(0.75) + 12(0.65)$
(C) $\frac{0.65}{15}+\frac{0.75}{12}$
(D) $(0.65)(0.75) + (12)(15)$

Ⓐ Ⓑ Ⓒ Ⓓ

73. What is the numerical value of the expression $3a^2 + 2b$, if $a = 2$ and $b = 3$?

(A) 12
(B) 18
(C) 31
(D) 42

Ⓐ Ⓑ Ⓒ Ⓓ

74. The main hot-air balloon used by Up-N-Away Tours is shaped like a sphere and has a diameter of 40 feet. How many cubic feet (rounded off to the nearest cubic foot) of hot air does the balloon hold? [The formula for the area of a sphere is $\frac{4}{3}\pi r^3$. Use $\pi = 3.14$.]

(A) 533　　(C) 33,493
(B) 16,747　　(D) 267,947

Ⓐ Ⓑ Ⓒ Ⓓ

75. Zoran buys five bags of seed per month in order to feed his two pet parakeets. If he is thinking of getting another parakeet, what proportion should he use in order to determine the number of bags of seed he'll need to buy per month?

(A) $\frac{5}{3} = \frac{B}{2}$　　(C) $\frac{3}{5} = \frac{2}{B}$

(B) $\frac{B}{3} = \frac{2}{5}$　　(D) $\frac{2}{5} = \frac{3}{B}$

Ⓐ Ⓑ Ⓒ Ⓓ

76. If Martin's ride to the beach takes 4 hours when he averages 40 miles per hour, how long would it take him to make the same trip if he averaged 50 miles per hour?

(A) 2 hours, 30 minutes
(B) 3 hours, 12 minutes
(C) 4 hours, 10 minutes
(D) 5 hours exactly

Ⓐ Ⓑ Ⓒ Ⓓ

77. It normally takes six landscapers a total of 4 hours to cut the grass at Wilkinson Stadium. If one of the landscapers were to call in sick, how long would the job take?

(A) 3 hours　　(C) 4.8 hours
(B) 4.2 hours　　(D) 5.4 hours

Ⓐ Ⓑ Ⓒ Ⓓ

78. "The product of x and y is subtracted from the sum of z and 4."

Which of following algebraic expressions expresses this statement?

(A) $\frac{x}{y} - z + 4$

(B) $\frac{x - y}{z + 4}$

(C) $xy - z - 4$

(D) $(z + 4) - xy$

Ⓐ Ⓑ Ⓒ Ⓓ

Answers and Explanations

66. The correct answer is (C).

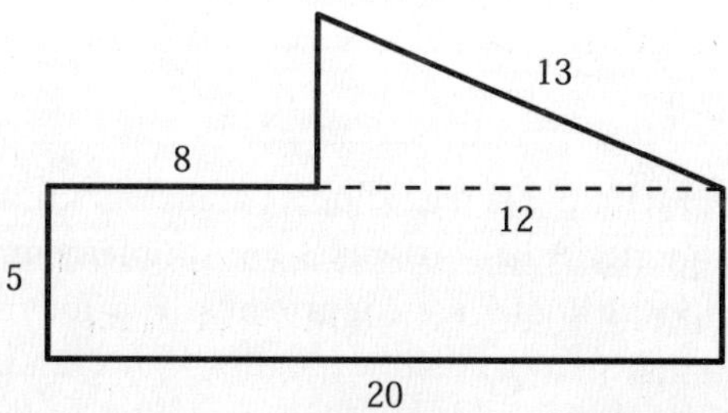

The irregularly shaped polygon looks funny, but it's really only a right triangle stuck on top of a rectangle. Therefore, you need to find the dimensions of the two smaller shapes. The height of the rectangle is 5, and the length of the rectangle is 20. The formula for the area of a rectangle is $l \times w$, in which l is the length of the rectangle and w is the width of the rectangle. Therefore, the area of the rectangle is 20×5, or 100 square units.

The trickier job is finding the dimensions of the triangle. Make things simpler for yourself and use some Stepping Stones. Since opposite sides of a rectangle are equal in length, the top of the rectangle is also 20 units long. That makes the base of the right triangle 12 units long (since the other length at the top of the rectangle is 8 units, and $8 + 12 = 20$. Since the triangle is a right triangle (and you now know two of the three lengths of the sides), you can use the Pythagorean Theorem to find the length of the third side:

$$x^2 + 12^2 = 13^2$$
$$x^2 + 144 = 169$$
$$x^2 = 25$$
$$x = 5$$

The area of a triangle is $\frac{1}{2}bh$, in which b is the length of the base and h is the height. The base of the triangle is 12, and the height of the triangle is 5, so plug these values into the formula: $A = \frac{1}{2}(12)(5) = 30$. Since the triangle's area is 30 and the rectangle's area is 100, the total area is 100 + 30, or 130 square units.

67. **The correct answer is (C).** The formula for the sum of the degree measures of a regular polygon is $180(n - 2)$, in which n represents the number of sides of the polygon. Since a pentagon has 5 sides, plug 5 in for n in the equation: $180(5 - 2) = 180(3) = 540$ degrees. If you didn't remember the formula, draw all diagonals from a single vertex. You'd find three triangles, each of which contains a total of 180°. 3(180) = 540°.

68. **The correct answer is (D).**

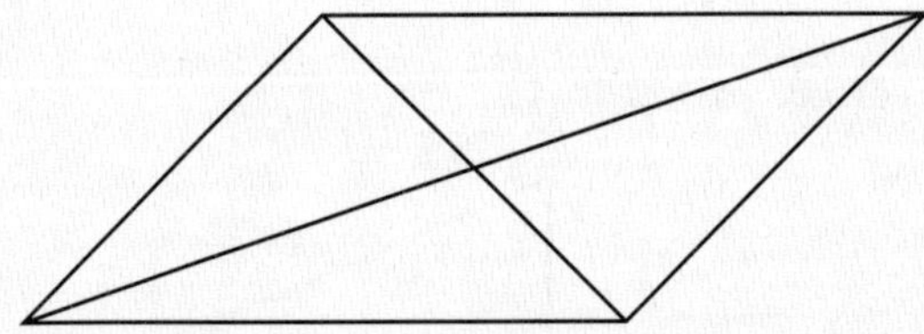

Each of the first three statements regarding a parallelogram is true; look at the example above as a guide. Adjacent angles are supplementary (that is, they add up to 180°), opposite angles are congruent (the same measure), and opposite sides are also congruent (the same length). However, the two diagonals are not the same length (that's only true for rectangles and squares).

69. **The correct answer is (B).** Each of these algebraic expressions must first be simplified using the distributive property of addition:

$$2(3a + 4b) = 2(3a) + 2(4b) = 6a + 8b$$

$$-3(a - 5b) = -3(a) - 3(-5b) = -3a + 15b$$

Now, combine the terms:

$$6a + 8b - 3a + 15b = (6a - 3a) + (8b + 15b) = 3a + 23b.$$

70. **The correct answer is (D).** The only way that the expression $\frac{2a+5b}{5b}$ can be simplified is to separate the numbers on top like this:

$$\frac{2a+5b}{5b} = \frac{2a}{5b} + \frac{5b}{5b} = \frac{2a}{5b} + 1.$$

This new form isn't much simpler than the previous form, and it doesn't match any of the other answer choices you've been given. Therefore, the term is already in its most simple form.

71. **The correct answer is (C).** Remember the rules of that word trick PEMDAS (or Please Excuse My Dear Aunt Sally): do all multiplication and division before any addition or subtraction. Leave the first x alone, and multiply the second term like this: $4(3x) = 12x$. Now, the expression becomes $x + 12x$, and you're free to add the two terms to come up with the final answer of $13x$.

72. **The correct answer is (A).** The amount of money you make selling a specific item is calculated by multiplying the price of the item by the number of items sold. In this situation, Rose's Café sold 12 muffins for \$0.75 each, so the dollar amount that was earned can be expressed like this: 12(0.75). You don't actually have to calculate how much that is, because the answer choices aren't simplified. Similarly, the dollar amount earned by selling doughnuts is 15(0.65).

73. **The correct answer is (B).** To solve this one, plug $a = 2$ and $b = 3$ into the expression, and then do the math:

$$3a^2 + 2b = 3(2)^2 + 2(3)$$

Now, remember your PEMDAS rule: E stands for exponents, and $2^2 = 4$, so $3(2)^2$ becomes 3(4), and the expression becomes 3(4) + 2(3). Now, multiply (the M in PEMDAS): 3(4) + 2(3) = 12 + 6. The final step is addition (the A in PEMDAS); since 12 + 6 = 18.

74. **The correct answer is (C).** Thankfully, the formula for the volume of a sphere has been provided (as is usually the case): $V = \frac{4}{3}\pi r^3$, in which r represents the radius of the sphere. Careful, though, because this one's a little bit tricky. If the diameter of the balloon is 40 feet, then the radius must be half of that, or 20 feet. (Did you plug in $r = 40$ by mistake and get choice (D) as an answer?) Plug $r = 20$ into the equation, and solve for V:

$$\begin{aligned} V &= \frac{4}{3}\pi r^3 \\ &= \frac{4}{3}(3.14)(20)^3 \\ &= \frac{4}{3}(3.14)(8,000) \\ &= 33493.33 \end{aligned}$$

When you round this off to the nearest cubic foot, as instructed, you get 33,493.

75. **The correct answer is (D).** Zoran needs to set up a proportion that relates the number of parakeets he owns to the number of bags of seed required to feed them. Two parakeets eat five bags of seed per month, and if he gets another parakeet, he'll have a total of three:

$$\frac{parakeets}{bags} : \frac{2}{5} = \frac{3}{B}$$

76. **The correct answer is (B).** The formula that relates speed (rate), time, and distance is: $r \times t = d$. The first part of the question tells you Martin rode for 4 hours (the t, or time) and his average rate was 40 miles per hour (the r, rate). Multiply these two together to determine the distance of the trip: $40 \times 4 =$ 160 miles.

    Now, we have to figure out the new time t if the rate is changed from 40 to 50. Since Martin is making the same trip, the distance is the same—160 miles. So plug $r = 50$ into the equation to figure out the new t:

    $$50 \times t = 160$$

    $$t = 3\frac{1}{5}.$$

    There are 60 minutes in an hour, so $\frac{1}{5}$ of an hour equals $\frac{1}{5} \times 60$, or 12 minutes.

77. **The correct answer is (C).** If the six landscapers each work for four hours (and are all working at once), then the total amount of time needed to completely finish the job is 6×4, or 24 hours of work. This 24 man-hours of work is required regardless of the number of people working on the project. So if one landscaper calls in sick, then the remaining five workers have to pick up the slack (and they will therefore have to work longer, because the sick worker isn't there to help). If five people have to work for a total of 24 hours, then they each must work for $24 \div 5$, or 4.8 hours.

78. **The correct answer is (D).** A product is the result of multiplication, so "the product of x and y" must somehow involve the term "xy." Therefore, you can eliminate choices (A) and (B). Also, a sum is the result of addition, so "the sum of z and 4" can be written "$z + 4$." The rest is a little trickier, since xy is "subtracted from" $z + 4$. Since "4 subtracted from 10" can be written "10 – 4," or 6, you can write this equation with the same thought in mind: xy is "subtracted from" $z + 4$ becomes $(z + 4) - xy$.

Hey, wasn't that a pretty thorough workout? Do you have your test tomorrow? The next day perhaps? Well, if it's any farther away than that, you can check out the sections you are unsure of and try the drill questions again. Repeat the cycle of studying the review sections and reworking these practice items to keep them fresh in your mind, and, more important, to keep fresh in the techniques you need to apply. Keep that up, and you're sure to succeed on your exit-level math test.

Break a leg! Maybe that should read: Break a Pencil! In simpler terms: Good luck on your test!

Notes

Notes

Notes

Notes

Notes